DKW

DKW

THE COMPLETE HISTORY OF A WORLD MARQUE

Siegfried Rauch
with Frank Rönicke

Schiffer Publishing Ltd
4880 Lower Valley Road • Atglen, PA 19310

Library of Congress Control Number: 2014948977

Type set in Adobe Caslon Pro/Helvetica

ISBN: 978-0-7643-4801-3
Printed in China

Published by Schiffer Publishing, Ltd.
4880 Lower Valley Road
Atglen, PA 19310
Phone: (610) 593-1777; Fax: (610) 593-2002
E-mail: Info@schifferbooks.com

Translated from the German by David Johnston.

This book was originally published under the title,
DKW: Geschichte einer Weltmarke,
© 2007 by Motorbuch Verlag, Stuttgart, Germany.

Contents

Foreword to the New Edition

In 1981, Siegfried Rauch, who joined DKW in 1937 and later became head of the company's Customer Service School, produced the book *DKW – The History of a World Marque*. The avowed (and enthusiastic) two-stroke engine and motorcycle specialist, whose postwar posts included technical director of the IFA in Chemnitz, head of customer service with Victoria in Nuremberg and, for many years, editor-in-chief of The Motorcycle magazine in Stuttgart, had written a marque history that was more extensive and self-contained than those of other companies at that time. And that is saying something, given DKW's broad and eventful history. The book became a bestseller that was produced in four editions, each revised, until 1994. Siegfried Rauch incorporated various corrections and additions into the last edition, which was ten pages longer than the first and reflected the ultimate results of his research and the information passed to him. The book is thus still just as timely today as the interest in the DKW brand. A new edition of this last version was therefore obvious to the author and the publisher, especially as no one else has tackled the complete history of the Saxon and later Bavarian manufacturer during the intervening period.

Two pages of color, with pictures from the DKW scene of the present and recent past, were added. They break up the events somewhat and make the book a contemporary and entertaining subject for the reader, while at the same time also an interesting reference book.

Frank Rönicke

The members of the DKW factory customer service school in 1938 behind the chassis of an F 1. Second from left: Customer service manager Wolf Doernhöffer. Second from right: Siegfried Rauch.

DKW – The Life's Work of Jörgen Skafte Rasmussen

Jörgen Skafte Rasmussen was born in Nakskow, Denmark on 30 July in the year 1878, the son of a ship owner and captain. It is unlikely that anyone could have predicted that the boy, who lost his father just one year later, would one day become one of the best known German businessmen and that the modest company he founded in Germany would become one of the largest motorcycle makers in the world in the 1920s and 1930s.

In Denmark he first completed an internship in preparation for the study of engineering. This he did at the renowned engineering schools in Mittweida and Zwickau; both cities were part of greater Chemnitz, an industrial city that was home to machine-building and textile industries known the world over.

After completing his studies, Rasmussen stayed in Germany – certain that the bigger country would offer his far-reaching talent and dynamic nature more opportunities than his Danish homeland. As became increasingly clear in the subsequent course of his life, Rasmussen was an extraordinary personality, capable of quick decisions and endowed with great spontaneity. With a good eye for his staff, for their character and abilities, he demanded of them the same effort that he gave to his company. He was imaginative in his technical planning and tireless in carrying it out.

In the beginning, however, the young engineer worked for the Rheinischen Maschinenfabrik in Dusseldorf for a short time and then in 1904 returned to Saxony, where, with his friend Ernst, that same year (also the year he got engaged) he established a company called Rasmussen & Ernst GmbH in Chemnitz (present-day Karl-Marx-Stadt). It designed and distributed steam boiler armatures and exhaust steam oil separators.

J.S. Rasmussen – born 30 July 1878, died 12 August 1964 – shown here circa 1930.

Foundation of the "Zschopauer Maschinenfabrik"

In 1907 Rasmussen also acquired a small shut down spinning mill near Zschopau (approx. 15km SE of Chemnitz) in the Erz Mountains with considerable property. With an eye towards future development, he soon acquired more land (at a price of about 10 Pfennigs per square meter!). There in the valley of the Dischau River, the "Zschopauer Maschinenfabrik," forerunner of the later "Zschopauer Motorenwerke J.S. Rasmussen AG" was founded. There Rasmussen manufactured the armatures that he had previously only distributed – until the First World War broke out in 1914 and this company too was forced to switch to the production of armaments.

Rasmussen frequently had to travel to visit authorities and suppliers in and around Chemnitz, and for this he employed a Wanderer-Puppchen, a small two-seat automobile made by the Wanderer factory in Chemnitz. With gasoline becoming increasingly scarce, he remembered a steam-powered car he had once seen in Denmark. He returned from a visit to Copenhagen with the car's designer, an engineer called Matthiesen, so that he could undertake the development of a steam-powered vehicle. Rasmussen suspected that as gasoline became increasingly scarce he would not be the only one interested in such a vehicle. Under Matthiesen's direction, beginning in 1917 the company produced prototypes of automobiles and trucks with steam drives. Within the company this development work was carried out under the abbreviation D.K.W. – *D*ampf-*K*raft-*W*agen (or steam motor vehicle), the first appearance of the trademark that would later become known the world over.

Interest in steam-powered road vehicles disappeared after the end of the war – gasoline was once again available in sufficient quantities. In Zschopau work on the steam-powered vehicle was halted. This did not mean the end of Rasmussen's association with automobiles, however. For the development work in his factory during the war was not his first contact with the automobile industry. He had himself been an automobile owner since 1904 and had a close relationship with Director Günther of the Chemnitz Presto Automobile Factory, with whom in about 1912 he established the Elitewerk AG in Brand-

Rasmussen (right) and colleagues in the early days in Zschopau (center Matthiesen, of the steam powered car, and left Ruppe, who developed the first DKW motorcycle).

"The Boy's Desire," the first DKW two-stroke, as a toy engine. With a bore of 22mm and stroke of 47mm, the engine (until now always given incorrectly) had a displacement of 18 cubic centimeters and produced approximately ¼hp. Open flywheel magneto.

The front crankshaft's cam plate served as an intake rotary vane plate, a centrifugally impinged valve as a speed limiter (like the Berini moped engines built by Auto Union in Rotterdam about 35 years later).

Erbisdorf near Freiberg, Saxony. Automobiles under the brand name Elite (and later Opel motorcycles) were made there until the mid-1920s.

In the first postwar years, however, Rasmussen saw little possibility of realizing his automobile plans in his factory in Zschopau. Things began looking up in 1918 when he was approached by a man, the son of an automobile maker in Apolda, Thuringia, who had made a name for himself as a designer, first in his father's company and later in his own automobile- and engine-building company in Markranstädt near Leipzig: engineer Hugo Ruppe. He proposed to Rasmussen that they make small two-stroke engines for various purposes. Rasmussen welcomed the proposal, even though two-stroke engines were then considered primitive and second-rate compared to the established four-stroke engine.

The first was a fan-cooled toy engine with a displacement of $18cm^3$ and an output of about ¼ horsepower. The engine, which was designed to compete with the small steam engines popular with hobbyists, had a number of interesting features. The small engines were sold in toy stores under the brand name D.K.W., which now stood for *D*es *K*naben *W*unsch (Boy's Desire).

"The Little Marvel"

Rasmussen of course realized that toy engines could not be the basis of an industrial company, the expansion of which occupied his thoughts night and day. Therefore the next developments followed quickly and new engines, again two-strokes, were created on Ruppe's drawing board. One, conceived as an "auxiliary engine" for the purpose of modernizing bicycles, initially had a displacement of 118cm^3 and produced 1hp. A second – with greater displacement – was designed to power machinery of all kinds in industry, trade and agriculture. Thus the company's future direction was staked out on two parallel marketing channels, in which the DKW brand would earn a worldwide reputation in the years to come.

Both engines, the bicycle auxiliary engine (for installation over the rear wheel) and a stationary pump unit, were first unveiled at the Leipzig Trade Fair in 1919 – the first of the auxiliary engines was delivered to a customer in Nuremberg in 1920. The company also concluded its first export agreement at the Leipzig fair – Bruno Cavani in Bologna became the first foreign DKW representative.

Rasmussen was not the only one to realize that bicycle motorization was a contemporary necessity given the economic situation after the lost war; bicycle auxiliary engines popped up everywhere in Germany in those years, and not all were two-strokes. Some were four-stroke engines and there were even a few twin-cylinder models. But unlike most of these rivals (a small reference booklet that appeared in late 1921 described more than twenty bicycle auxiliary engines), the Ruppe design (apart from the fact that it was built with a high quality level) had one decisive advantage: in the crankcase there was a primary reduction gear wheel which made possible a driving pulley on the engine that was sufficiently large and a pulley on

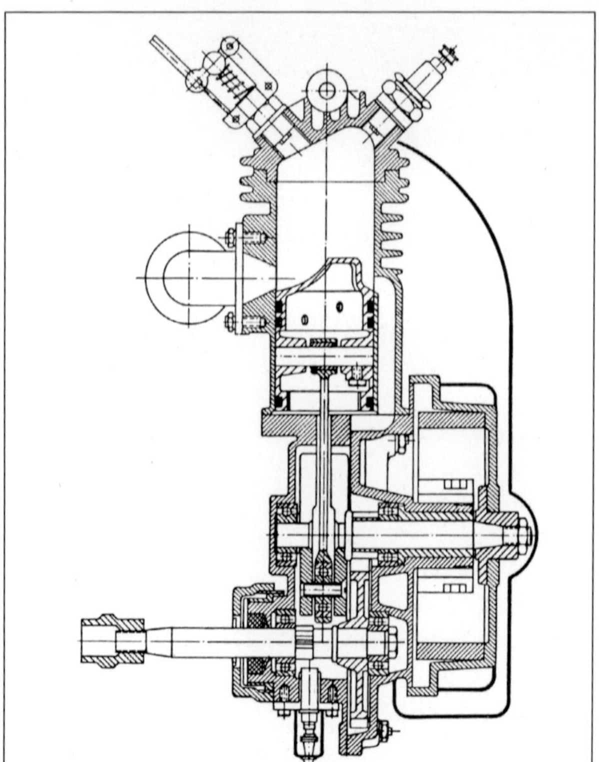

This cutaway drawing depicts the Type M auxiliary and integrated engine of 1919, known as "The Little Marvel" (here with removable cylinder head), designed by Hugo Ruppe. It had a displacement of 118cc (50mm bore and 60mm stroke) and produced about 1hp. Primary gear reduction 1:3. On the outside of the case the breaker operated by tappets from the countershaft.

Also designed by Ruppe, this stationary engine was unveiled at the Leipzig Fair in 1919 and was used to power a water pump. The horizontal, fan-cooled engine, of which no technical details have survived, is said to have produced 5hp. It was also the "running board engine" of the first miniature car built in Zschopau (see photo page 17).

Above: **The DKW auxiliary bicycle engine above the (belt-driven) rear wheel of this bicycle (already reinforced and equipped with front wheel suspension), which is now in the two-stroke museum in Augustenburg).**

Right: **A further development of the DKW auxiliary engine (1920) with injection (instead of the original float) carburetor, rear wheel with cable operated pulley block brake.**

the rear wheel that was not too large. This benefited both the small engine's torque and the life of the v-belt that delivered power to the wheel.

The engine made in Zschopau soon justified the third iteration of the trademark DKW – "*D*as *k*leine *W*under" (The Little Marvel). And from one end of the country to the other, people smiled at the advertising slogan "DKW, the little miracle, runs uphill like many do down."

For a brief time there was a danger that Rasmussen would be forbidden to use his popular trademark: the Deutschen Kabel-Werke, which for a longer time had been using the abbreviation DeKaWe, filed suit because of the phonetic similarities, and an injunction was granted. But despite this, Rasmussen was able to dispense with the trademark DGW ("Das Grosse Wunder," or The Big Marvel), which was in fact used for a short time, for the cable company was interested in providing the Zschopau factory with tires.

DKW integral engine (still without blower) in a production chassis.

The stationary engine … and "The Little Mountain Climber" were touted in these advertisements. The car at least, however, was probably never sold to customers.

Soon after production began, in addition to delivering his auxiliary engines to private customers and manufacturers, Rasmussen also began selling them with bicycles as complete packages. In the process he was forced to learn the hard way what others would repeatedly encounter in later years: even a combustion engine as small and light as his was not suitable for long-term use in a normal bicycle. What counted then as later was to motorize the rider, not the bicycle. Rasmussen came to this realization very quickly, as did all of the large and small manufacturers, at home and abroad, using the by then universally proven DKW engine: reinforced special chassis were proving better suited to the requirements of motorization, indeed they even permitted an increase in engine displacement and a power increase to 1.5hp. The option of fan cooling represented another important advance over most of the competition.

Among the manufacturers of motorized bicycles that used DKW engines (and in some cases in competition) was the well-known designer Neumann-Neander (right). Here he is seen in front of an "Ultra Lightweight" with the fan-cooled 143cc DKW engine. The small racing machine, which weighed 28.5kg, reached 85kph!

After the Berlin designer Eichler developed the scooter-like Golem bicycle with backrest seat, which was then built in Zschopau for a short time (see page 36), in 1922 DKW brought out the Lomos motorcycle with back rest seat. Its handling characteristics were far superior to those of the Golem – it can be seen as the true forerunner of the motor scooter (it was also later sold by Eichler in Berlin).

Golem and Lomos

A new design was added to the Zschopau model range in 1921: the Golem was a motorized bicycle with small wheels, a low, comfortable seat, and the 1hp engine (see illustration on page 36) mounted horizontally in a tubular frame – it was an early stage on the path to the scooter, but with less than satisfactory handling characteristics. The solution came the following year in the Lomos, which was designed by the Berliner Eichler. Described as an "armchair motorcycle," it had the fan-cooled 1.5hp engine under the seat, with a rear wheel swing arm suspension, and exhibited much better handling characteristics than the Golem. By that time Hugo Ruppe was no longer in Zschopau. He had parted ways with Rasmussen and set up shop in Berlin, where he began producing an engine that he had designed in Zschopau ("Bekamo"), but which at the time had seemed too costly to Rasmussen. Always full of ideas throughout his life, Ruppe did not return to Zschopau until after the Second World War (but not to DKW) and died there in 1946, when the occupying power planned to dismantle the DKW factory down to the last light switch and blow it up.

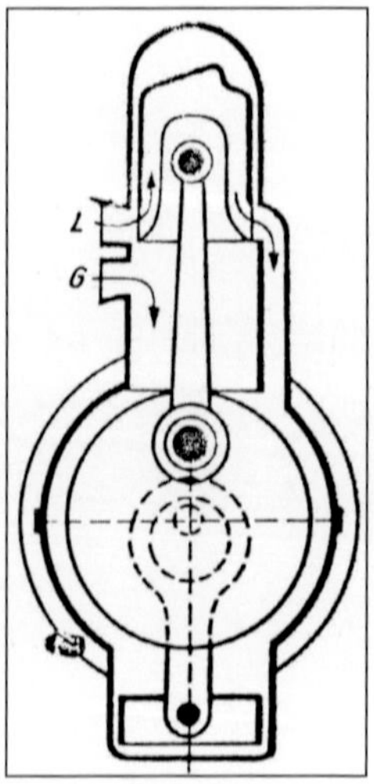

The picture shows the interesting Bekamo engine built by Hugo Ruppe in Berlin (at the Berlin Klein-Motoren AG) after he left Zschopau. The engine probably seemed too complicated for production at Zschopau. With a displacement of 148cc, the engine produced an astonishing 5.5hp at 3,800rpm. Noteworthy features included the opposed auxiliary pump in the crankcase and the scavenging air controlled by the piston (later cast in one piece) (L = scavenging air, G = fresh charge). The opposed auxiliary charging pump was later adopted for racing engines in Zschopau.

As Ruppe was leaving, two new employees began their careers with DKW. One was Dr. Carl Hahn, age 28. Rasmussen hired him on the special recommendation of his friend, the Jöhstadt pump manufacturer Flader. Hahn was supposed to take some of the load off Rasmussen in the fields of marketing and advertising. Dr. Hahn subsequently filled this role for decades. The charm of his Austrian homeland was combined with a tenacious willingness to work, an almost fanatical belief in the technical advantages of and the future opportunities for the two-stroke engine, paired with a rare power of persuasion which he fully employed at all times for the DKW brand.

The other was Hermann Weber, a young engineer trained at the Chemnitz National School (now the Technical Institute). Rasmussen envisaged him as head of the then still small design department (which did not prevent him successfully taking part in many races on DKWs, together with manager Blau and head of testing Sprung). All of the motorcycles created in Zschopau in the years that followed until the bitter end in 1945 showed his signature as chief designer (he died in the late Forties in Russia, where he, along with the later director Hoffmann and five other employees were forced to help build a Soviet motorcycle factory).

The beginning of motorcycle development by DKW in 1922-23: Hermann Weber's "Reichsfahrt Model" with fan-cooled 142cc engine (1.5hp), here with the very effective "Steigboy" muffler made by Leipzig designer and manufacturer Friedrich Boysen, in which two partial flows of exhaust gas collided with each other.

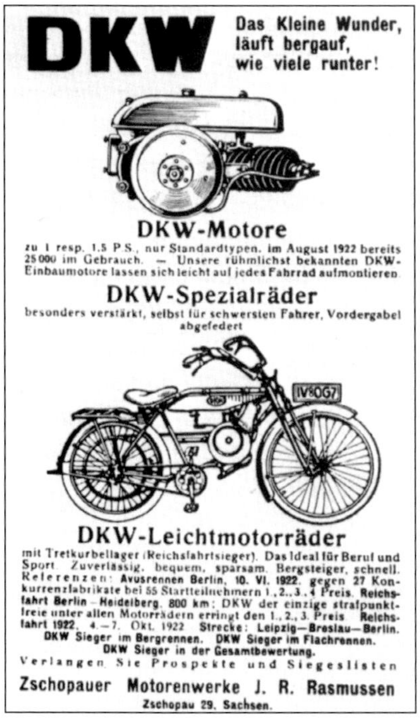

Advertisements and flyers like these were used to promote DKW (now without periods) all over the country, an innovation in the industry. Right: After Dr. Hahn joined the company DKW placed greater importance on intensive sales propaganda and a comprehensive customer service organization.

Reichsfahrt Model

Weber's first work was a light motorcycle, which had the 1.5hp engine mounted in the frame triangle with the cylinder immediately behind the steering head. It still did not have a multi-speed transmission but did have the interesting "Lomos clutch" (see page 37), available with or without foot pedals. As soon as the very first examples of this new model became available, the men from Zschopau, led by Weber, began competing in large and small races and reliability contests. And after three of the vehicles achieved a spectacular success in the "ADAC-Reichsfahrt" against competitors with machines of up to 8hp, Weber's promising new creation was given the attractive name "DKW Reichsfahrt Model."

This designation revealed a trend that would also be inextricably linked to the DKW brand in the future: Rasmussen was firmly convinced of the value of sporting use for technical advancement as well as that of racing victories for product advertising in the motorcycle sector. A growing number of factory and private riders therefore began using DKW machines in the widest variety of competitions, initially with vehicles that were almost identical to production standard. This situation remained unchanged until 1927, when August Prüssing joined DKW and established a racing department of a significant size, which was largely separate from the series design and production organization.

For the time being, however, Rasmussen and his employees were proud not just of their sporting success, but in particular of the steadily rising production. In Zschopau they were able to celebrate the completion of the 10,000th DKW engine in August 1921 – by July 1922 this figure had reached 20,000 engines and 2,000 DKW vehicles. The ratio was shifting more and more in favor of complete vehicles (motorcycles), even though the "stationary engine" sector likewise grew steadily in importance.

For the development of new DKW motorcycle models was proceeding rapidly. The end of 1923 saw the addition of the first models (ZM with tubular frame and SM with pressed steel frame) intended to replace the Reichsfahrt model in the product line of the company which that year had become a joint stock company called Zschopauer Motorenwerke J.S. Rasmussen AG (with Rasmussen as chief shareholder). They were powered by newly designed engines installed in the center of the frame. The cylinder was arranged vertically and the engines had a displacement of 175cm^3, output of 2.5hp, and a one- or two-speed transmission with clutch, later also with kickstarter. In 1924 the company in Zschopau was able to celebrate its 50,000th completed unit, the newest of which was just coming off the production line.

The factory complex also grew in all areas as production and employment numbers grew: not only had an entire complex of sheds and buildings (under which there was a tunnel through which the Dischau flowed) grown up around the building and additions that had once housed the spinning mill and then Rasmussen's armature plant. It had also become necessary to build a large administration building. The seven-storey structure was erected on the slope of the Dischau Valley. The structure was integrated into the countryside, with its two upper stories and the main entrance on the road leading to the factory, which ran up the hill.

(Roughly opposite the administration building was the "Finkenburg," which was owned by Rasmussen. Its splendor was maintained by the tenants, and guests often including employees and visitors to the factory.)

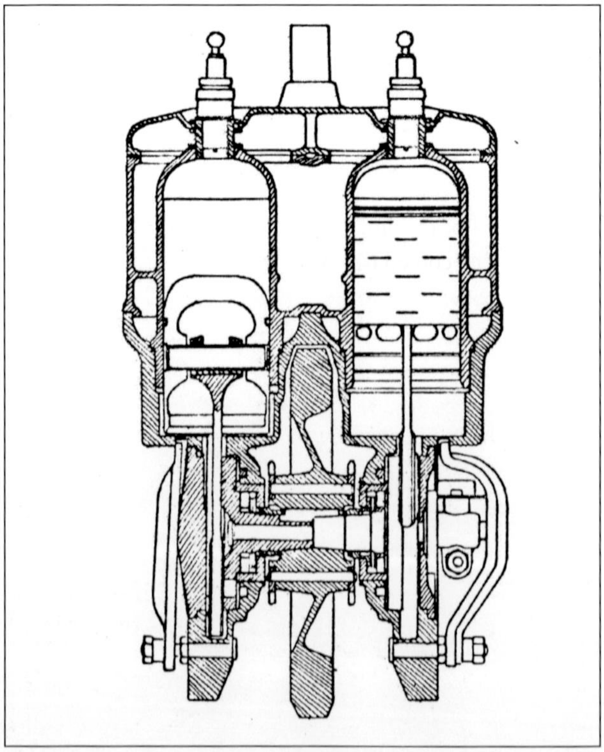

This cutaway drawing shows the design of the Scott twin-cylinder two-stroke engine. It probably played a not insignificant role in DKW's decision to also develop twin-cylinder two-stroke engines, however without adopting the central downthrust with its advantages (and disadvantages).

The LM – A Bestseller

The bestselling LM with "balloon tires" arrived in 1926. It was initially powered by a 206cc two-stroke, kick-start engine producing 4hp (the Sport produced 4.5hp). When the displacement requirement for a driver's license was reset at 200cc in 1928, the management at Zschopau, which had receive prior warning, was ready. Thanks to its structural flexibility, it had available sufficient quantities of cylinders and pistons with a diameter of 63 instead of 64 millimeters and was thus able to offer an LM model with a displacement of 198cc – which was no less powerful than the original version and did not require a driver's license – more quickly than the competition.

In the second half of 1926 the number of employees at DKW's Zschopau factory was 1,600, daily production consisted of 100 motorcycles and 130 engines. 1926 also saw the start of roller bearing production, and construction of a three-wheel transport vehicles, which can be seen as the forerunner of the later Framo, was also begun.

1926 was also a fateful year for Rasmussen and his Zschopau factory for another reason: the well-known race driver Pätzold from Cologne had given an impressive performance on an English Scott motorcycle at the (already traditional) Marienberg race (on the triangular course Marienberg – Heinzebank – Wolkenstein). Riding the liquid-cooled, twin-cylinder 600cc machine, he had run away from the brand new 750cc BMWs. Rasmussen had become acquainted with the type in Denmark during the war. Rasmussen took possession of the motorcycle after the race – his managing director Blau personally drove it to the factory. Subsequent study confirmed that the DKW engine then under development was very probably justified, despite gloomy predictions. It was a 500cc engine, a twin-cylinder like the Scott, but it was initially air-cooled. Rasmussen and his team were convinced that the field of motorcycle two-stroke engines in no way had to remain limited to single-cylinder designs.

Apart from additional single-cylinder models with 200, 250 and 300cc engines in various performance and equipment stages (as well as frame variations), from 1927 there were also DKW twin-cylinder motorcycles with 500 and 600cc air- and later liquid-cooled engines. (Liquid cooling was adopted because, at that time, two-strokes everywhere, including in Zschopau, were made almost exclusively with deflector pistons, which had less then ideal thermal characteristics. As performance increased, air-cooling reached the limits of its effectiveness.) The twin-cylinder models initially had separate three-speed gearboxes and later linked units, and the air-cooled 500 produced 12hp, the liquid-cooled version 15hp and the likewise liquid-cooled 600 18hp – the latter two were also best suited for sidecar motorcycles.

One of the very few photos of the "Little Mountain Climber," showing it during an anniversary parade in Zschopau – the DKW auxiliary bicycle engine sits on a display mount. The horizontal, fan-cooled stationary engine can clearly be seen on the running board. It probably drove the rear wheels by means of a clutch and (two-speed?) transmission (for otherwise it would not have been able to manage the route between Zschopau and Chemnitz, where the author saw it himself on several occasions in those days). The boy in the sailor suit was Rasmussen's youngest son Arne.

DKW Twin-Cylinder Engines

With the twin-cylinder engine, however, Rasmussen now had the proper power plant for a small car he had long had in mind. At the end of 1919 in Zschopau (in the Kaisersaal – which, a little excessively, was for a short time called the "car body factory," even though it was mainly used to make the flywheel ignition systems for DKW engines), the company experimented with a small four-wheel vehicle on Rasmussen's personal initiative. Its load-bearing plywood body (no chassis frame) was relatively narrow, with the two seats arranged in tandem. Its small air-cooled single-cylinder engine was mounted on the left running board and powered the rear wheels by means of

The "Little Mountain Climber" – a tandem two-seater with load bearing body (built in the Kaisersaal subsidiary enterprise in Zschopau and powered by a 5hp stationary engine mounted on the left running board with chain drive to both rear wheels). Contrary to other accounts, the vehicle was an independent Zschopau experiment and definitely not an SB (Slaby & Beringer) car by Dr. Slaby of Berlin.

a chain drive (an arrangement later used by the Grade Wagen and the Hanomag "Kommißbrot").

As absurd as such a design might appear today, an experimental car of this type was used by the company for years. This first DKW automobile was probably never sold to the public, even though it was featured in DKW advertisements for a time with the optimistic title "The Little Mountain Climber," probably to gauge buyer interest.

Since 1919 Rasmussen had had contacts with the designer Dr. Slaby, son of the founder of Telefunken in Berlin. Immediately after the war he had constructed a small, primitive single-seat automobile powered by an electric motor – he did not even have the four bicycle-size rubber tires he needed when Rasmussen met him on the streets of Berlin one day. But the idea fascinated him, and impulsive as he was, he ordered 100 of the little cars from the company Slaby & Beringer (which Dr. Slaby had founded because of the lively interest shown in his design from other quarters).

Rasmussen displayed the electric car (along with his auxiliary bicycle engine and the DKW stationary engine) at the Leipzig Fair in 1919 – and concluded deals for almost 1,000 vehicles. This led to his entry into the Slaby & Beringer company and the purchase of larger quarters in Berlin. A Japanese importer was particularly interested and placed further orders. Unfortunately, however, inflation placed the small company in an increasingly

Dr. Slaby in his first self-built electric car, as Rasmussen first met him in Berlin in 1918 or 1919. Note the "ersatz tires," which were sold for use on bicycles in the early years after the war (with small compression springs between the hub and travelling rim) and the tiller steering.

A photo of an SB Car (Slaby & Beringer), a miniature electric car sold in 1919-21. Note the rear wheel brakes (there was no Ministry of Transport in those days!).

This photo shows a fifty-vehicle series of SB electric cars, ready for shipment to Japan. By this time Rasmussen was already part owner of the Slaby & Beringer Company of Berlin.

The two photos here show the SB single-seat car powered by the 142cc single-gear DKW engine, circa 1923-24. Its trellis frame was planked with varnished strips of ash. The suspension consisted of one cross leaf spring front and rear, which was later typical of DKW automobiles (from Spandau as well as Zwickau).

The P 15, the first DKW automobile from Spandau – with load-bearing plywood body covered with synthetic leather and a front-mounted 600cc twin-cylinder engine with dry clutch, three-speed transmission and rear-wheel drive.

perilous situation, and even the adoption of a single-seater powered by a DKW engine instead of the electric motor could not prevent the company from going bankrupt in 1924. It was taken over by Rasmussen, who later moved the operation to Spandau, into the (initially only rented) factory rooms of the Deutschen Industriewerke AG and installed Dr. Slaby as technical director of what was now his branch works in Spandau.

Under Dr. Slaby the only series production activity was the making of *Elektro-Droschken* (electric cabs), a joint production by DKW, AEG and AFA (batteries). Rasmussen also continued experimenting with miniature cars and, in 1924 at the Berlin Automobile Exhibition, unveiled a small car powered by a rear-mounted DKW engine with belt drive. It did not go into production, however.

Not until twin-cylinder engines with greater power became available from Zschopau (in 1927) were the conditions right for a "proper" automobile as envisaged by Rasmussen. The first DKW automobile, an open two-seater (Roadster), was unveiled in 1927-28, first at the Berlin Automobile Exhibition. Later the car also had two "auxiliary seats" in the rear. It had a load-bearing plywood

Plant director Dr. Slaby (right) demonstrated the first four-seat sedan made in Spandau to Rasmussen (center of photo) on the occasion of his fiftieth birthday (in 1928). On the far left (in festive cutaway) is Schüttoff, sent by the Chemnitz motorcycle industry to wish Rasmussen well on his birthday. His Schüttoff factory also used DKW engines and was later taken over by Rasmussen (after the production of motorcycles ended, the Schüttoff factory on Rößler-Straße in Chemnitz became the Auto Union-Elektrowerk).

body covered in imitation leather with wooden ribs, the 600cc twin-cylinder engine mounted longitudinally in the front. The liquid-cooled engine had a dry clutch and three-speed transmission plus a Cardan shaft and differential at the rear wheels. It gave rise to the various three- and four-seat models from Zschopau, first with twin-cylinder engines then with four-cylinder two-stroke engines in a V arrangement from Zschopau, the wide variety of three- and four-seat models up to the "Schwebeklasse" (1934) and various versions of the "Sonderklasse" (1930 and 1937). All were made in Spandau.

Above: Rickenbacker eight-cylinder in-line engine, produced in the Scharfenstein factory.

Below: The Zwickau (or Dresden) model, a large automobile built in small numbers in the Audi factory in Zwickau (after the six- and eight-cylinder engines obtained from America could not be sold to other car makers).

Automobile Engines from the USA

During a study trip to the USA in 1927, Rasmussen had purchased all of the production facilities for six- and eight-cylinder engines of the defunct Rickenbacker Automobile Factory and had them moved to the recently acquired branch facility in Scharfenstein (other American machine tools were used to augment the machinery in the Zschopau factory). The new facility was to produce engines and supply them (as integrated engines that were rational to produce in large numbers at reasonable prices, as the company had already done with DKW two-stroke engines) to automobile makers who lacked the facilities to produce their own engines. This plan failed, however, not least because of the serious economic crisis then beginning. Rasmussen therefore accepted an offer from the State Bank of Saxony and took over the Audi works in Zwickau, which had fallen into financial difficulties. Prototypes of new Audi models (Dresden and Zwickau types) were then made there using the six- and eight-cylinder engines from America, which from 1929 were offered at relatively reasonable prices. But this was no more successful – and so Rasmussen found himself forced to use other production to utilize the Zwickau factory to capacity. The small Audi 5/30 – nothing more than a Spandau car, normally powered by the DKW four-cylinder two-stroke engine, but with a Peugeot 1100 four-stroke, four-cylinder engine installed – in 1931 represented another attempt. This automobile also failed to achieve success.

The three Rasmussen sons: Hans (later head of the Framo factory in Hainichen), Ove (later head of the Zöblitz Metal Works, after the war owner of the Rasmussen GmbH in Maintal near Frankfurt) and Arne (later head of the experimental department in the Framo factory and after the war active in the experimental section at Fichtel & Sachs in Schweinfurt); here they are seen with the first DKW front wheel drive car, with which Ove entered the Eib Lake race in 1931 and despite the still-experimental power plant (with no reverse gear) was able to demonstrate the superiority of front wheel drive.

DKW Front-Wheel-Drive Car

In 1930 in Zwickau, development began of a small car that would – Rasmussen assumed – better suit the steadily deteriorating economic situation. The original plan called for it to be equipped with a 350cc DKW two-stroke and have front wheel drive, however the first prototypes (early 1931) had the (transversely-mounted) 500cc twin-cylinder motorcycle engine. When Rasmussen's son Ove entered it in its first race on Lake Eib, it had a motorcycle gearbox and therefore had no reverse gear. The cleverly designed, low-slung two-seater immediately demonstrated its potential, and the interest generated by the car with its compact drive unit (consisting of the liquid-cooled twin-cylinder engine with Dynastart system, three-speed transmission with reverse gear and differential) at the Berlin Automobile Exhibition in 1931 led Rasmussen to anticipate good sales. An unusually low price was a particular incentive to buy. It was anticipated that production in the Zwickau plant would begin quickly.

The start of series production was delayed, however, and high startup and materials costs exacerbated the Zschopau company's financial situation, which after previous good years had become strained.

In 1927 DKW produced and sold 27,000 motorcycles. This figure rose to 43,000 in 1928 and to 60,000 in 1929 (a quite astonishing development), but beginning in 1930 motorcycle sales figures began dropping rapidly due to the

The DKW front wheel drive car on display at the Berlin Automobile Exhibition for the first time in 1931.

Dr. Hahn (above with hat next to the tree trunk) demonstrated the DKW front wheel drive car to DKW dealers at dealer conferences all over Germany.

economic crisis: still 36,000 in 1930, but then to 12,500 in 1931 and 11,000 in 1932.

Just as the motorcycle business grew in leaps and bounds until 1929, DKW's parent plant in Zschopau grew into a group of companies. The goal was for Rasmussen-owned companies to provide as many of the necessary vendor parts and intermediate materials as possible. In 1920 the former "Kaisersaal" in Zschopau became the Rota factory that produced flywheel ignition systems. Then some ten years later, like the Dyna motorcycle ignition and headlight systems, production was moved to the DKW factory in Chemnitz (Rößlerstrasse, former site of the Schüttoff motorcycle factory, purchased by Rasmussen in 1928). In 1922 Rasmussen founded the Zöblitz Metal Works, which delivered turned and formed parts, armatures and motorcycle brake hubs to Zschopau. In 1923 Rasmussen, together with his assistants Blau and Figura, established the Framo Works (initially in Frankenberg, later in Hainichen). Three- and later four-wheel delivery vehicles powered by DKW engines were built there, along with saddles and pillion seats, carburetors and armatures. The Scharfenstein branch plant, which had been acquired from the former Moll Auto Company, a small manufacturer in Chemnitz in 1925, produced sheet metal components, stamped and pressed parts (such as tanks, fenders, license plates and frame components). In 1927-28 it also began making household and commercial refrigerators plus (temporarily) the previously mentioned six- and eight-cylinder engines for Audi. Light metal, malleable iron, grey cast iron and drop forged parts came from the group's own foundries in Annaberg, Erla and Wittigsthal. Rasmussen had previously gained a foothold in Berlin (apart from the previously mentioned branch plant in Spandau) by investing in the Prometheus gear factory.

Assembling (now on an assembly line) the successful LM 200 in the DKW factory's newly built big assembly hall in 1926-27.

Facing page:
Top: Assembly of motorcycles in the DKW factory in Zschopau (in the foreground the Reichsfahrt model, left the new ZL model still without drive unit). *Bottom*: Assembly of the ZM model (with two-speed kick-start engine) in the DKW plant in Zschopau in 1924.

Below: Inflation currency issued by the DKW company in 1923.
Right: Refrigerator made in the DKW factory in Scharfenstein.

The first milestone in autumn 1921 (still small-scale): the 10,000th DKW engine, behind it operations manager Höppner.

Subsequent milestones were more lavishly celebrated with the participation of the entire workforce, as evidenced by these consumption vouchers issued to mark the completion of the 20,000th (1922) and 50,000th (1924) DKW engines.

DKW – The World's Largest Maker of Motorcycles

The Rasmussen group of companies reached its apex in 1929. Since 1928 DKW had been the largest manufacturer of motorcycles in the world, but despite its marketability the widely diversified overall program of the Zschopau engine works was not spared the economic crisis overtaking Germany. When, in 1931, quantities of DKW motorcycles began piling up in the factory courtyard of the Zschopau works and the various outsourcing sites in the Erz Mountains, series startup of the front wheel drive car was delayed, and the dealer exchange system with its extensions of credit from the State Bank of Saxony becoming a serious burden, the Rasmussen group of companies found themselves in a precarious financial situation. Then a difference in opinion over business policies caused the relationship between Rasmussen and Dr. Hahn, his closest colleague, to become clouded. The State Bank of Saxony, however, delegated Dr. Richard Bruhn as its representative from the board of directors to the management of the Zschopau engine works.

When, after the startup difficulties were overcome and production of the new DKW front wheel drive car, of which a four-seat version was already in preparation, began, the car already had the 600cc engine producing 18hp. This engine also powered the various Reichsklasse models made until the Second World War, while the Meisterklasse models built in parallel from 1933 had the 700cc twin-cylinder engine which produced 20hp. Apart from detail improvements to the engines and various changes to the chassis (unlike the twin- and four-cylinder rear wheel drive cars made in Spandau, at that time the DKW front wheel drive cars had chassis frames on which were mounted the synthetic-leather-covered plywood bodies predominantly used or the sheet steel bodies of the convertible and luxury models) the front wheel drive cars were built essentially unchanged until the early years of the war (from 1932 in the Auto Union program).

The shut-down textile factory near Zschopau in the Dischau Valley, acquired by Rasmussen in 1907.

The first extensions to the DKW factory. Among the projects worked on there was development of the steam-powered car.

Overall view of the DKW factory, looking towards the seven story back side of the complex. The administration offices were located on the upper floor.

Hermann Weber, born in Chemnitz on 11 March 1896, died Kazan, Russia on 23 February 1948, senior engineer and chief designer of the DKW factory in Zschopau. His design bureaus were not only responsible for the development of all DKW motorcycles (from the Reichsfahrt Model to the NZ 500) and all DKW racing machines, but also all stationary engines and all twin- and four-cylinder automobile engines made by DKW.

The administration building at the top of the complex, a more modest view from the road to Marienberg.

View of the narrow factory courtyard, which was closed off at the front by an adjoining building which, among other things, housed the experimental department. Still present between the two new tall buildings is the old building from the beginning days of the DKW factory.

The DKW complex in its ultimate state, as it appeared at the top of the company's letter paper. The caption reads "The biggest motorcycle factory in the world."

A photo of the actual complex in the narrow valley of the Dischau River, which was channeled below the factory and flowed into the Zschopau. The low-rise building in the foreground was home to the DKW racing department, the empire of August Prüssing and his men.

In addition to his three sons Hans, Ove and Arne, Jörgen Skafte Rasmussen also had a daughter – Lise. Like her brothers, she felt a close connection to the DKW life's work of her father.

End of the workday at the DKW factory in Zschopau. At that time about 6,000 men were employed there and in the branch plants in the Erz Mountains.

While the rear wheel drive DKW cars were made in Spandau until the war and the engines for them in Zschopau, construction of the chassis and assembly of the front wheel drive cars (in significantly greater numbers, for the DKW cars in the Reichs- and Meisterklasse stood in second place in the German Reich's registration statistics in the last years before the war) took place in the Audi plant in Zwickau. Complete engine assemblies were delivered from Zschopau – by outside carriers, because, to the end, the Zschopau factory did not have its own rail connection – while the Spandau factory daily sent production plywood bodies (and special bodies made by outside body makers) to Zwickau (by state railway).

With the front wheel drive car (whose 700cc versions had the freewheel feature that had proved itself in the rear wheel drive Spandau models), DKW finally had a "second leg." And if fifty years later almost 70% of all newly registered passenger vehicles in the Federal Republic are front wheel drive cars and front wheel drive has successfully conquered the world market up to the medium class, it should not be forgotten that it was Rasmussen's initiative that first brought this logical propulsion system to use in mass production.

This initiative made 1932 a decisive year – decisive for DKW engines and, as it would later turn out, for the development of the fast running two-stroke engine worldwide.

The DKW Loop Scavenging System

As stated earlier, with increasing engine power per liter, towards the end of the 1920s it was becoming increasingly clear that the thermal problems associated with the standard single-piston two-stroke engine with its transverse scavenging caused by the deflector piston limited its potential performance improvements – and it was inferior to the four-stroke, especially because of its fuel consumption. In the long run not even the mechanical simplicity of the two-stroke ("The Engine with Just Three Moving Parts") could not compensate for these disadvantages.

It is true that Rasmussen had opposed any "complication" of his engines even in Ruppe's time, and the opposed auxiliary piston to raise conveyed volume and with its rpm and power proposed by Ruppe (which he later successfully realized in his Bekamo engines) therefore seemed to him to involve too much effort. But as he repeatedly encountered the advantages of the twin-piston two-stroke (like those made for years by the Puch factories in Austria, in particular) he decided to bring the well-known designer Arnold Zoller into his circle of employees. Zoller had made a name for himself both through his rotary superchargers and his work with twin-piston two-stroke engines, and by 1931 (after DKW twin-piston racing engines had immediately demonstrated their superiority) the first prototypes of the coming production models with Zoller-type air-cooled, twin-piston two-strokes were running. Their introduction into series production was imminent – both in the motorcycle and automobile sectors.

Then Rasmussen stumbled across the doctoral dissertation by engineer Herbert Venediger of Wurzburg about the possibilities of improving the economy of fast-running two-stroke engines. Venediger's documentation also included examinations of the "loop scavenging" system patented by Dr.-Ing. Adolf Schnürle, an employee of the Klöckner-Humboldt-Deutz Company. This enabled the use of a piston with a flat bottom, like those used by a standard four-stroke engine, eliminating the deflector piston with all its disadvantages, without the complication of the earlier single-piston engine (as represented by the twin-piston design). Again it was Rasmussen himself who recognized the possible solution to the development-limiting two-stroke problems and who immediately hired Dr.-Ing. Venediger and brought him to Zschopau to head

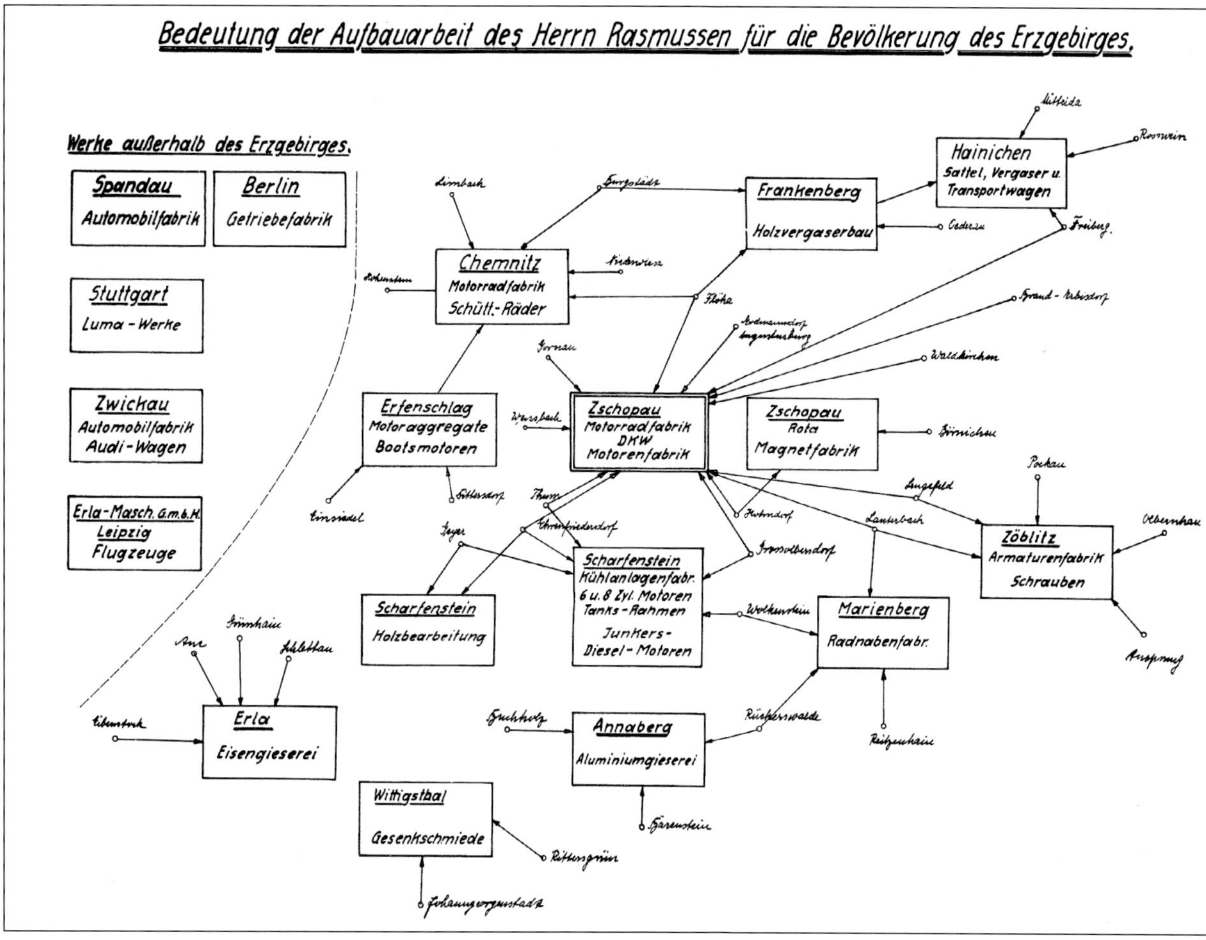

This chart shows the drainage area of the central Erz Mountains with the many towns from which workers came daily to Rasmussen's factory.

the development and experimental department. And in turn, it took an unbelievably short time for Dr. Venediger and the Zschopau engine designers led by Hermann Weber to convert the entire DKW engine program to loop scavenging and flat pistons. Zoller's twin-piston design (which Zschopau abandoned) was, however, reserved for the DKW racing engines.

Rasmussen had no more "invented" loop scavenging than the two-stroke engine, or front wheel drive and freewheel. But he had "found" them at the right time thanks to his intuitive sense and his willingness to take risks. The correctness of his decision with respect to the acceptance of loop scavenging was proved not only by the subsequent development of DKW engines and their rising sales compared to their four-stroke competition in later years after the economic crisis was passed in the early Thirties: wherever two-stroke engines were built in the world, especially for use in motorcycles, their makers tried to get away from deflector pistons and, whenever possible, adopt flat pistons. This was provided that they did not go over to the twin-piston design, for the Schnürle license acquired by Rasmussen was so comprehensive that it was almost impossible to build a flat-piston two-stroke whose scavenging process did not infringe on the Schnürle/DKW patents. The result was years of patent litigation (to which Dr. Venediger, as the most prominent expert on the subject, had to devote much of his time). When the patents expired after the Second World War, there were no manufacturers of two-stroke motorcycles anywhere in world that did not build their motorcycles with flat pistons and loop scavenging – in some cases slightly modified.

That DKW and the Rasmussen group of companies, like the German economy as a whole, found themselves in a difficult (though never really dangerous) financial situation during the period of this new technical success has already been said. Six million unemployed were only

Right: Dr.-Ing. Adolf Schnürle, whose loop-scavenge patent acquired under license from Auto Union formed the basis for further development of the DKW two-stroke engine and later, after the patent expired, influenced two-stroke development the world over.

Far right: Dr.Ing. Herbert Venediger, who in 1932 was hired by Rasmussen and brought to Zschopau as head of research and development. In a very short time, in cooperation with Hermann Weber, he converted the entire DKW two-stroke program (with the exception of the four-cylinder engine) to loop scavenging. His special knowledge was decisive in winning the patent lawsuits filed by competitors with respect to the reverse scavenging technology.

one sign of a situation that was becoming more dangerous from day to day, especially in the German motor vehicle industry, as the following figures illustrate:

The entire German motor vehicle industry (not counting supplier companies) employed:

1928	83,751 workers
1929	80,037 workers
1932	34.392 workers

Production of automobiles:

1928	108,029
1929	96,161
1932	43,430

Motorcycle production showed a similar trend:

1928	160,782
1929	195,086
1932	36,272

Materials consumption by the motor vehicle industry was:

1928	624 million
1932	140.3 million

The situation of the motor vehicle industry in Saxony at that time was the same as that of the motor vehicle industry in Germany (and similarly in all of German industry). At the urging of the State Bank of Saxony, which was strongly involved in the industry there, Rasmussen had taken over Audi in 1928, but now another Saxon automobile maker, namely the Horch works in Zwickau, was in such distress that the end was ultimately just a matter of time. The large luxury cars built there had been especially hard hit by the crisis. But the State Bank of Saxony, buffeted by a large number of bankruptcies in the Saxon economic zone, was convinced that it could not cope with a collapse by Horch. And if that happened, the Rasmussen group of companies – along with many other companies in Saxony – would inevitably be drawn into the maelstrom that would follow, especially the DKW factory.

Auto-Union – "A Union Born of Necessity"

The state bank therefore approached Rasmussen with the suggestion that the HORCH factory be liquidated and that Dr. Bruhn be involved. But this seemed an impossible solution given the thousands of work places that would be lost and the already difficult internal political situation. Together with Dr. Bruhn, Rasmussen therefore developed the plan for a joint venture, which was to include the:

Zschopauer Motorenwerke AG,
AUDI-Werke AG, Zwickau,
HORCH-Werke AG, Zwickau.

To this consortium of companies, which, with the approval of the state bank, was named Auto Union AG on 29 June 1932, was added by purchase and lease the automobile division of the Wanderer-Werke AG of Chemnitz, so that all of the automobile factories in the Free State of Saxony would be combined in the new company. Rasmussen's Zschopauer Motorenwerke was the incorporating company (and the actual backbone of this union born of necessity, which could not have survived without the parts of the Rasmussen group that were brought in). After the merger, its headquarters were moved from Zschopau to Chemnitz.

When Auto Union was founded, its board of directors consisted of:

Dr. Richard Bruhn for the commercial and fiscal field, Ing. Jörgen Skafte Rasmussen for the technical division, Klaus Detlof von Oertzen (previously on the board of directors of the Wanderer-Werke) as sales director, in particular the four-stroke program.

Deputy members of the board were:

Dr. Carl Hahn for sales of the two-stroke program, Ing. William Werner (to date on the board of directors of the HORCH-Werke.

The establishment of the Auto Union was based on a time-based plan that envisaged the reprivatization of the individual plants as soon as the economic situation improved.

Conditions underwent a fundamental change, however, when the new government took over on 30 January 1933. For the motor vehicle industry – as for the German economy as a whole – it was positive; not so for Rasmussen.

The officers of the state bank involved in the foundation of Auto Union were relieved of their posts and Rasmussen was unable to force his claims for reprivatization – the reinvigorated state bank, under new management, and the political changes prevented that. But even in his position as technical member of the board of directors he had no impact. In part due to political influences (although Rasmussen was no opponent of the new regime) there were growing differences of opinion among the board members, which ultimately resulted in Rasmussen being placed on leave by the supervisory board in 1934. He never returned to Auto Union. Instead, on 31 December 1934 his service contract was terminated without explanation or compliance with terms.

DKW without Rasmussen

A subsequent lawsuit would not be heard by a proper court. In 1938 a trial in a court of arbitration at least ended "on orders from the top" with a settlement, on the basis of which Rasmussen received partial compensation but no satisfaction. Instead, that same year on his sixtieth birthday he received an honorary doctorate of engineering from the Dresden Technical College.

Rasmussen, together with his three sons, busied himself until almost the end of the Second World War with the family's remaining companies that had not been absorbed by Auto Union, especially the Framo-Werken in Hainichen and the Metallwerk Zöblitz. He had moved to Sacrow near Berlin in 1938, where together with Ing. Petersen he worked on new projects (under Hermann Weber, Petersen had played a large part in the development of DKW racing motorcycles and later at Framo participated in the development of a two-stroke, twin-piston engine for a delivery van). Rasmussen was in Flensburg when the war ended. In 1948 he returned to his Danish homeland, where he was once again active with his youngest son Arne – for the Danish company DISA – in preparation for the planned (but never realized) production of motorcycles.

Prototype of the Danish DISA motorcycle developed in Rasmussen's design bureau in Copenhagen (did not go into production).

Jörgen Skafte Rasmussen died in Copenhagen on 12 August 1964. He had remained a Danish citizen; but his entire life's work had been dedicated to the building of a multilayered German industrial group, with the Zschopauer Motorenwerken and the DKW automobiles and motorcycles it produced at its core, which became the basis and in large part the financial backbone of Auto Union (even though before the war the DKW division was regarded in-house as the "Erz Mountain Cinderella" – but without which there would have been no postwar Auto Union in West Germany!).

But the creation of this valuable foundation was not the only service done by Rasmussen that would reach into the future: he and his enthusiastic core of colleagues had not only made DKW the largest producer of motorcycles in the world from 1928 until the Second World War – in doing so they also created the conditions which allowed the two-stroke engine – often denigrated as "not fully adequate" – into a power plant that is an integral part of modern technology, and not just in the field of motorcycles.

Jörgen Skafte Rasmussen at eighty years of age – still full of ideas and interested in technical events of the day.

From the DKW Auxiliary Bicycle Engine to the Largest Motorcycle Factory in the World

The production of motorcycles in Zschopau can be roughly divided into three eras. The first, beginning in 1921 with the bicycle auxiliary engine, extended over the scooter-like experiments Golem and Lomos to the first light powered bicycle, the Reichsfahrt Model (which could not deny its origins from the "auxiliary engine" but which nevertheless became a great sales success). Then came the first "true" motorcycles, with single-cylinder engines and two-speed gearboxes in the crankcase area or with separate three-speed gearboxes, with or without flywheel fan cooling, plus twin-cylinder models, air- and liquid-cooled, and with these also the first (also built as single-cylinder models) true three-speed block engines. This era saw the switch from belt to chain drive, from high-pressure to balloon tires, from tubular to pressed steel profile frames and from the pocket to the saddle tank. All of the engines had mixture lubrication (with various mixture ratios depending on the design), very soon had mufflers, and some were delivered with flywheel magneto ignition, some with battery/coil ignition and DKW DC generators – and all of the engines of this era had cross-flow scavenging and deflector pistons. On the last single-cylinder model (Block 350) the intake was not controlled by the underside of the piston, as on all previous (and subsequent) engines, but instead by a reed valve.

The second era began with the introduction of loop scavenging in 1932. The first model with this feature was the Block 350, the others – with 100 (RT), 200 (KS and SB) and 250, 350 and 500cc (SB) – followed immediately afterwards. In 1935-36 the pressed steel profile frames (except for that used in the RT models) were lengthened and delivered with longer, more shapely tanks. For several years there were the SB 200 A and 500 A with electric starter (DKW Dynastart). Foot shifting was not yet a standard feature, but was probably retrofitted to several models (with very long, shifting travels).

The third and last Zschopau era was the NZ series (created under the influence of Richard Küchen). It began with the twin-cylinder NZ 500, which entered production just before the start of the war, and was supplemented by the newly conceived RT 125, which became a huge success. All of the machines of this era had chain primary drive, the NZ models four-speed foot shifting coupled with the tank-mounted hand shifter, and the NZ 500 was the first DKW production machine (apart from the Lomos) with rear wheel suspension. The most important technical details accompany the following photos from the years 1921 – 1945.

Production of motorized two-wheelers began in the DKW factory in Zschopau in 1921 with the 118cc (50x60 bore/stroke) 1hp auxiliary bicycle engine. The engine, with a horizontal, airstream-cooled cylinder, initially came with a floatless carburetor, which was later replaced by a float carburetor. It had a flywheel magneto ignition with external breaker and a 1:3 reduction in the crankcase (resulting in a 1:10 mixture lubrication). The engine was sold both to dealers and private customers for mounting over the rear wheel, however very soon it was limited to special reinforced frames with front-wheel suspension. No clutch, belt drive to pulley on the rear wheel.

The Golem, a motorized two-wheeler with backrest seat, first appeared in 1921, similar to a motor scooter with a comfortable seat, sprung front fork and small wheels. It, too, had the bicycle engine, but with a cone type clutch and chain drive to the rear wheel.

It was probably the unsatisfactory handling characteristics of the Golem (which people still remember) that led to the development of the Lomos the following year. The larger 142cc (55x60 bore/stroke), 1.5hp engine with fan cooling was mounted directly beneath the backrest seat (with fuel tank in the back rest). The (larger) rear wheel was belt-driven with a manually adjustable starting clutch ("Lomos clutch"). The rear wheel was also sprung (swing arm with encapsulated compression springs). There were three versions of the frame, with the upswept footboards serving as mudguards: a double cradle frame, welded plate box frame and – amazingly – a cast Elektron alloy frame.

DKW Reichsfahrt Model with a 142cc, 1.5hp engine mounted in the special chassis' frame triangle. It was available with the Lomos clutch (1922-23).

The "Lomos clutch" consisted of two pulley halves that were adjustable towards each other. They could be moved far enough apart so that, when the engine was running, the belt could rest on the pulley rotating on the crankshaft with no power being transmitted to the rear wheel. If the two pulley halves were then moved closer together by operating a lever or a helix thread section (visible in the photo), the belt was picked up, initially with slippage – it was engaged. Supposedly this clutch with its variable pulley diameter also served as a "torque converter" – but this function was of course problematic, because there was no synchronously adjustable thrust plate. Nevertheless, the Lomos clutch was the forerunner of later belt drives (such as that found in the DKW Hobby-Roller in the postwar period, for example). There was a ratchet in the front of the dome-shaped housing mechanism for insertion of a starter crank!

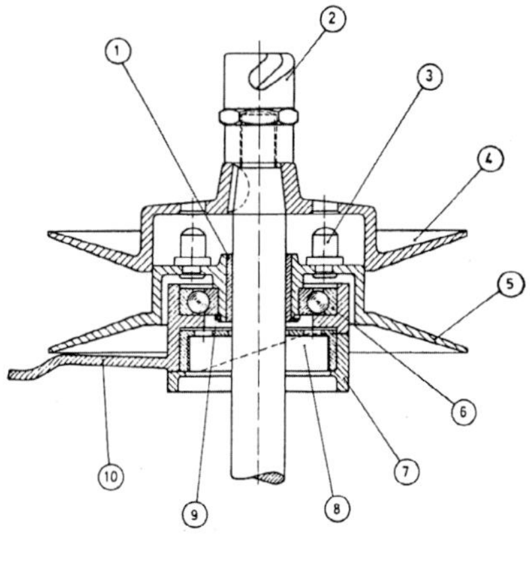

1 = Lagerbuchse, 2 = Anwerfkurbel-Ratsche, 3 = Mitnehmerbolzen, 4 = feste Riemenscheibenhälfte, 5 = axial verschiebbare Riemenscheibenhälfte, 6 = Druckstück, 7 = Lagerflansch, 8 = Verschiebestück, 9 = Druckleger, 10 = Betätigungshebel.

Far left: The single-speed engine with cooling fan as used in the Reichsfahrt Model also powered the DKW ZL light motorcycle, albeit installed vertically and delivered with the Lomos clutch (the photo shows an original machine prior to restoration – note the clutch lever control rods).

Left: Cutaway drawing of the Lomos clutch: 1. Bearing bushing, 2. Starter crank ratchet, 3. Driving pins, 4. Fixed pulley half, 5. Axially adjustable pulley half, 6. Thrust piece, 7. Bearing flange, 8. Sliding section, 9. Pressure switch, 10. Operating lever.

The DKW Model ZM was also built in 1924-25. The newly designed 175cc engine (59x64mm bore/stroke) producing 2.5hp at 3,000rpm was mounted in the tubular frame of the ZL. The vertical cylinder was cooled by the already familiar flywheel fan. A manually operated two-speed gearbox was housed in the crankcase area (resulting in a 1:10 mixture), and on the main shaft there was a cork disk clutch. This engine also had a kick tarter with external ratchet mechanism Note the long running boards.

The "Steel Model" (SM) was built in parallel with the ZM in 1924-25 and the forward frame element also served as the exhaust pipe. The power plant was similar to that of the ZM model. The latter's metal running boards were, however, replaced by aluminum footboards that also served as footrests for the passenger.

The Model E 206 appeared in 1926-26 with the two-speed engine having a bore and stroke of 64mm (206cc). It was housed in a new steel tube frame with significantly improved shape and handling characteristics. A kickstarter was available as an option. Also known as the LM, this model also gave rise to the ...

... Model E 200 (LM 200), which became DKW's next big sales success. Its engine initially produced 4hp at 3,500rpm, later 4.5hp at 4,000rpm. It was largely similar to the LM 206 – except for having a bore reduced by 1mm, which allowed the machine to qualify for a tax break. The change was inspired by a new law that took on 1 April 1928 and eliminated the tax on all motorcycles up to 200cc. And as Zschopau had learned of this important rule change in time, it was able to ready sufficient quantities of cylinders and pistons for the 63mm version. DKW was thus the only motorcycle company in a position to sell new machines on the day the new fiscal valuation took effect.

In 1927 DKW introduced to the market the first model (Z 500) powered by the 497cc air-cooled twin-cylinder engine (68x68 bore/stroke) producing 12hp at 4,000rpm and with a separate three-speed gearbox. The machine was not in production long, however, for despite the fender shield that served as a wind guide plate, the designers in Zschopau were unable to get a grip on the thermal difficulties (which extra manual lubrication did nothing to correct). As a result, the air-cooled version was replaced that same year by ...

... a liquid-cooled version with an almost identical tubular frame (which was sufficiently long). It also had a separate gearbox and two clumsy balcony radiators mounted on the forward frame. The company claimed a power output of 15hp at 4,000rpm.

Two more new models appeared in 1928-29 – E 250 and E 300 – which were offered as the Sport 250 and the Sport 300. Both had vertical, single-cylinder engines with displacements of 245cc (68x68mm) and 300cc (74x68mm) producing 5 and 8hp at 3,500rpm. The engines were equipped with the E-carburetor used for years by DKW and made by Framo. This unit, a needle valve carburetor with float chamber arranged concentrically to the mixture chamber, had two Bowden operating cables: one for the throttle valve, the other to change the needle valve position. Both models had tubular frames, three-speed gearboxes with kickstarter and chain-chain power transmission to the rear wheel.

Instead of a steel tube frame, the DKW ZE 200 models (198cc with 4hp and ZE Luxus also with 186cc but an output of 4.5hp, both at 3,000rpm) had a frame, including front fork, which was made entirely of sheet steel, a design that would dominate DKW motorcycles until 1936. The power plant was the fan-cooled two-speed of the earlier models but with increased power, and the rear wheel was driven by a belt (chain drive on more powerful models). The E 200 also saw the introduction of the saddle fuel tank. Contrary to common practice, the 200s wee painted fire-red, which resulted in the model being nicknamed the "Blood Blister."

While the previous ZE models had clearly been conceived with the economic situation and the reduced buying power in Germany in mind, this trend was all the more evident in the next two models offered in 1930 and 1931: the ZIS and the Volksrad. Both had almost the same chassis and engine as the E 200, but were "scaled down" in the details and lacked fan cooling (the directly-operated belt-pulley block brakes on the rear wheel show what the designers had been forced to eliminate). But while the ZIS model still had the two-speed gearbox with clutch and kickstarter, the buyer of a Volksrad had to get by without a kickstarter and be satisfied with a single gear.

Response to the cheap versions was obviously poor, for in 1931 two new three-speed models appeared from Zschopau. The Luxus Spezial 200 was unveiled at the end of 1930. It had a displacement of 192cc and produced 4.5hp at 3,500rpm, was equipped with a Framo E carburetor and flywheel ignition without ventilator. It also had a separate three-speed gearbox with kickstarter, chain drive to the rear wheel and armature handlebars.

The Luxus 300 model differed from the smaller motorcycle mainly in its power plant. The engine was of similar design but had a displacement of 292cc and produced 8hp at 4,000rpm.

By 1931 the company had obviously decided to emphasize technical quality instead of price in appealing to customers, for this year saw the arrival of the visually appealing Block model motorcycles. The smallest was the Block 200 with side-mounted carburetor on the forward-sloping cylinder, with battery-coil ignition, gearwheel primary drive, three-speed gearbox and kickstarter in a light metal block – all in the pressed steel chassis with sheet steel armature handlebars.

While the Block 200's engine produced 6.5hp at 4,000rpm, despite its similar design the power plant of the Block 300 (which also arrived on the market in 1931) delivered 8.5hp at 3,500rpm. Because of the greater cylinder width the carburetor was placed on a gooseneck behind the cylinder.

The Block 350, which was outwardly almost identical to the 300, also appeared in 1931, but its 342cc engine (76x76 bore/stroke) delivered 11hp. The position of the carburetor was unusual: it was located on the (rather large) crossover cover. And beneath it sat the secret to this motorcycle: the intake was not controlled by the bottom edge of the piston, instead a reed valve arrangement that was responsible for this powerful engine's excellent draft. Incidentally the 300 and 350 Block machines had ball and socket shifting.

In 1931 DKW also restored twin-cylinder machines to its program and likewise offered block engines with three-speed gearboxes and gearwheel primary drive: the 14hp 500cc air-cooled version (Luxus Sport 500) which, while it had a flywheel ignition on the right side, also had a DC generator on the left side of the engine. The 1931 twin-cylinder models also had ball and socket shifting.

In 1931 DKW added two single-cylinder motorcycles (still with deflector piston engines) to its program alongside the big single- and twin-cylinder machines: the 125- and 175cc models were light, reasonably-priced, steel tube frame machines with striking optics. Thekm 125 (50x60mm bore/stroke) delivered 3hp and had the old two-speed gearbox concept (which is why, like the larger version, it had to use the 1:12 mixture). But it had no kickstarter and had to be push-started. Its larger sister (shown in the photo) produced 4hp from its 174.8cc engine (59x64mm hub/stroke).

The TM 200 model (here an example painstakingly restored by Ing. Michael Heise) was built in small numbers in 1932. It was the last DKW production motorcycle with the gearbox separate from the engine, but the first with battery ignition (Luma) and twin-port exhaust system.

But the DKW fan could also once again have liquid cooling (standard on DKW racing motorcycles): the Sport 500 model's 500cc twin produced 18hp. The two radiators of the original model were replaced by a much more elegant combined "balcony" radiator – and the three-speed gearbox sat in a two-dimensional tube frame.

For those not satisfied with the 18hp of the 500, the 600cc (74x68mm bore/stroke) Super Sport 600, seen here, was also available. Its engine delivered 20hp.

And for those who preferred a motorcycle-sidecar combination (very many at that time), DKW dealers offered just such a combination using the 600cc DKW, which was best suited to this role.

After this model (RT 2½ PS), all subsequent DKW motorcycles were built with loop scavenging, the RT in several development stages, but all with flywheel magneto ignition, three-speed gearbox and tubular frame, 50mm bore and stroke, 98cc displacement. (the 2½ PS version could be recognized by the shift lever on the gearbox housing and coil springs in the front fork). Year of manufacture 1934.

The RT 3 PS (RT 100) was introduced in 1937 with a more efficient, but basically unchanged, engine and gearbox. The front fork now had Neimann rubber shock absorbers, hand shift lever recessed on the tank.

Close-up photo: the RT 3 PS' engine-gearbox block. The kickstarter did not fold, and the decompression valve in the cylinder head was only available on the police and competition model.

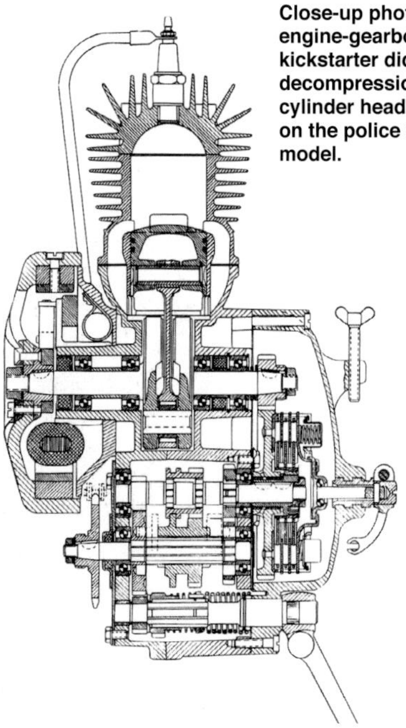

Cutaway drawing of the RT 3 PS' engine block.

KM 200 – year of manufacture 1934, 63x64mm bore/stroke, 198cc, 6hp at 3,500rpm. Flywheel magneto ignition, tubular dry battery for parking light. Pressed steel frame, single-port cylinder.

KM 200 – year of manufacture 1934, 7hp double-port engine with battery/coil ignition. Hand-shifted three-speed gearbox, pressed steel frame, short tank.

KM 200 – year of manufacture 1935, 7hp double-port engine with three-speed gearbox, but with lengthened pressed steel frame and longer tank (like SB).

Engine-gearbox block of the 1937 KS 200 7hp. Unlike the SB models, the KS 200's crankshaft had no drive shock absorber, therefore there was no cap for the shock absorber at the front of the casing cover on the left side. The kickstarter was not foldable.

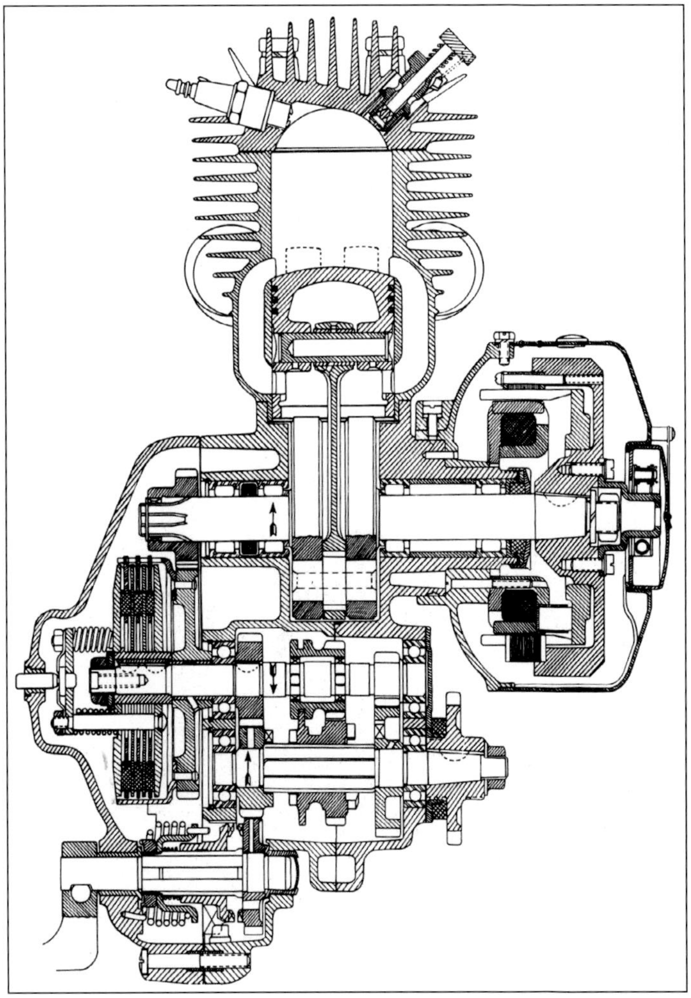

Cutaway drawing of the KS 200's power plant. Unlike the SB 200 (60x68mm bore/stroke), all KM and KS models had a bore of 63mm and a stroke of 64mm = 198cc. The KM 200 had flywheel magneto ignition until the change was made to battery ignition.

SB 200 – year of manufacture 1934, 7hp engine (60x68mm bore/stroke, 192cc), still with short pressed steel frame with short tank.

SB 200 – year of manufacture 1934, from the drive side. Shock absorber cap on the front of the drive case, beneath which were located the gear wheel primary drive (with drive shock absorber) and the multi-plate clutch. Folding kickstarter. The ignition coil, as on all models of the KS/SB series, is in the "coil box" on the battery mount – together with the ignition/light switch and the DC generator's regulator/switch combination (left side).

Engine-gearbox block of the SB 250, year of manufacture 1933 (68x68mm bore/stroke, 247cc, 9hp at 3,500rpm). Combined foot/hand shifting. Ignition setting window on the generator cap.

SB 350 – year of manufacture 1934. Overall design similar to that of the SB 200/250, but 76x76mm bore/stroke, 342cc, 11hp at 3,500rpm. Short pressed steel frame and tank.

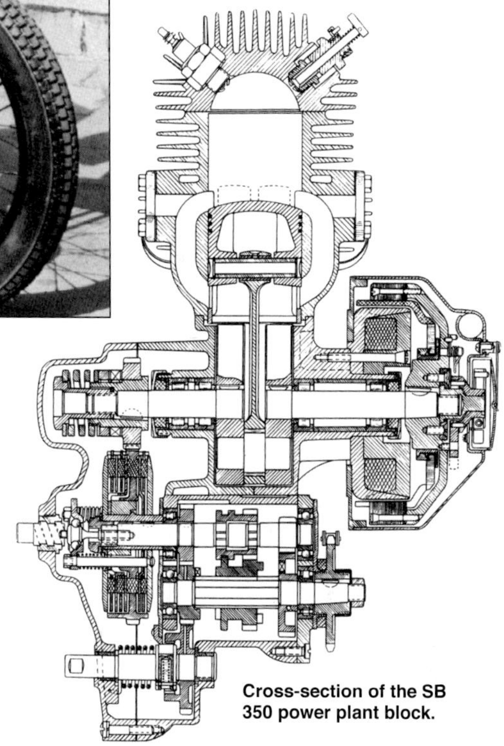

Cross-section of the SB 350 power plant block.

Close-up photo: the combined foot-hand shifter available (for sports purposes and police use) on the SB 350 – an unfavorable arrangement with the foot brake lever on the same side.

SB 350 – year of manufacture 1936 – same specs as the previous model, but with long frame and larger, more slender tank.

Luxus (Luxury) version of the SB 500 with electric starter (Dynastart) and twin headlights. 15hp twin-cylinder engine, 494cc, 68x68mm bore/stroke, three-speed gearbox in the engine block. Year of manufacture 1935 – still with the short frame and small tank.

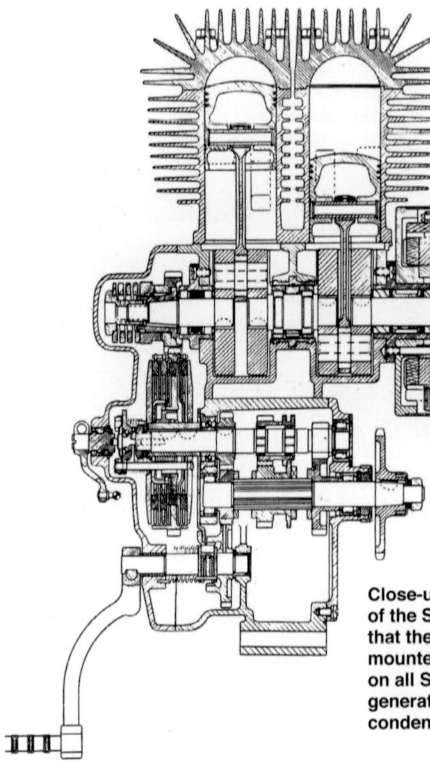

Cross-section of the SB 500's engine block.

Close-up photo: Engine-gearbox block of the SB 500. It can clearly be seen that the gearbox housing was flange-mounted to the engine case, as it was on all SB models. The bulge on the generator cap is due to the second condenser.

SB 500 (with electric start and twin headlights, designation SB 500 A). Technical data the same as the SB 500, but with longer frame and corresponding tank. Year of manufacture 1936.

Hermann Weber's masterpiece: the DKW RT 125, which entered production in 1939, then, because the German military did not want it, was not made for years – until it was realized that an infantryman could better handle such a light and lively vehicle than one of the big machines such as the initially favored NZ 350. Then production could not keep pace with demand – suddenly the motorcycle was needed everywhere and there were fantastic plans as to what could be done with the little thing. The end of the war put an end to all these ideas. But the RT 125 did not really hit its stride until after the war – when it became the most copied motorcycle in the world.

The design layout of the cylinder and casing was uniquely successful, and the graceful tubular frame blended perfectly.

These two photos of a cutaway model show the interesting interior of the 125cc engine block: the disproportionately large internal flywheel masses, the primary drive (roller chain once again instead of gear wheels), the multi-plate clutch with cork-coated plates, the three-speed gearbox with the original foot shifter (which was not a product of the design department but of one of the in the experimental section) – and the graceful small generator with breaker and condenser under the cover cap. Today one would surely smile at the small size of the cooling fins, the tiny intake cross-section and the puny transfer ports, as well as at the chain in the primary drive, no longer feasible with today's powerful engines – but then, in 1939, it was an acknowledged masterpiece.

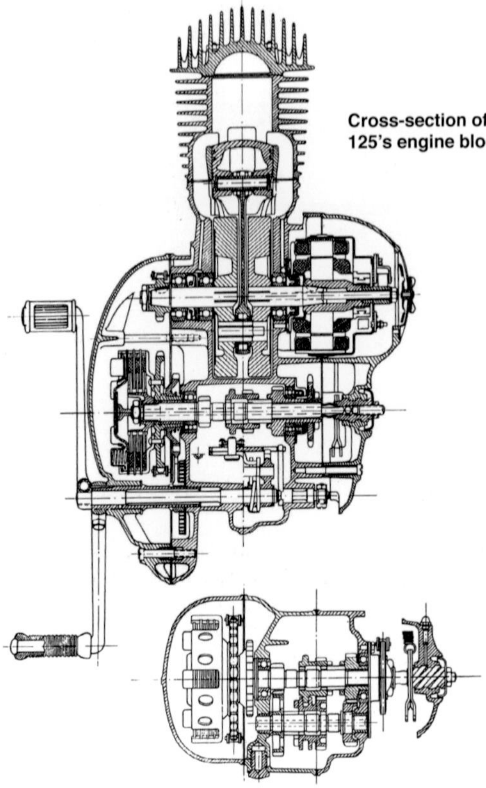

Cross-section of the RT 125's engine block.

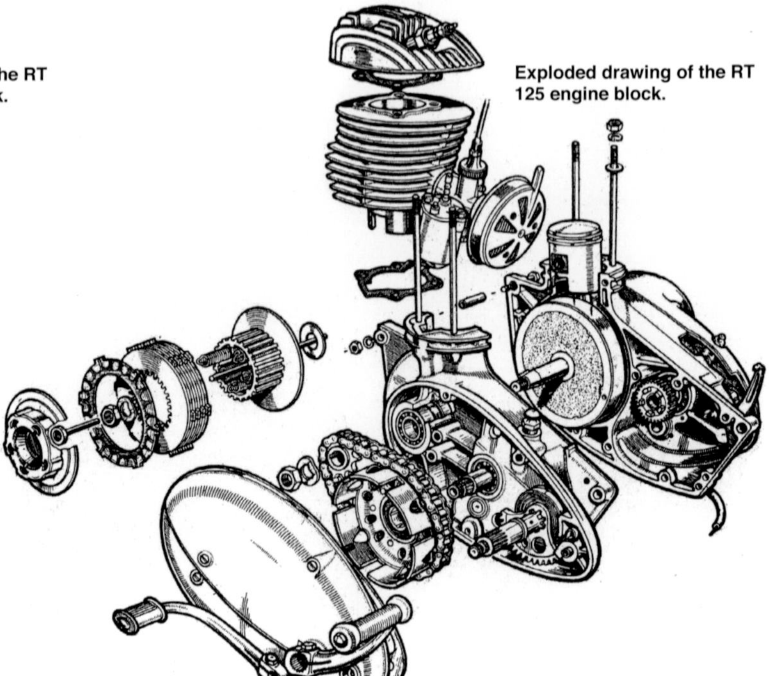

Exploded drawing of the RT 125 engine block.

The NZ 250, which was introduced in 1936-37 – the NZ models replaced the SB series as well as the RT 125 and RT 100. The typical shape of the engine case (and many other features on these machines) went back to the work of Richard Küchens. The NZ engines, the first DKW engines to go into production with a four-speed gearbox, also had a chain in the primary drive as this ran more quietly than the previous gear wheels. The engines (NZ 250 with 68x68mm and 247cc, from which resulted 9hp at 4,500rpm) were not highly specialized racing engines – they were quite simply refined engines for utility machines, which were a joy to ride. But the actual highlight was not contained in the power plant – instead it was the two-dimensional center frame made of two identical halves butt-joined and welded together, forming the center piece of an absolutely twistable box frame. The only impediment to production was the fact that welding could only be done after midnight – because the energy demand was so great, the last of the good residents of Zschopau had to have turned out their lights to prevent the electrical generating system from overloading and breaking down.

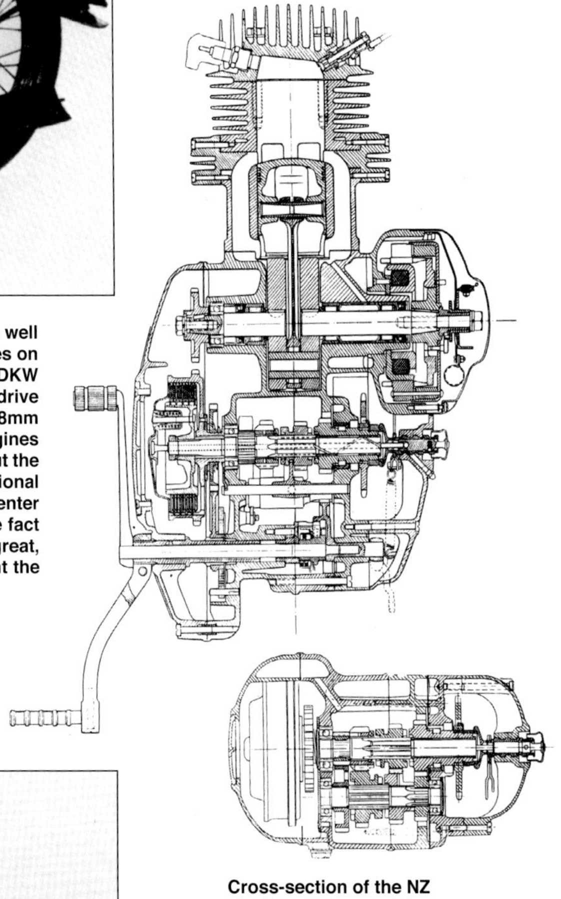

Cross-section of the NZ single-cylinder models.

Outwardly the NZ 350 was almost identical to its little sister. But with 343 cubic centimeters, which resulted from a bore/stroke of 72x85, the engine produced 11.5hp at 4,000rpm.

The shapely engine block of the NZ 350. During the war the NZ 350's case was switched to grey cast iron, and the cover over the transfer ports was deleted because, for the first time, precise casting meant that the control slots no longer had to be reworked.

Below left: On the NZ models the ignition and light switch was relocated from the coil box (still present) to the fuel tank. The (long-throw for contemporary loads) trapeze front fork – with 120mm front wheel caster – made a not insignificant contribution to the NZ's good road-holding ability. The hand shifter on the tank was coupled to the foot shifter. *Right*: A great deal of effort went into designing the saddle and its suspension. Shortly before the Kaiserdamm Exhibition, where the NZ models were supposed to be shown for the first time, the use of chrome for the tank sides was forbidden. A change to light metal was made more or less overnight: it was sprayed using a special process and then polished to a high gloss. It looked almost as good as chrome – and stood up to normal riding use. *Below*: The concentric arrangement of the foot shifter and kickstarter shafts was patented by Auto Union – no one could copy this elegant arrangement during the life of the patent.

The last flagship of the Zschopau DKW motorcycle fleet: the twin-cylinder NZ 500, few of which were delivered in Germany (although 1,500 were received by the Madrid City Police after a fierce competition with Moto Guzzi and Harley). The engine had a bore/stroke of 64x76mm, the engine produced 18.5hp, and, for the first time on a DKW production motorcycle (apart from the good old Lomos), there was a rear-wheel suspension with long swing arms (of joined pressed steel sections) and telescopic cylinder, similar to the design used with success on the company's racing machines. Handles allowed the rider to switch from solo to two-up riding.

The NZ 500 seen from the primary drive side.

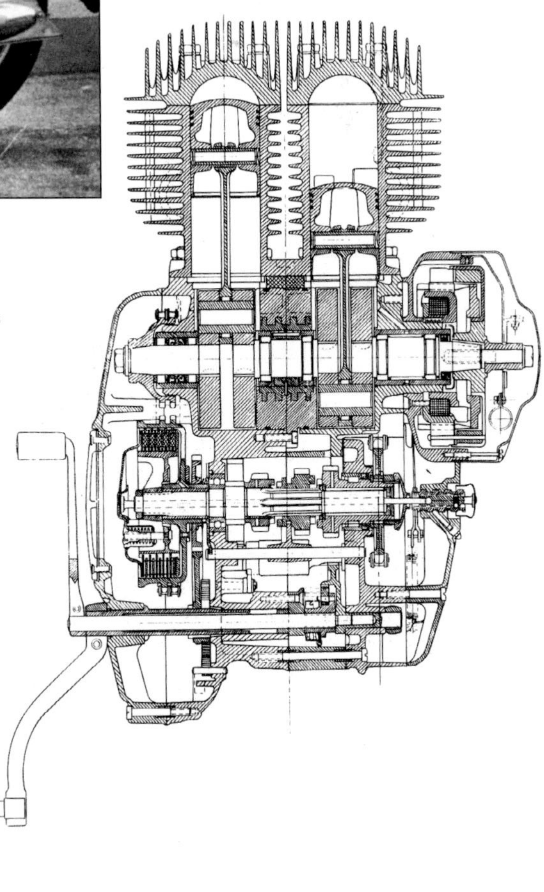

Cross-section of the NZ 500 engine block.

During the war DKW developed this "Hummel" (Bumblebee) to compete with the Saxonette (a rear wheel hub engine) brought out by Fichtel & Sachs just before the war. The 32cc engine produced 1.5hp and it was envisaged that it could be fitted to any bicycle simply by changing the rear wheel (the old dream of the "motorized bicycle"). After the war a new factory to be built in Chemnitz was to have produced several thousand of these bumblebees per day. Instead, after the war the drawings made their way to England, where the Hummel was built as the Cyclemaster – and later under license by Rabeneick. All that remained was the name: in the DKW-Moped from Ingolstadt (see page 203).

The Breakthrough: the DKW Loop Scavenging System

With a daily output of several hundred engines and motorcycles, by 1928 the DKW factory in Zschopau had become the largest motorcycle factory in the world. DKW engines were also sold to numerous manufacturers in Germany and abroad for use in motorized bicycles as well as to companies that used them to power agricultural and construction machinery. And, finally, twin- and four-cylinder DKW engines were used in the DKW automobile program. All of these engines were fast-running gasoline engines, two-strokes with crankcase pre-compression (not the four-cylinder) and slot-control of the gas exchange through the (deflector) pistons, with mixture formed in the carburetor, mixture lubrication, magneto or battery ignition, air or liquid cooled. Their maximum power per liter was 22-30hp, their specific consumption at best was just under 500 g/PSh.

They had become a significant rival to the traditional four-stroke, especially in the production of motorcycles, as the following comparison of the annual production of motorcycles in Germany shows:

	1925	1926	1927
Large motorcycles	48,000	46,000	72,000
Four-strokes	32,000	22,500	32,000
Two-strokes	16,000	23,500	40,000
Small motorcycles (under 200cc)	7,100	3,900	11,500

In 1925, therefore, twice as many four-strokes were manufactured as two-strokes. About 80% of the four-strokes installed in large motorcycles had displacements between 400 and 600 cubic centimeters. After virtually no change in numbers in 1926, production in 1927 clearly showed the trend of future development: while the production of two-stroke motorcycles almost doubled, that of four-stroke machines only rose by fifty percent.

In 1928 there were twelve significant two-stroke engine manufacturers in Germany. Their products were all single-cylinder designs except for one (DKW 500), the majority with a maximum displacement of 300cc. And while the mentioned 500cc DKW engine was a twin, in the four-stroke field up to 600cc the single-cylinder engine still dominated.

The latter fact alone, however, documented that the possible uses of the fast-running two-stroke gasoline engine were primarily limited to small displacements. The shortcomings of the two-strokes of the day – high fuel consumption, overheating and power per liter that was only slightly higher than that of four-strokes despite twice the number of cycles at the same rpm – became increasingly apparent as displacements increased. In this respect, therefore, technical two-stroke development was at a dead end, despite the sales development shown by statistics.

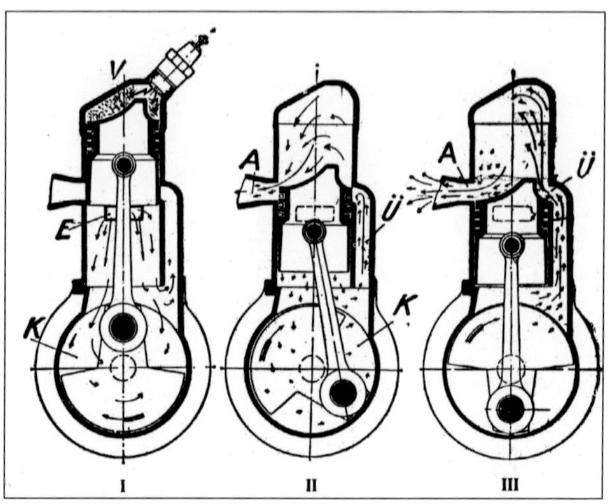

Functional schematic of cross-flow scavenging with deflector piston.

Two-Stroke Modifications

It was not surprising, therefore, that the manufacturers of two-stroke engines (and others trying to find constructive ways of bringing the essential superiority of the mechanically-simple two-stroke to bear, even with greater cylinder volumes, and with better economy) sought ways of improving them.

There were many proposals, some of which were patented and saw practical use, for example engines with various types of differential or auxiliary pistons, two-stroke engines with poppet valves for controlling the intake and/or exhaust, with reed or rotary slide intake control – and there were also designs in use on the production line which were supposed to result in improved guidance of the gas flow during gas exchange in the cylinder. Most important, however, was the so-called twin-piston two-stroke, of there were various designs, whose uniflow scavenging was also supposed to result in an improvement of the scavenging and charging process in the cylinder and (in some cases) also cause an asymmetric control diagram.

But all these modifications of the original object, the single-piston two-stroke with piston controlled slots and crank chamber pre-compression, meant increased manufacturing and operating complication (and rise in costs), which at least partly offset the advantages gained with respect to engine power per liter, economy and operating reliability. Especially for DKW, which had based its future program entirely on the two-stroke system and whose mass production program was also dependent on future superiority over the four-stroke engine (development of which was not stagnating) – and that this superiority would also be underlined by racing successes and attract a broad circle of purchasers, and finally that

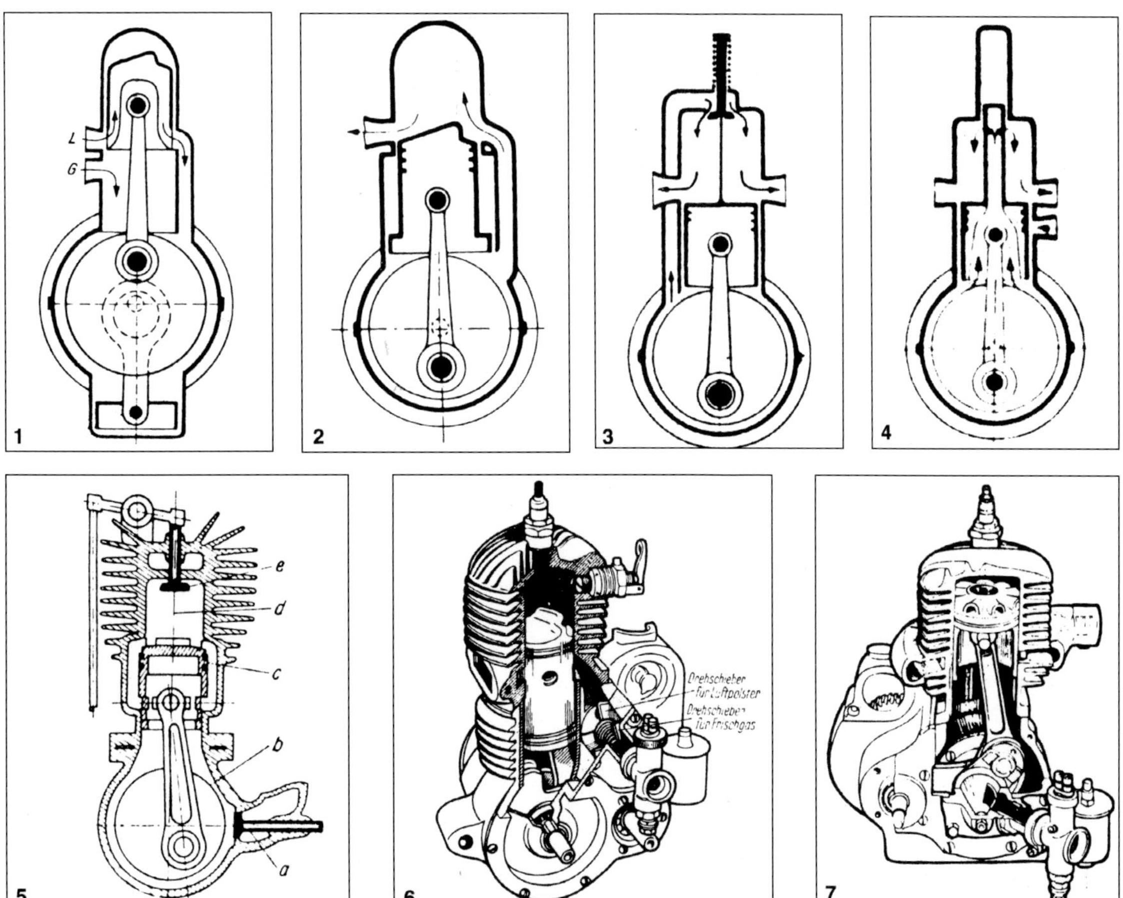

Two-stroke designs from the 1920s:
1. Bekamo engine with opposed auxiliary pump piston and fresh charge intake through the double-walled working piston. 2. Dunelt stepped piston engine. 3. Vis engine with piston-rod-controlled relief valve. 4. Schliha engine with uniflow scavenging. 5. Orionette engine with poppet valves for intake and exhaust. 6. Ermag engine with slide valves for air and charge intake. 7. Dolf engine with conical slide intake valve and fountain scavenging.

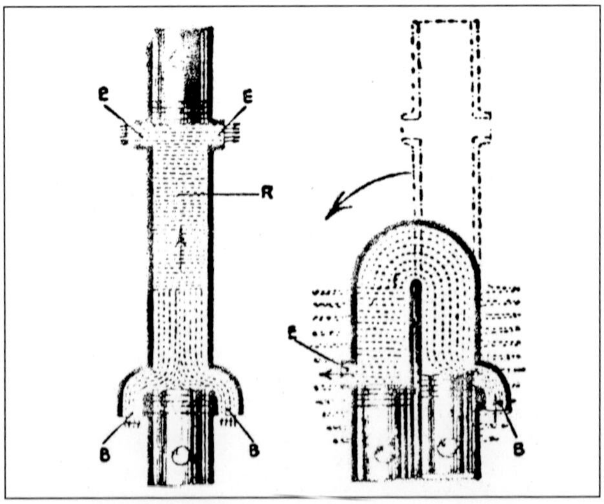

One must imagine that the U-cylinder engine (double-piston engine, right) was created by folding the counter-piston engine shown on the left (as built in Prüssing's design bureau after the war and previously by Junkers).

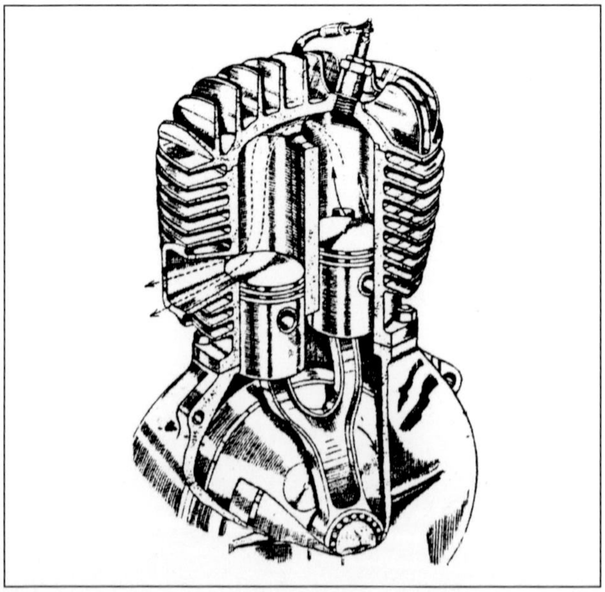

Double-piston engine with fork connecting rod, made by Puch for many years.

the four-stroke was becoming a serious competitor in the automobile sector, it was vitally important that the barriers standing in the way of further development of the two-stroke be cleared away.

In 1929 in Zschopau they had already equipped the 350cc single-cylinder engine with the reed valve intake control already used in the Austrian Titan engine (and in principle, although of different design, previously in the German Grade two-stroke aero-engine). With its help, at least it was possible to achieve an asymmetry in the control diagram on the intake side and thus achieve a better filling in the lower rpm range and reduce fuel consumption – even such a piston-independent intake control was unable to overcome the thermal difficulties that stood in the way of an increase in power per liter.

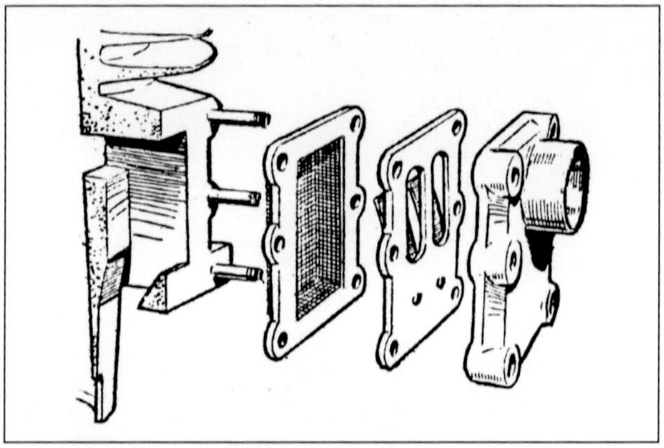

Reed inlet valve on the Austrian Titan engine.

Reed inlet valve of the DKW Block 350 (final version before the switch to loop scavenging).

Zoller and His Twin-Piston Engines

More promising were the experiments that Arnold Zoller of Switzerland had been carrying out for years with his two-stroke engine designs. On the one hand they made use of the twin-piston design, while on the other the crank chamber pump was replaced by a special charging mechanism, a rotation (rotor) compressor. An asymmetry of the control diagram was achieved for the intake, scavenge and exhaust processes by the (Zoller patented) connection of a second connecting rod to the main connecting rod.

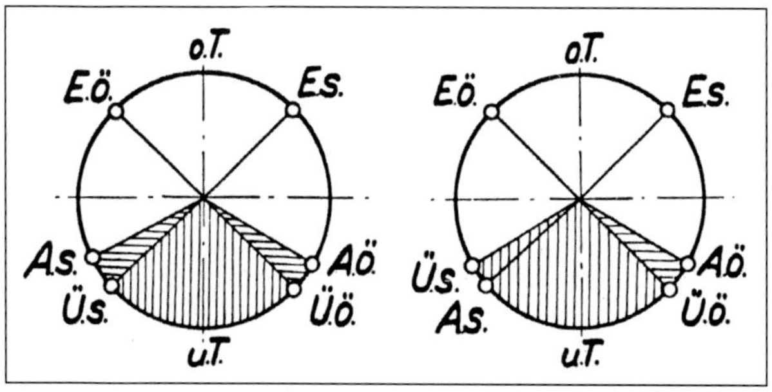

Two-stroke engine control diagram; left symmetrical – the exhaust port remains open by the amount of same crank angle (As) after the closing of the transfer slot (Üs), as it was before bottom dead center prior to opening of the transfer slot; right asymmetric, here too the exhaust port (which is necessary) is opened by the transfer slots, but when the pistons move upwards again it remains open after bottom dead center when the exhaust port is already closed.

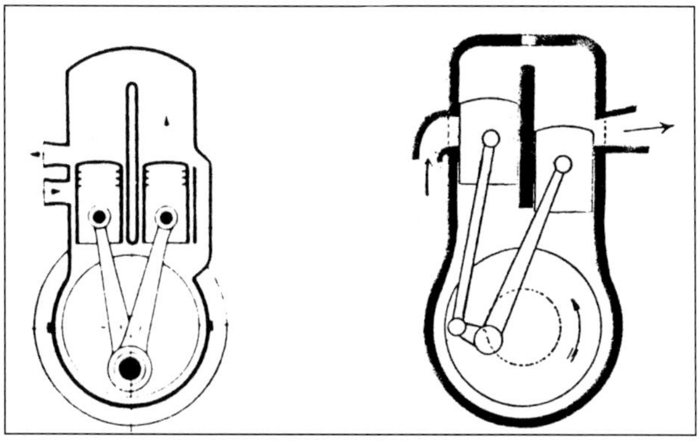

While two separate connecting rods work on the crank pin in the Hirth double-piston engine (left), the Zoller-type double-piston engine (right) has a slave connecting rod attached to the bottom of the main connecting rod, thus enabling greater control angle asymmetry.

Rasmussen too had become aware of Zoller (who at the beginning of the 1920s took part in the development of a car model for the Zwickau factory while working in Horch's design bureau in Berlin) and his work on two-stroke engines, and then in the second half of the decade he hired him to work in Zschopau. New motorcycle engines with double pistons and the "Zoller connecting rod" (as the combined connecting rod was commonly known, even though such linkages had been known prior to Zoller). The experimental models were already under test, and a step-by-step conversion of production (including the twin-cylinder engines for DKW cars) was scheduled for 1932. It must appear questionable whether Rasmussen was very pleased about this development, for the complication would of course have made his engines more expensive to manufacture.

Then at the end of 1931 he came across a publication that Engineer Herbert Venediger had written on earning his doctorate of engineering at the technical college in Munich titled "Improving the Power and Economy of Two-Stroke Carburetor Vehicle Engines." Rasmussen immediately recognized that there was a man who, after the more or less empirical development stages of the past years, would be in a position to scientifically tackle the solution to the existing problems of the two-stroke engine with deflector pistons.

The first discussions were held before 1931 was over, and at the beginning of 1932 the now Dr. Venedig began working in Zschopau as head of development directly under Rasmussen.

One chapter in his dissertation based on his own extensive studies of two-strokes was a very precise examination of the scavenging methods for two-stroke engines: uniflow scavenging, reverse circulation scavenging and cross-flow scavenging were analytically compared – and in conclusion reference was also made, relatively briefly, to loop scavenging. This process had already proved itself in large machine construction, was entirely possible for vehicles engine construction and was undoubtedly also advantageous. Venediger went on to say about loop scavenging that it had "curiously not yet been tried."

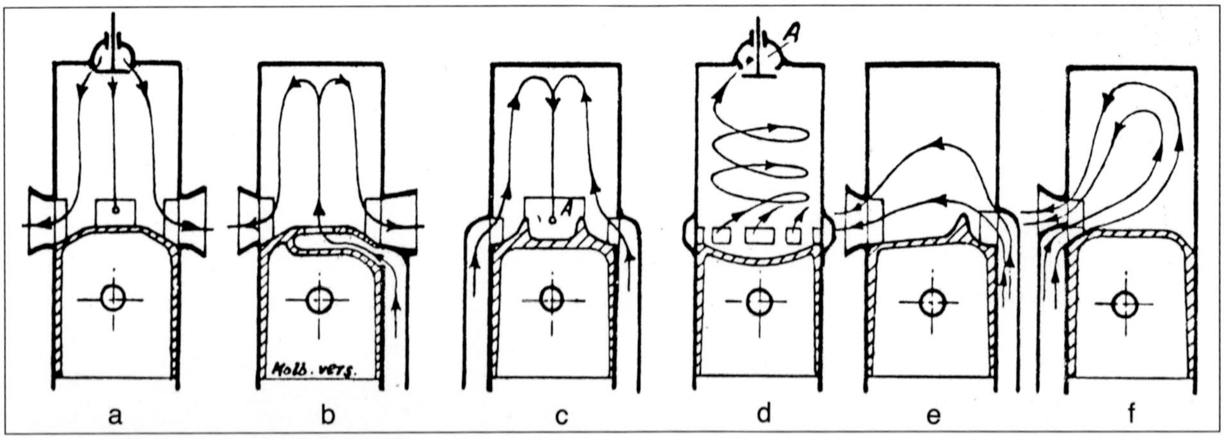

Two-stroke scavenging: a = uniflow scavenging (with valve in head), b = fountain scavenging, c = steep flow scavenging with deflector piston, d = eddy current scavenging (with valve in head), e = cross-flow scavenging with deflector piston, f = loop scavenging.

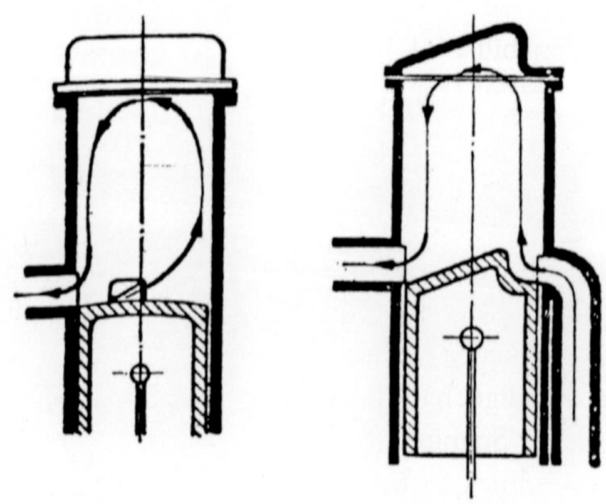

Above: Schematic of cross-flow scavenging with deflector piston.

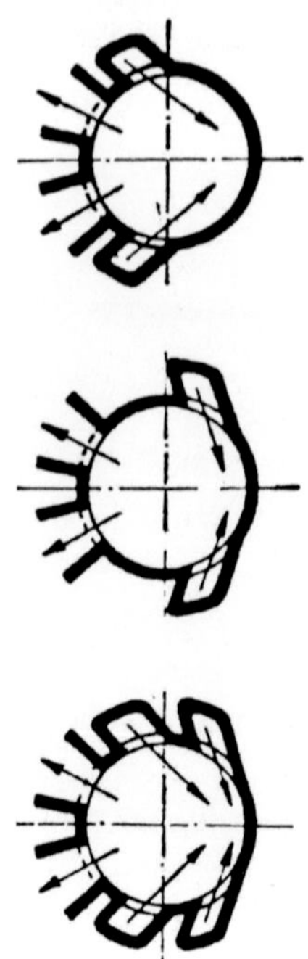

Row left: Loop scavenging with flat pistons as per the Schnürle patents 511 102 (1924) and 520 834 (1925).

The Solution: Loop Scavenging

Zschopau quickly helped out. As the first constructive designs were being drawn up and test bench experiments with DKW engines with the aforementioned loop scavenging were being carried out, negotiations were already under way with the man on whose loop scavenging patents (issued in 1924 and 1925) the Klöckner-Humboldt-Deutz held the general license: Professor Adolf Schnürle. As it turned out, in Deutz they were not interested in using the licensing right in gasoline engine construction and were prepared to allow Schnürle to issue licenses for his loop scavenging patents in this sector.

In 1932, therefore, Rasmussen (and the AUTO UNION, of which the DKW complex was by then a part) concluded an exclusive license contract with Prof. Schnürle for the use of the Schnürle loop scavenging system based on Patents 511,102 and 520,834, restricted to two-stroke gasoline engines.

At that time Dr. Venediger had listed the advantages of loop flow scavenging over cross-flow scavenging with deflector pistons then in use as follows:

1. Significant increase in engine power per liter;
2. Considerable reduction in specific fuel consumption as a result of improved scavenging and charging effectiveness;
3. Possibility of raising compression as a result of more favorable combustion chamber shape, the

reduced heat-absorbing piston surface area and improved cylinder scavenging;
4. Reduction in piston weight and resulting increase in engine speed;
5. Reduction of piston clearance on account of the reduced heat level and improved running smoothness;
6. Extended operating life before overhaul on account of piston rings remaining non-binding longer;
7. Reduction in acceleration time for the power plant, more favorable bearing wear;
8. Less frequent use of the transmission, which can also be more favorably staggered;
9. Improved running at low speed and idle;
10. Possibility of increasing cylinder capacity as a result of Points 4-7.

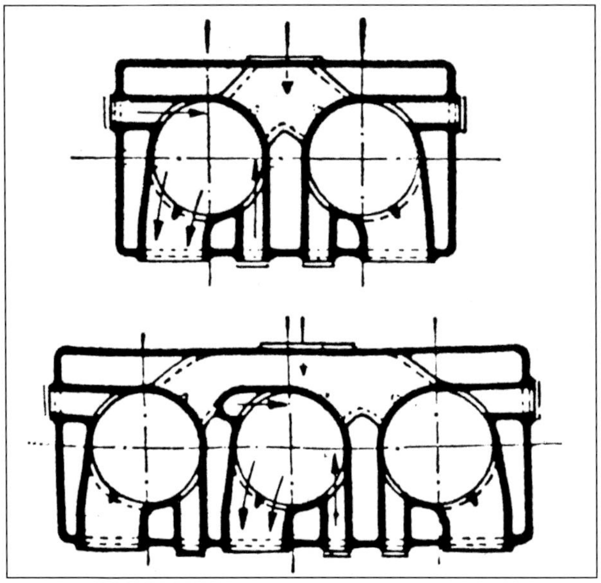

Scavenge port arrangement of DKW twin-cylinder (above) and three-cylinder (below) engines with loop scavenging.

It seemed of particular importance to him that, because of the more favorable thermal conditions, it would be possible to significantly increase not only top end performance but also continuous output and to open up the area of higher rpm for continuous use.

Dr. Venediger had always emphasized as an important fact about the Schnürle loop scavenging system that, "as a result, as all four uses of the scavenging flow have a fixed guide on the cylinder wall or on the piston, the scavenging method is usable at any desired engine speed, and, with respect to the good exploitation of the working stroke, in particular also for fast-running engines."

In the shortest possible time DKW began converting from the cross-flow scavenging previously used to loop scavenging and thus from deflector to flat pistons. The first motorcycle with loop scavenging to appear in the DKW program was the Block 350 – outwardly recognizable (and thus differing from the last engine with deflector pistons still in use in the Block 250) by the location of the carburetor – not on the side of the cylinder, but (as temporarily on the reed valve model) on its backside. The two scavenge ports typical of the loop scavenging system now took their places on both sides of the cylinder.

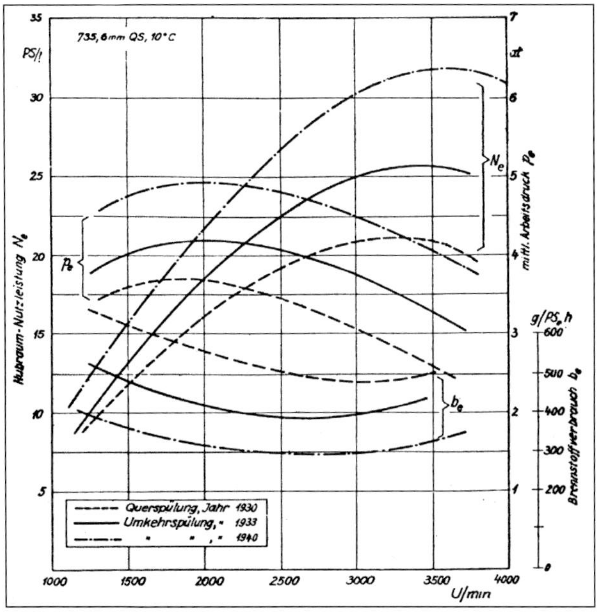

Characteristic curves of fast-running two-stroke gasoline engines with cross-flow and loop scavenging in two development stages. The differences in power, torque and fuel consumption may be clearly seen.

Conversion of the other engine programs, including automobile and stationary engines, took place rapidly.

After Dr. Venedig's arguments had been accepted, all that remained of Zoller's work was the new twin-piston racing engine. He had made it clearly understood that the cost of the twin-piston design would only be justified if the crank chamber pump was replaced by a special boosting mechanism or supplemented by an auxiliary pump, with whose help even an overcharge could be achieved. Without this, it would be inferior to a loop scavenge engine with just one piston.

Incidentally, a logical consequence of these considerations was a double-piston automobile engine created in Zschopau in 1932, the result of a cooperative effort by Dr. Venediger and Zoller. It was a four-cylinder V-configuration with a displacement of 1160cc. It operated with a Zoller rotary piston compressor with a conveyed volume of 1.9 liters and produced 50hp, equivalent to a displacement performance of 43hp. It powered an AUDI front wheel drive chassis until trials were halted. On the other hand, conversion of the existing V-4 circulating pump engine (for the Sonder- and Schwebeklasse cars), which used deflector pistons and cross-flow scavenging, was not done; they obviously shied away from the completely new design which would have made required the installation of symmetrical scavenge ports between the charging pump and working cylinders.

Arnold Zoller left Zschopau in 1932 and established his own design bureau where he worked to develop his supercharger (including for an engine made by the automobile maker Röhr). He died in Darmstadt in 1934.

Lawsuits over Loop Scavenging

With the new loop scavenging system, the DKW engines were suddenly far ahead of all the competition and the advantage over four-strokes was reestablished. For without any mechanical complication, it was now possible to increase power output without thermal difficulties, especially in the piston; the refined running of the engine was unmistakable. Most importantly, however, fuel consumption dropped – to below 400g/hp right away and in the course of further development to less than 300g/hp in the first years of the war – at peak load. This was a reduction of 40% – in the area of the four strokes of that time. It should also be taken into consideration that the partial load consumption of two-stroke engines was not inconsiderably lower than full load consumption.

But then the unavoidable happened: the two-stroke competition of course wanted to get away from deflector pistons, away from uneconomic cross-flow scavenging, and up to the technical standard of DKW engines. But as incomprehensible as it must seem to many, who regard previous trademark rights on scavenging concepts, that Schnürle could receive such comprehensive protection on his loop scavenging system – no matter what the competition came up with to get around the Schnürle patents – the DKW lawyers won every legal battle concerning this matter. Even though in some cases not until years later: whoever, for example Zündapp with the tri-flow scavenging system devised by Richard Küchen, believed that they were not colliding with the DKW trademark rights found out, in some cases from Germany's highest judges (Zündapp lost the trial before the Reich Court in Leipzig), that nothing could be done against the Schnürle patents – and had to pay DKW license fees.

The exception was the various kinds of cross-flow scavenging, which differed fundamentally in principle from loop scavenging. This was used, for example, by Fichtel & Sachs, Villiers of England and later the Ardie two-strokes. Such engines could be made without penalty – but without achieving the quality of the loop-scavenging engine. Not until after the Second World War, when the DKW/Schnürle patents were negated, could all two-stroke manufacturers produce their engines with Schnürle loop scavenging – and there were none that did not take advantage of this opportunity, both in Europe and Japan. And even where other designs and scavenging systems had proved themselves (for example Puch's double-piston

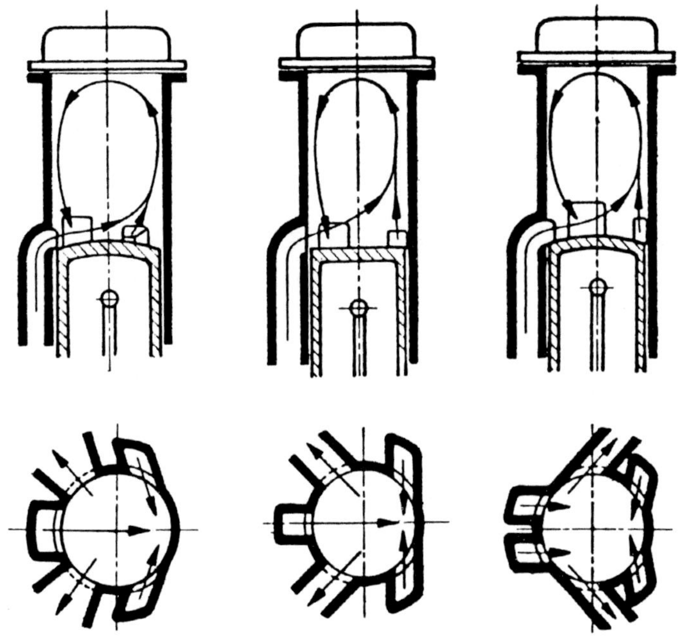

Loop scavenging systems developed by Dr. Venediger in Zschopau. In 1935 he and Auto Union were given protection by patents 685 173 and 716 989.

engines in Austria), the economic advantages of loop-scavenging resulted in its introduction.

Loop-scavenging was a decisive factor in the present dominant position of the two-stroke engine in motorcycle construction (especially since motorcycle racing's ban on boosting systems). For even the most modern scavenging systems with four, five or six scavenge ports are nothing more than modified loop-scavenging systems.

Dr. Venediger, who conducted extensive investigations into countless scavenging systems in Zschopau, was certainly not the last ro recognize the possibilities of modification. As a result of these experiments, he patented new scavenging methods (see drawing), which in tests at Auto Union's central experimental department demonstrated even better results in terms of performance and fuel consumption than the Schnürle loop-scavenging system. Auto Union left these trademark rights in the drawer, however, so as not to undermine their own arguments with which they had won the patent lawsuits.

Dr. Venediger and Rasmussen shared a mutual respect; Venediger stood by his boss in the early years of the Auto Union, when others thought it opportune to anticipate his departure and attuned themselves accordingly. Dr. Venediger left DKW in 1940. After the war he continued working on two-stroke engines in Germany and America. In 1947 he published one of the first new textbooks to appear in postwar Germany, about *Two-Stroke Scavenging – especially Loop Scavenging*. Every two-stroke designer should be familiar with it. To this day none of the fundamental conclusions to be found there have been made obsolete.

The Two-Stroke as a High Performance Engine: DKW Racing Engines 1920-1940

From the beginning, in Zschopau there was the conviction that sporting competitions with motorcycles were beneficial for two reasons and therefore necessary: first, because racing victories provided the victorious marque with good direct advertising among the spectators and then could be exploited in media advertising; second, because the stresses that the vehicles and engines had to withstand in racing could provide experience that sooner or later would also benefit the development of production models. As long as he was in control of the DKW marque, Rasmussen clung to this conviction – then, after his departure, the development and use of DKW racing engines and machines so intensified that racing engine technology differed more and more from production models. The second of the two named benefits thus withdrew more and more into the background (the racing department had become a small factory unto itself) – but all the successes by DKW motorcycles in national and international races proved a valuable advertising tool: with its production machines DKW was not only the largest producer of motorcycles in the world, its racing machines also made it the most successful motorcycle maker in the world.

By 1939, the Zschopau two-stroke racing engines hade become superior to the four-stroke, which had previously dominated the racing scene, even though they were almost as complex mechanically and had considerably higher fuel consumption. But no one asked about that in those days – all that mattered was the two-stroke motorcycles' superior acceleration and top speed.

In 1922 numerous DKW racing machines were appearing, especially in road races – as here on the Avus; the engine, equipped with flywheel fan cooling (and therefore usually more durable than the competition), was already mounted in the frame triangle of specially reinforced bicycles – predecessor of the Reichsfahrt Model.

The Reichsfahrt Model was used in many sporting competitions, especially by private riders. The rear wheel was belt-driven – some machines had pedals, others foot rests.

In the Beginning There Was the Reichsfahrt Model

DKW engines became involved with racing sport very early: company and many private riders competed in circuit and mountain races on closed roads with the first machines, which were still very similar to bicycles but now carried the two-stroke engine in the frame, instead of over the rear wheel as an auxiliary engine. Then, in 1922, the Reichsfahrt Model, so named after its sensational success against much more powerful motorcycles in the ADAC-Reichsfahrt road race across Germany, began reaching customers in large numbers. Some had the 118cc engine, others the 150cc power plant. Slightly modified examples of the production machine began participating in growing numbers in road and paved track races and other motorcycle competitions, in many cases without foot pedals.

Power came from a pulley (1:3 reduction) in the engine case with drive belt; the engines were initially cooled by the airstream and were later fan-cooled, which was the source of many problems, and the interrupter located on the bottom of the engine case and operated by the reduction shaft by means of a tappet was replaced by one in a protected position under the flywheel cover. These machines had neither a clutch, a starter nor a multispeed gearbox (except for a few later examples with the so-called "Lomos clutch") – but despite their simple design the small, light vehicles repeatedly demonstrated their superiority, even against more powerful competition.

Otto Voight of Pratau near Wittenberg was one of these private riders.

Arthur Geiss of Pforzheim began riding the Reichsfahrt Model in 1924 and won many significant competitions.

Right: Increased performance led to liquid cooling. Here Meister Sprung on one of the fist racing machines with a small radiator saddled over the upper tube.

With continued development and the inevitable performance increases, the fan cooling of the deflector piston two-stroke was no longer adequate. It was therefore given a shrouded cylinder and a small radiator, initially a pannier type, slung over the upper frame tube in front of the (larger) fuel tank. It was a thermosiphon liquid cooling system without pump (which, by the way, was retained until the last supercharger machine built in 1939). The floatless carburetor, which was difficult to adjust, was soon replaced by a float carburetor. These engines produced 5hp at 3,500rpm. These machines were ridden by DKW racing motorcyclists until 1924.

An example of this DKW racing machine is preserved in the Two-Wheel Museum in Neckarsulm. It is still based closely on the concept of the Reichsfahrt Model but has a liquid-cooled cylinder and head (not removable) from the standard production stationary engine. The machine in the photo on the left was ridden in races by chief designer Hermann Weber, as were the later ARE (175cc) and ORE (250cc) racing models.

The First Charging Pump Engines

New DKW racing machines conceived by Hermann Weber and intended for the then very relevant class up to 175cc made their appearance in 1924. They were the first specially designed racing machines and differed significantly from the production types (which consisted of the ZL, ZM and SM models). They were true small motorcycles that made an organic impression – and a good image on the racetrack.

The engine, with vertical liquid-cooled cylinder (still without removable head) was mounted in an open-bottom, two-dimensional tubular frame – with the bottom closed by the engine case and a malleable iron transmission cross beam – with integral tank. An open-running roller chain led to the hand-shifted (English) Sturmey-Archer three-speed gearbox with cork plate clutch, then a second chain to the rear wheel. In front of the fuel tank, the front of which was shaped to match the radiator, was the honeycomb radiator which was attached by clamps to the top and front frame tubes – high enough compared to the cylinder to permit an unimpeded flow of coolant. The twin-port cylinder was mounted on the crankcase in such a way as to result in an original arrangement of the exhaust pipes (horizontal as far back as the rear axle), with one straight back the other curved (see photo at top of page 68).

Hermann Weber (right) with Meister Sprung after victoriously completing the 1925 Winterfahrt.

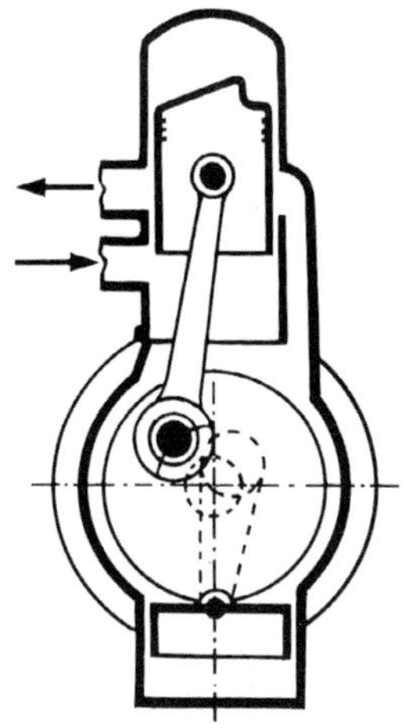

More charge in the cylinder was needed if revolutions and thus power were to be increased. Then they remembered the counter-running auxiliary pump in the crankcase suggested by Ruppe and equipped their racing engines with it.

The highlight of the new engine, however, was the auxiliary pump located under the engine case, which went back to a proposal by Ruppe. Driven by a cam connecting rod from the crankshaft and working in opposition to the main piston, a small, ultra-short-stroke piston increased the engine's intake volume by about 40%. The result was an increase in engine speed and top-end performance – admittedly at the cost of higher fuel consumption, for thanks to the asymmetrical piston control of the scavenge and exhaust ports, in the lower engine speed ranges at least, even more unused fuel-air mixture was spewed from the exhaust than before.

In 1926 an improved version of the machine on which riders Weber, Sprung and Friedrich (Chemnitz) had achieved great success in 1925 appeared. It had the type designation ARe 175. The engine, which retained the counter-running pump piston, had a new cylinder with removable (grey cast iron) cylinder head. Its two exhaust flanges were on the front, resulting in a symmetrical arrangement of the exhaust pipes – higher compression and a modified control diagram plus larger gas passages brought a further increase in performance to approximately 12hp at 4,600rpm. A limited number of these special machines were provided to DKW dealers involved in racing. Wherever they appeared, they were the undisputed masters of the 175cc class until 1931. The machines, which were designed in the production design bureau, were assembled by special personnel along with the production models (which by 1927 also included twin-cylinder machines).

The first DKW charging pump racing engine (with auxiliary pump located low on the engine case) with side-facing exhaust flanges and consequent layout of the exhaust pipes.

DKW charging pump machines in a road race: Müller (Zschopau) and Friedrich (Chemnitz). Their machines have the same style of radiator and exhaust pipe arrangement. At the top of the photo on the side of the road is Zehnder of Switzerland on a Zehnder, next to him Ernst (Breslau) with an AJS, and at the very bottom a rider with an English Blackburn-Motor.

The 175 racing engine later received a newly-designed cylinder (but still with a non-removable grey cast-iron head), whose two exhaust flanges were located at the front. Power to the rear wheel was delivered by a three-speed racing gearbox with hand shifter.

Among the successes achieved by this machine was the international record in the 175cc and below class over an hour on the Berliner Avus under rider Arthur Müller from Zschopau in 1926 with an average speed of 106 kph, and the European Championship under rider Henkelmann at the Nürburgring in 1927. The riders of these machines included names like Walfried Winkler and Arthur Geiss, who later became famous, and the previously named Henkelmann, Goldbach, Gelsenkirchen and Goldbach of Frankfurt.

In 1927 Rasmussen and Dr. Hahn felt it appropriate to place the escalating production of racing machines under a central leadership in a dedicated racing department. For this task he brought from Berlin a man who had made a name for himself as a maker of two-stroke engines as auxiliary power plants for gliders: August Prüssing. Nevertheless, the design of racing machines remained under Weber's direction and, initially, the production of parts remained largely within the framework of series production. But assembly was already being carried out in the new racing department, which grew steadily and later also offered the opportunity to produce racing sport machines for private riders in limited numbers, selling them at home and abroad.

For years factory and private riders dominated the 175cc class with this model (ARe engine identifiable by the exhaust flanges). Flywheel of cast Elektron alloy.

Inspired by the success of the 175s, in 1928 an engine was experimentally fitted with the liquid-cooled cylinder of a 250cc stationary engine. Under Walter Winkler this prototype was immediately able to demonstrate its superiority over foreign contemporaries. And as interest in the 175 class was already waning and the quarter-liter class was gaining priority, a 250cc racing engine was designed and given the type designation ORe 250. Although its basic design was similar to that of the 175cc engine, there were external differences from its smaller predecessor: the case was reinforced, the auxiliary piston pump was larger (and, again by a cam connecting rod, driven by the other crankcase side, causing the charging pump cylinder to move more to the right). The cylinder – with significantly enlarged porting – could be recognized by a large ribbed scavenge port cover on the backside and its light metal cylinder head. It had two threaded exhaust ports (because the flange mounting on the 175's cylinder was too rigid and caused pipe breakages). Elektron alloy was used for the engine case and the large external flywheel that carried the permanent magnetic ring. In the

Partially cut away charging pump engine with displacement of 175cc (ARe 175) with removable cylinder head – this is the ultimate light-metal version. The short-stroke pump piston was moved by an eccentric tappet.

This was the no less successful ORe 250, essentially similar in design to the 175, recognizable by the large ribbed scavenge cover and the exhaust clamping nuts.

Drive side of an ARe 175 with light metal head. Unlike the later 250 models, it has a small scavenge cover.

very beginning the engine produced 14hp at 5,000rpm; like all the previous models it employed a needle valve float carburetor mounted on the side of the cylinder, with mixture lubrication (Castrol 1:12-1:15) plus open chain drive with a three-speed Sturmey-Archer or Hurth gearbox with close gear spacing and a multi-plate clutch with cork inserts. There was no kickstarter.

Hermann Weber, the chief designer, rode the machine himself (the last time he did so, for Rasmussen then forbade him to continue racing) – in addition to Walfried Winkler, Arthur Geiss, Arthur Müller plus Hans Winkler and Gmelch of Munich. They were later joined by Ewald Kluge, who gained two-stroke experience on a privately owned English Dunelt racing machine before he moved from Dresden to Zschopau (and like Walfried Winkler later settled in Adelsberg near Chemnitz, the "racing driver village"). In 1927 and 1928 Walfried Winkler became the German road master on the ORe 250. Its engine produced 17hp at 5,000rpm in 1930, and almost 18hp at 5,300rpm in 1932.

Left: For its time, the ORe 250 engine was an inspiringly beautiful piece of two-stroke engine design. The crankcase and the charging pump cylinder (with cylinder liner) were also made of cast Elektron alloy. ***Right***: A beautifully restored ORe 250 – only the cover cap on the carburetor intake is not true to the original style.

The Arrival of DKW Twin-Cylinder Racing Machines

DKW had had a twin-cylinder production motorcycle since 1927, initially air-cooled and later liquid-cooled. It was an obvious choice to produce a racing version, if only for its advertising value. This happened in 1928 – essentially by combining two 250cc single-cylinder engines to produce the PRe 500 twin-cylinder. The initial version was envisaged with two charging pump cylinders – in a V arrangement under the engine case for space reasons – but this was soon replaced by a single cylinder in the center of the engine case. Its tappet-operated short-stroke piston was dual-function – the top for one cylinder, the bottom for the other. The working cylinders each had just one exhaust port. The performance of this engine, equipped with just one Amal TT carburetor, which again powered the rear wheel via a separate Burman or Hurth four-speed racing gearbox and chain-chain drive, produced 28hp at 4,000rpm in 1928, 34hp at 5,300rpm in 1930, and 36hp at 5,400rpm in 1931-32 (when the model was abandoned). These performance increases were in part due to the progressively developed favorable lag of the charging pump compared to the main pistons. It had a crank angle of 36° (like the 250cc single-cylinder) – surely one of the first examples of the correctness of the theory that modern internal combustion engines were fluid flow, rather than positive displacement machines. At the time, it is unlikely that anyone suspected the decisive effects this theory would have on the later development of high-performance two-strokes.

The new DKW 500 entered its first event in 1927, the 24-hour race on the Opelbahn. Ridden by the team of Sprung and Müller, it was a complete success. Its average speed over the 2300 kilometers was 96kph. An even more impressive result was achieved in 1928, when the

After twin-cylinder engines were added to the DKW production program, it wasn't long before the racing department also forged a weapon for the struggle in the 500cc class against the four-stroke competition: cutaway model of the PRe 500 engine with light metal cylinder head and double-action, cam-actuated auxiliary pump at the bottom on the crankcase.

For whatever reason – at that time DKW was not particularly interested in the 350cc racing class. But there was already a PRe 350 engine, a liquid-cooled, charging pump engine. Here Hans Winkler (Munich) has just won an ice track on Eib Lake with it, much to the joy of his DKW boss (beside him).

The 500cc engine and the DKW half-liter racing machine saw action under many riders Sunday after Sunday. Here is one of these machines (with production-style "balcony radiator" – not as elegant a solution as on the single-cylinder racing machines). The rider is Niemeck of Hamburg.

There was also a dirt track racer with the 500cc twin-cylinder charging pump engine.

Spectacular crash by Toni Bauhofer's 500cc charging pump DKW during a circuit race in Königsbruck in 1931.

Chief designer Hermann Weber (center) as class victor at the Inselberg races in 1925.

machines ridden by Zündorf and Stegmann finished one-two against the BMWs of Stelzer and Henne in the Avus race – from then on there was a duel almost every Sunday between BMWs and DKWs of the later King Class, so called because of their attractiveness.

There were also individual examples of this twin-cylinder machine with a smaller 350cc engine. In the very first race in which one of these machines took part, Meister Sprung took second place in the Eilenrieder Race of 1928 – but further development of the PRe 350 was abandoned. It would be almost ten years before DKW again showed interest in this class.

Twin-Piston Engines as Development Perspective

By 1931-32 DKW was forced to realize that it could not achieve the increases in performance necessary to compete with the four-strokes (development of which had not stood still) with the previous single-piston concept with symmetrical control diagram.

At that time (see page 59) designer Arnold Zoller, who had been also been involved with two-stroke engines for some time, was working for DKW. He used the twin-piston design (which by then was well-known and had been used by various designers and manufacturers), for which he had developed an articulated connecting rod, which later became commonly known as the "Zoller connecting rod." This concept made it possible, in contrast to the single-piston engine, to achieve an asymmetrical control diagram – the diagram asymmetry could also be varied with the aid of different connecting rod linkages.

The DKW stable during the salad days of the charging pump machines – at Eilenriede Park, 1929. From l. to r.: rider Barthels, Walfried Winkler, Winkler (Munich), Meister Sprung, Klein (Frankfurt), Niemeck (Hamburg), Xaver Gmelch (Munich), behind him racing director Prüssing, Friedrich (Chemnitz) and Arthur Geiss. In the middle (with hat) Director Blau (Zschopau). The motorcycles here were entered in the 175-, 250- and 500cc classes.

Zoller was using what Prüssing and Weber also immediately recognized: with the asymmetrical control diagram it was possible to prevent the performance-limiting (and consumption raising) flow of precious fresh gas through the exhaust by the scavenge port remaining open after the exhaust port had closed. Indeed it was even possible to achieve an overcharging of the twin-cylinder provided a sufficient charging volume was available.

Zoller himself had not come to the twin-cylinder two-stroke because of the possibility of using this design to build high-performance two-strokes. Instead, together with the rotary blower he had developed, he wanted to make such an engine that was ultimately so variable that it could get along without a gearbox, like a steam engine. It was Zoller's fate that he was always forced away from his actual objective and forced to build high-performance two-strokes (for example, the Berlin racing driver Macher drove a DKW race car in which two Zoller twin-cylinder, twin-piston engines, with a Zoller supercharger between them, had been combined to create a one-liter racing engine; see page 121).

Prüssing, however, took up Zoller's ideas and, in agreement with Rasmussen and chief designer Weber, converted the entire DKW racing engine development program to twin pistons. One can envisage such an engine (see page 58) by imagining one long cylinder bent in the middle to form a U with two originally opposed pistons, which, with parallel vertical cylinders, were joined by a cylinder head with shared combustion chamber and working on a common crank pin via two separate or combined connecting rods. In one cylinder is the scavenge port, in the other the exhaust port, so that the inflowing fresh charge must push the burnt old gas before it, preventing it from escaping prematurely through "short circuiting" (as possible in a single-cylinder engine). The mentioned asymmetry of the control diagram further improves these conditions.

Right: Soon after the first privately owned 250cc twin-piston racing machines began entering international races, the French magazine Moto Revue – known for its outstanding content – published these detail drawings of the DKW charging pump engine.

Below: Designer Arnold Zoller, who brought the twin-piston engine to Zschopau and began experimenting with rotary superchargers there.

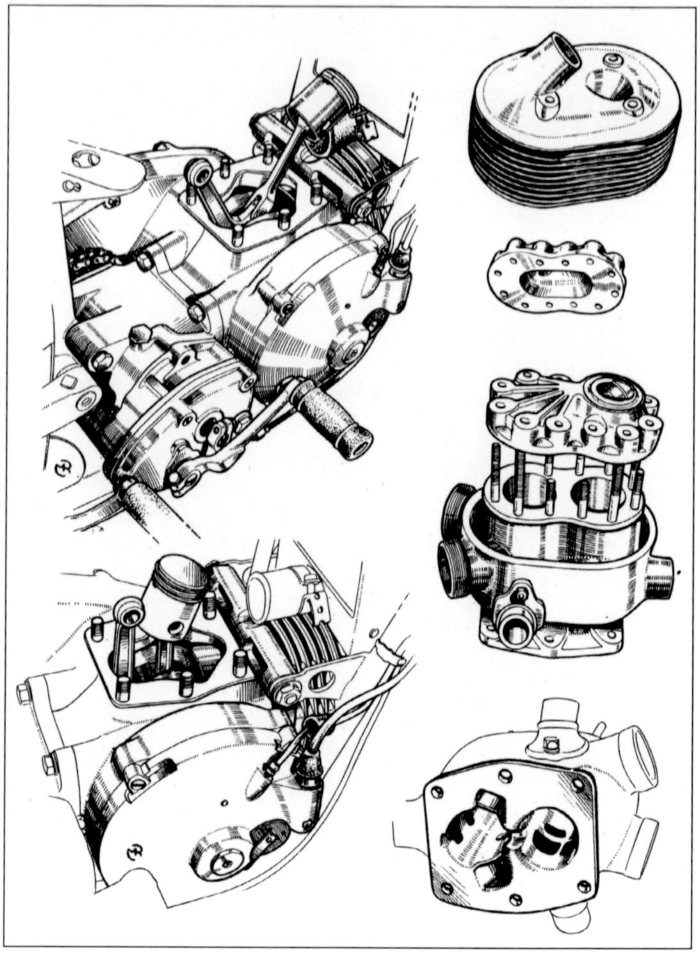

The team in Zschopau saw too many difficulties in the added development of a Zoller-type supercharger as a boosting mechanism for the new twin-piston racing engine they were working on. They therefore reverted to the piston supercharger, but – originally, as per the previous modality, they only wanted to use it to increase the crank chamber loading volume – not to serve as a supplement to the crank chamber pump, but instead to charge directly into the front cylinder with its head. In order to keep the scavenge line as short as possible, the charging pump cylinder was arranged in front of the engine with its piston (because of its considerably greater diameter), actuated by two tappet connecting rods, at right angles to the vertical main cylinder. And as the short-stroke pistons did not appear suitable for port control, intake control was achieved by a system of reed lamella (with which DKW had gained experience on the 350 production engine). Two carburetors pressurized the reed valve in the charging pump cover and delivered the fuel-air mixture. As the crankcase remained free of fresh charge and thus oil in this concept, instead of the simple mixture lubrication that had proved its effectiveness even in racing engines, the engine had to work with a fresh oil pump lubrication system. Nevertheless, oil was added to the fuel (though the mixture was only 1:50) to quasi-lubricate the upper part of the cylinder.

Walfried Winkler on one of the first reed valve machines.

The first DKW twin-piston design, the URe 175/250, was created in 1933-34. In this case (with two 40 or 47.5mm bore and 68.5mm stroke) the detected favorable lead (not lag!) of the charging pump amounted to 34° crank angle, the scavenge ports in the front cylinder remained open for (limited) overcharging 15° after the exhaust port closed.

The 250 engine (which was the most important) immediately reached its maximum performance of 22hp at 4,200rpm. Especially impressive and important, however, were the power and torque curves – such favorable engine acceleration characteristics were never achieved with another control system, as a comparison of the curves in the diagrams (page 84) shows.

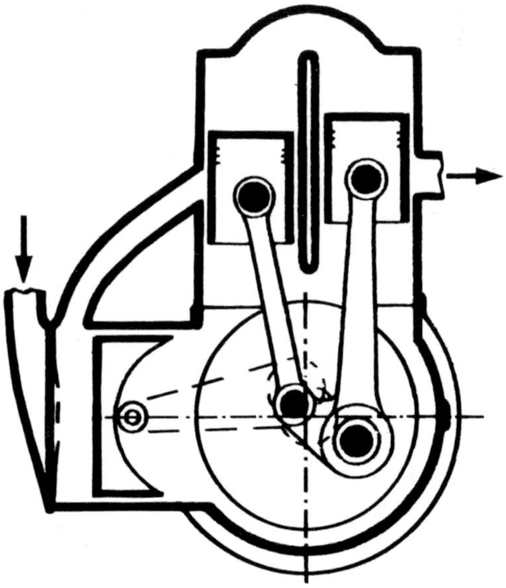

Functional diagram of the twin-piston factory racing engine with reed valve intake control in the charging pump space, which was independent of the crankcase.

The reed valve system responsible for this characteristic remained an ongoing problem child however: after many trials, Swedish watch spring steel was finally found to be the relatively best-suited material for the reed plates, which at higher revolutions simply "couldn't keep up," which meant that the intake openings in the pump cylinder opened and closed erratically causing frequent

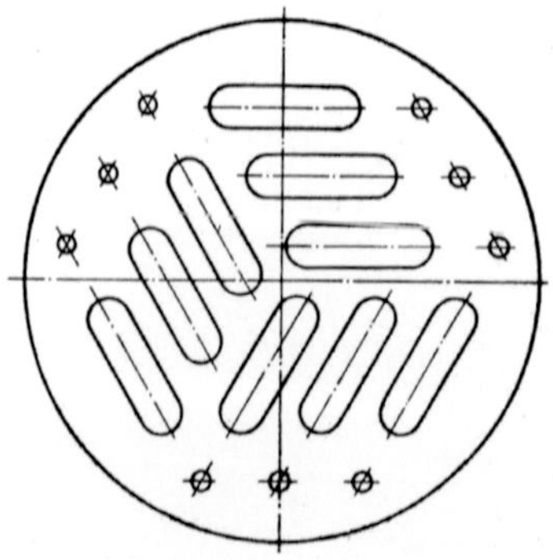

Arrangement of intake reed valves on the URe 250's engine.

The twin-piston machines ridden by the company riders were initially built with the engine case of the SB models and even had their kickstarter. The altered function of the charging pump made it necessary to use separate lubrication (one can see the oil pump in the extension of the crankshaft).

This is what the URe 250's power plant looked like in 1935: still with block gearbox but modified cylinder with ribbed light metal water hood separate from the (bronze) cylinder head. Double cradle frame with radiator between the forward tubes (still without rear wheel suspension).

In 1937 the cylinder and radiator were arranged vertically, and the rider was given typical DKW rear wheel suspension with guided swing-arm based on the Benelli design. Flywheel magneto ignition with external flywheel made of Elektron alloy. Separate four-speed gearbox.

breakdowns, and revealing the wild fluctuations in the stroboscope when revolutions reached the critical level.

But the power, which in the course of further development was increased to just under 24hp, revealed the correctness of the chosen path. A further increase in power (which was absolutely vital in the face of stiff competition from contemporary four-strokes) was only prevented by the reed valve control, which limited engine speed to 4,800rpm. As well, it became necessary to abandon the charging pump arrangement, which caused severe vibration at higher rpm. It was also found that the connecting channel between the charging pump and the front working cylinder was still too long.

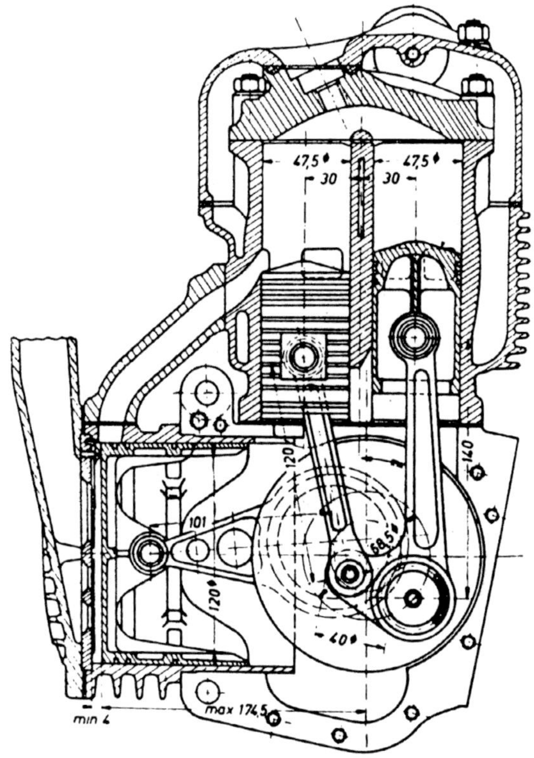

Sectional drawing of the DKW 250cc reed valve engine. The separation of the cylinder head and water hood may be clearly seen, likewise the arrangement of the charging pump.

The Big Success: The Rotary Slide Two-Fifty

As a consequence of these considerations, after an interim solution in 1936 (see page 78) with a chain-driven charging pump arranged vertically in front of the engine with its own crank drive and the reed valve system on the cylinder cover (and short scavenge passage to the working cylinder) in 1936 – which failed to produce the desired success because the shortcomings of the reed valve system remained – in 1937 the company took the decisive step. Instead of the reed valve in its cylinder cover, the charging pump, again in a vertical arrangement with its own crank drive, was given a rotary slide valve with two Amal-TT carburetors attached to its sides. The charging pump was driven by the engine crankshaft via radial tooth gears, as was the rotary slide valve (total of seven gear wheels!).

The new engine design, which bore the type designation ULD 250, immediately delivered more power than the reed valve engine, plus absolute operating reliability despite increased engine revolutions, making the added cost of the two gear wheel drives appear justified.

The rotary slide valve machine immediately became famous, and from 1937 to 1939 riders Kluge, W. Winkler and Petruschke rode it to success after success. In addition to the European Championship, in 1938 Kluge also won the German Grand Prize in Hohenstein-Ernsttal plus the grand prizes of Belgium, Holland and Hungary, as well as countless mountain races; most impressive of all, however, was his victory in the Lightweight TT on the Isle of Man in 1938. (Schorsch on his BMW won in 1939, but he was

In 1937 the reed valve engine produced approximately 24hp at 4,500rpm with outstanding acceleration characteristics – but problems with the reed valves prevented the further necessary increase in peak power.

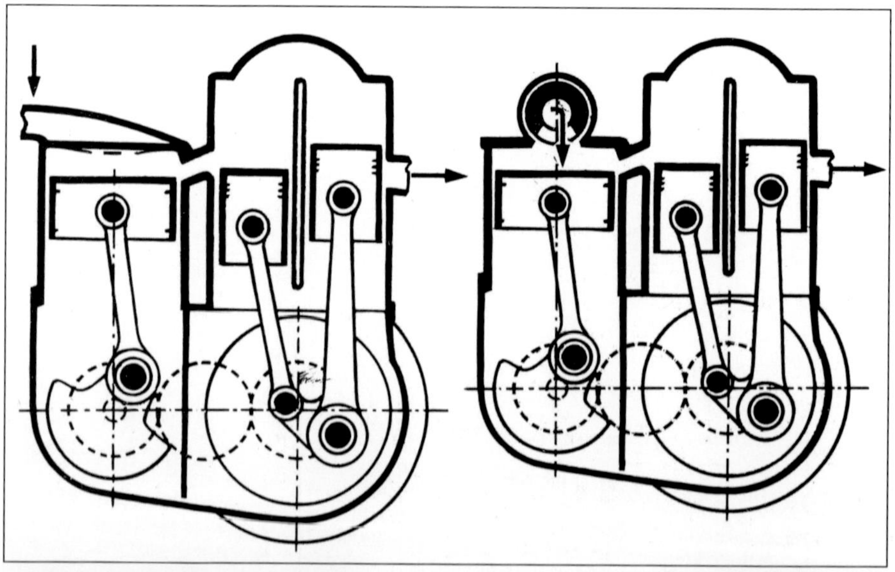

Left: Interim solution: reed valve intake in separately powered piston charging pump (first used in TT 37).

Right: Functional diagram of the rotary intake valve twin-piston engine (first used at the 1937 Grand Prize in Spa).

The switch to rotary intake valves and separate gear-driven piston charging pump took place in 1937 (see functional diagram above right).

not the first German to win a TT on a German machine, as is sometimes claimed. Instead it was Ewald Kluge, who won on the DKW a year earlier.) Incidentally, Kluge entered seventeen races with the DKW 250 rotary slide valve machine and won them all.

Not until 1939 did this machine meet its master in the new Italian Moto Guzzi with supercharger (the victory by an Italian single-cylinder Benelli at the 1939 Lightweight TT was obviously not only a question of the superior engine performance of the twin-cam four-stroke, but also of its English rider Mellor's greater familiarity with the course – especially important given the catastrophic weather conditions).

In terms of charging, the rotary slide valve control system was vastly inferior to the reed valve control system in the lower and medium engine speed ranges, but from 5,000rpm the power curve of the rotary slide valve machine continued to rise and at 6,000rpm the 250 rotary slide valve engine produced more than 28hp.

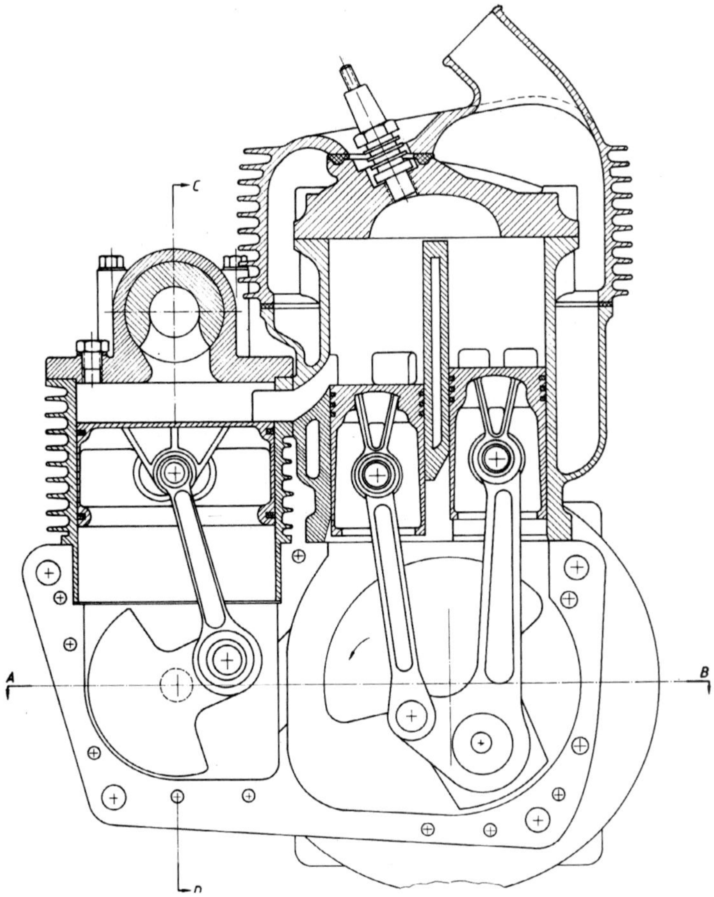

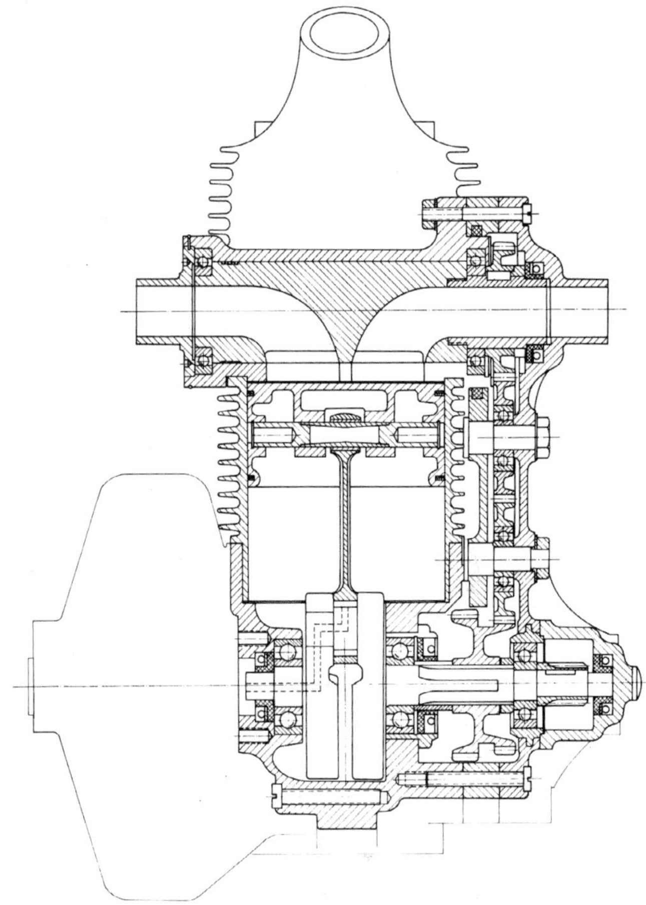

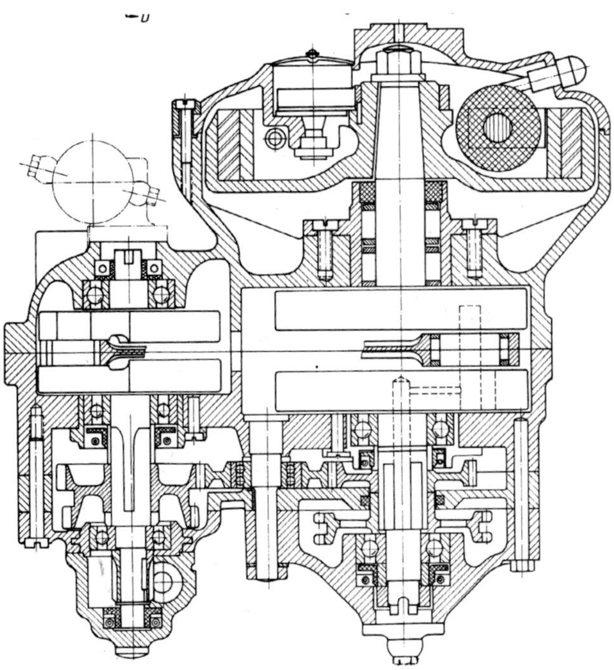

This (original) sectional drawing of the DKW ULD 250/1937 rotary intake valve racing engine (with which Ewald Kluge also won the English TT in 1938) reveals the integration of the individual components: the twin piston arrangement with compact combustion chamber over the (critical) partition, the articulated connecting rod ("Zoller connecting rod") with the slave connecting rod's slide bearings, separately-mounted cylinder head with water jacket extending down the side, the forward-mounted charging pump cylinder, whose own crankshaft is gear-driven by the engine, on top the rotary intake valve (supplied by a carburetor on each side), likewise gear-driven, plus the (DKW's own) flywheel magneto ignition with flywheel bell housing, which carried the permanent ring magnet and was open on the outside – but with a Bosch interrupter!

The period of DKW superiority, national and international, began in 1937 with the rotary intake valve machine, ridden by Walfried Winkler, Ewald Kluge (in photo) and Petruschke. The crowning success was Kluge's victory in the English TT in 1938.

The 250cc rotary valve engine from the ignition side – twin-tube chassis with rear wheel suspension, vertical cylinder and radiator, two carburetors at the rotary valve intake.

The drive side of the rotary valve engine with exposed primary drive to the separate four-speed gearbox. Ventral oiler for supplying the engine and charging pump with fresh oil.

Ewald Kluge on a victory lap with the rotary valve DKW at the Lightweight Tourist Trophy on the Isle of Man in 1938.

A Supercharger Becomes Necessary

The threat posed by supercharger-equipped, one- and multi-cylinder Italian four-strokes, which first appeared in 1938 and became clearly evident in 1939, forced the designers in Zschopau to initiate new and radical development work so that the lead the company had achieved could be maintained. Whereas in 1933-34 work had concentrated on replacing the single-piston engine, which had reached the limits of its potential, with the twin-piston engine, the objective now was to replace the oscillating piston supercharger, whose large moving masses limited engine speed to about 6,000rpm. In 1939 the Zschopau two-strokes were still equal to the Italians in acceleration – but peak power was lacking. If engine revolutions were to be increased to improve power, it could only be achieved with a rotating charging device, a rotary supercharger. The Roots blower, then favored in

View of the first version of the four-piston supercharger machine (US 250), still with the previous version of the encapsulated magneto ignition.

Right: Ewald Kluge with the supercharger machine during training for the Eilenriede race in 1938.

Below: Ing. Herbert Friedrich, who played an important part in the development of the supercharged engines and the supercharger.

racing car design, did not seem suitable for the purpose at hand for a variety of reasons. Instead they decided on a so-called rotary blower, initially with free-rotating blades. It consisted of a cylindrical housing in which turned a cylindrical rotor eccentrically mounted in the side covers. The rotor had radial slots in which steel blades could slide. When the rotor was set into rotation, centrifugal force moved them outwards to the housing wall. Free-rotating bearer rings made of bronze were embedded in the housing on both sides of the rotor. The blades lay against these and in this way were kept about 0.2mm from the housing wall, preventing the blades from touching the housing, rubbing away the film of oil and seizing. Changes were also made to the engine: the 250 with the previous two pistons was now given four and two separate combustion chambers and therefore became a true twin-cylinder. The rotary blower was attached directly to the front of the engine case, the fuel-air mixture drawn in by the blower (supercharger) was fed through the crankcase, which served as a pressure balancing chamber, to the two scavenge cylinders (as a result of which the engine could again be operated with simple mixture lubrication, mixture

The 250cc supercharged DKW (US 250) from the drive side – exposed primary drive.

Left: The US 350 (350cc supercharger machine) in its second configuration with modified supercharger and encapsulated primary drive.

Below: Functional schematic of the DKW 250/350/500cc twin-piston engines with supercharger.

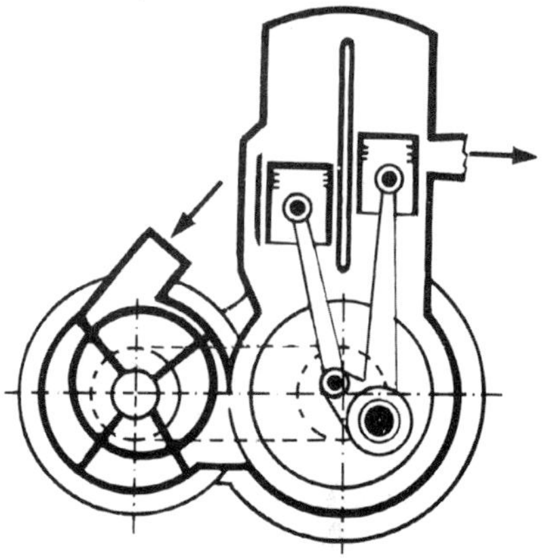

ratio 1:18). As the supercharger continuously drew in a fresh charge, it needed no intake valve at the entrance to the blower, which in its first version was powered by the crankshaft via a chain.

Though the performance achieved with the supercharger engine was encouraging (almost 35hp at 6,500rpm, roughly 25% more than the last rotary valve engine), the supercharger was the source of many headaches. Contrary to theoretical expectations, there was wear-inducing slippage between the powered blades and the free-spinning bearer rings. As a result, after a short running time the blades touched the case wall that very abruptly caused the supercharger to freeze. The designers in Zschopau were therefore forced to carry out redesign work that affected both the supercharger and the engine (which was also being produced in a 350 version).

Heiner Fleischmann, who moved from NSU to DKW, was chosen to ride the 350cc supercharger machine and in his first races with it showed how well he got on with this motorcycle. Right: Fleischmann with the 350cc supercharger machine during the Hamburg City Park Race in May. He led his class for most of the race, but because of two stops to replace spark plugs he fell back into second place. In the boxes (with cap) is racing fitter Kurt Haase, left (the second) master Electrician Rudolph, who was present at every race.

The supercharged machines (here the US 350) also offered a different look than the original model from the right side: the flywheel magneto ignition (with the heavy flywheel) was replaced by a new racing magneto ignition with a light internal rotor, developed by the Auto Union DKW electrics factory in Chemnitz.

With respect to its function, the redesigned blower was identical to the first. But the rotor, which was still mounted excentrically in the case, was now hollow, and the blades were individually mounted in anti-friction bearings on a shaft in the rotor aligned centrally in the case. The blades were fed through slots in the rotor and because of their central mounting were always kept wear-free at a small, precisely measured distance from the case wall, regardless of the revolutions of the supercharger and the centrifugal forces acting on them. The development of this supercharger and the engines was in the hands of racing engineer Friedrich, who – as the last "remainder" of the racing department shut down when war broke out in 1939 – was still able to bring these projects to a successful conclusion.

For even though there were no more problems with blades making contact with the case of the modified supercharger, difficulties arose with the rotor. The high degree of volumetric efficiency achieved by the new version of the supercharger (up to 75%) required the minimum possible gap between the rotor and case where they almost touched. A certain elasticity of the rotor led to an increase

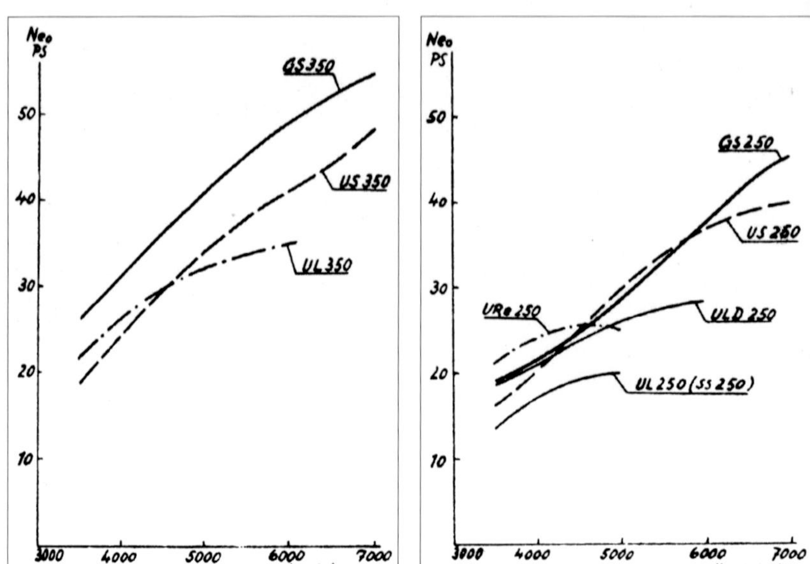

These two diagrams offer a good impression of the performance development of the 250 and 350 DKW racing engines (the GS 250 and 350 power curves refer to the counter-piston two-stroke engines developed under Prüssing's direction in a Soviet design bureau in Chemnitz after the war and described elsewhere).

The principal parts of the 500cc three-cylinder supercharged engine, temporarily put together. With respect to supercharger development, the US 500 engine was further back when development work had to be abandoned during the war.

in diameter at high revolutions, and this after a certain time to fatigue fractures. (This was also the reason why the rotary valve machine had to be entered at the Saxon Ring in 1939 instead of the supercharger version. As expected, it was defeated by the Moto Guzzi with its higher top speed.) The potential performance of the new four-piston machine was demonstrated by Heiner Fleischmann at the Hamburg City Park races in 1939, where he achieved lap times that were close to those of the 500cc supercharged BMWs. The supercharger withstood this relatively short race, and the DKW only finished second because of ignition difficulties and a blown crankshaft seal.

As previously stated, engineer Friedrich was able to continue working on the supercharger and by mid-1941 (when even the last experimental work on racing engines had to be suspended) brought it to full stability. While there was no opportunity to prove this at the time – there was some years later, and under circumstances that few could have imagined in 1941.

In any case, the supercharger engines in their final development state in 1941 produced just under 40hp at 7,000rpm in the 250cc version and 48.5hp in the 350. One example each of the 250- and 350cc engines was also completed for record attempts (which never took place); the produced 50hp from 250 cubic centimeters and 60hp from 350 – albeit with alcohol fuel (which was allowed for record attempts).

In the course of supercharger engine development a 500cc version was also in preparation, and the first experimental engines had already been fitted when war broke out. It was a three-cylinder (six-piston) engine whose basic design was identical to that of the 250- and 350cc variants, but with a correspondingly longer supercharger (and as the initial version was understandably expected to have even more difficulties than the shorter version for the smaller four-piston engines, development of this interesting 500cc three-cylinder engine was initially shelved pending the solution of the supercharger problems.)

Taken after the war when a motorcycle racer from Zwickau came into possession of the remaining parts of a US 500 engine and wanted to complete it, this surely unique photo gives an interesting impression of this new development – even if only individual parts. Particularly noteworthy is the layout of the three-cylinder block (the heads are missing), which is enclosed by the water jacket, as were the heads by the (ribbed) water hood. The crankshaft is still missing the articulated connecting rod. The long supercharger rotor gives some idea of the difficulties inherent in this configuration.

Development of the Twin Piston, Two-Cylinder Engines

After the 250cc engine demonstrated the superiority of the twin-piston design over the single-piston engine in 1933, the Zschopau racing department also began development of a parallel development for the half-liter class. After the PRe engine reached the limits of its success, it was succeeded by the UL 500, with which Rosemeyer, Bauhofer, Ley and Mansfeld, as well as Bodmer and Herz, were able to achieve success. Although there were experiments with 500cc four-piston engines with reed and rotary intake valves (ULM and ULD 500) on top of the cylinder cover and a charging pump in front of the engine (see pages 88-89), DKW decided in favor the mechanically simpler arrangement of a double-action charging pump low on the case and intake control by the pistons of the working cylinder, with the pump piston powered by the crankshaft with excenter.

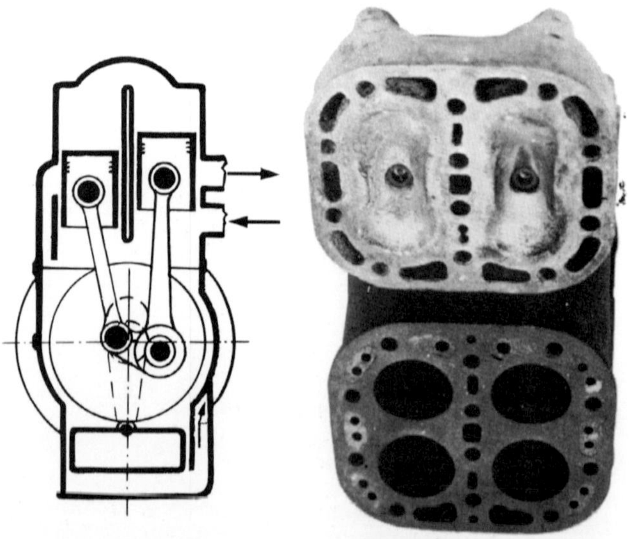

Design schematic of the twin-cylinder double-piston engine as built in 350- and 500cc versions for solo machines and 600- and 700cc units for sidecar machines. On the right the cylinder head and block.

After a brief testing period, this machine was first entered in competitions in 1934 under riders Bauhofer, Rosemeyer and Ley and immediately achieved total success. Bauhofer won at Eilenrieder in new record time and became Eilenrieder champion. That same year Ley was able to win the German Grand Prize in Hohenstein-Ernsttal.

Understandably, the chassis underwent constant changes and improvements hand in hand with continued development of the 250cc twin-piston engine. The final and most decisive change was the switch to rear wheel suspension (a swing arm suspension with shock cylinder just in front of the axle socket, which had outstanding stiffness and was made similar to a Benelli design). The photos illustrating the various development stages of the four-liter racing machine also show the changes that the suspension underwent in order to achieve a level of road-handling ability that allowed the ever-increasing engine power to reach the road and enable the rider to achieve the attainable speeds without risk.

Experience from the first season forced the designers to improve the new 500cc racing machine's road-handling ability. Once again the photos shows how the chassis was

In 1934 the 500cc racing engine was also converted to the double-piston design, meaning with four pistons. Precompression took place in the crankcase, whose intake volume, like the PRe 500 before it, was significantly increased by a huge double-action charging pump. The photo shows the first version of the UL 500 from 1934.

Left: Toni Bauhofer on the UL 500 used in 1934-35 – still with the two-dimensional tubular frame which was only forked underneath, and the DKW-typical radiator (as in the days of the single-cylinder deflector piston engines). *Right*: Bernd Rosemeyer also rode the first version of the UL 500 (identifiable by its radiator) after he left NSU and began riding DKW machines successfully in long-distance races (2000km ride, Six Day Race and others).

adapted to cope with increased engine power by lowering the center of gravity, reducing the weight of the radiator and changing the shape of the fuel tank – and not last by introducing new full hub brakes made of cast Elektron alloy (for a time the rims were also made at least in part of Elektron to save weight wherever it seemed possible). For the liquid cooling system and its contents were just as much a weight handicap compared to the competition's lighter air-cooled four-strokes as the considerable quantity of fuel that had to be carried – the result of the great thirst of this high-performance two-stroke.

In order to also achieve success in the two sidecar classes then advertised, four-piston charging pump engines were produced based on the UL 500, initially with a displacement of 600cc, later 700cc. The DKW combinations ridden by Kahrmann, Babl, Braun and later Schumann used the chassis of the 1934 solo machine until 1935, when a special chassis was introduced.

The UL 500, whose road handling was anything but satisfactory, was redesigned for the 1936 season. It received a completely new double cradle chassis, between whose forward tubes the radiator was installed. The engine was also improved, with increased power (note the modified cylinder head). There were also 600- and 700cc versions of this engine (for sidecar machines).

H.P. Müller prepares for the start of a race on the new UL 500.

An experiment in building a 500cc four-piston engine with a twin-cylinder gear-driven piston charging pump with reed valve intake control and two carburetors was abandoned (see schematic of the single-cylinder experimental version on page 78). Its type designation would have been URM 500.

Above: **This experiment was also not adopted (the rebuilt rarity is now in the Two-Stroke Museum in Augustusburg); instead of reed valve intake control in the twin-cylinder charging pump of the 500cc engine (see page 88), this ULD 500 was to have used a rotary slide valve (as on the very successful ULD 250, see page 78).**

The right bearer of the twin-tube frame was beefed up and it extended to the rear axle to enable a sufficiently sturdy sidecar mount – this arrangement resulted in the motorcycle and sidecar frames forming a single stable unit. Otherwise the chassis was largely similar to that of the 1936 solo machine with the radiator mounted between the front tubes, sloped forward at approximately 15 degrees.

The attempt to cushion the front fork of the UL 500/1934 with the help of Neiman rubber elements in place of a coil spring was quickly abandoned.

In 1935 the machines used in motorcycle-sidecar races still had the complete structure of the 1934 solo 500cc machine.

In 1936 the sidecar machines received the chassis and engine of the modified solo version.

Probably the only DKW motorcycle-sidecar combination (ridden by Schumann) to survive the war is now in the possession of the Hercules Factory in Nuremberg (currently in the Two Wheel Museum in Neckarsulm. Unfortunately it is not complete).

The four-piston engine of the Schumann sidecar machine. In the body mount cover, on whose exterior the tachometer drive is mounted, is an added crankshaft outer bearing, which picks up the primary chain.

This DKW motorcycle-sidecar combination, here ridden by Kahrmann and Fulda, has the new frame that caused the sidecar and motorcycle chassis to become one rigid unit.

This drawing gives an impression of the described asymmetrical motorcycle frame, whose continuous lower tube running to abeam the rear axle also formed the mainframe element of the sidecar chassis.

An Interesting Experiment

After the road-handling problems caused by the higher weight of the half-liter machine were found to be worse than those of the smaller models, at the initiative of racing engineer Franz Ischinger, in 1935 an experimental model was built with the frame made of sheet metal instead of tubes and the fuel tank as an integral component. To achieve an very low center of gravity, a special version of the four-piston engine was made with a horizontal cylinder block and a double-action charging pump mounted at 90 degrees to it. The flywheel ignition with its relatively heavy flywheel was replaced by a gear-driven Bosch standing magneto (with rotating permanent magnet inductor and fixed ignition coil), which resulted in significantly improved acceleration values. A mounting for a rotary slide intake valve in the engine case was envisaged, but the engine was only entered in races with piston-controlled intake valves. The machine, which was

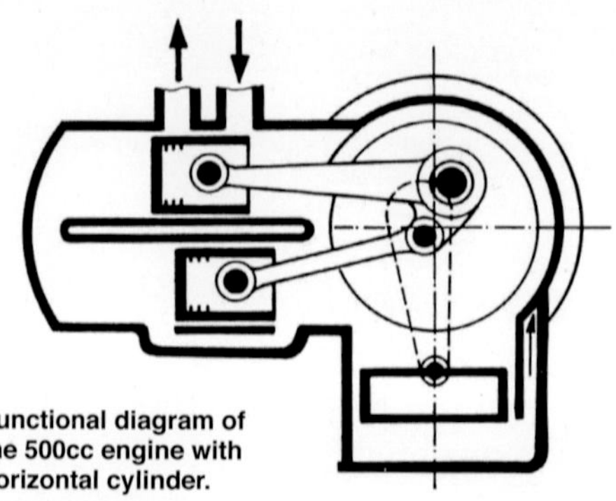

Functional diagram of the 500cc engine with horizontal cylinder.

Below: This sheet metal frame was created in 1935 on the initiative of Franz Ischinger. Its lower center of gravity resulted in better riding characteristics, and a larger fuel tank was supposed to better match the two-stroke engine's thirst for fuel. For this purpose the engine was designed with a horizontal cylinder block with a charging pump projecting downwards from it at a ninety-degree angle. The heavy magneto ignition was replaced by a chain driven standing magneto, and as well the installation of a rotary slide valve on the engine case was envisaged (clearly visible in the photo). The fuel tank's capacity was increased to 40 liters, and the road handling and initial acceleration of the machine (which was considerably lighter than the normal tubular frame version) were impressive. Below right: H.P. Müller with the sheet metal frame machine; one can see a relatively light steel flywheel – which was then experimentally deleted (except for the hub needed to drive the magneto), resulting in a further improvement in the engine's ability to rev during acceleration.

approximately 25kg lighter than the tube frame version, also had a better top speed – and most important it was easier to handle and handled the road very well.

Internal differences of opinion (and the fact that the brawny and reckless Mansfeld achieved good success with the modified tube frame 500) led to the cancellation of the experiments with the "sheet metal machine" (and, incidentally, later to the departure of Ischinger – who was responsible for the production of DKW motorcycles by Auto Union in Ingolstadt after the war – to the Auto Union racing division in Zwickau.)

Entry into the 350cc Class

In 1937 DKW decided to reenter the previously neglected 350cc class after Mr. Moore, former head designer at Norton who had come to Neckarsulm in 1929, failed to defeat the British machines that dominated the class, in particular the original Nortons, with his Norton-like NSU single-cylinder engine. An enlarged version of the successful 250cc ULD, the reed valve engine, was originally considered, and the drawings were already complete when it was decided to build the 350 engine on the basis of the 500 in order to have it ready sooner. The new racing engine therefore became the ULD 350.

With a bore of 39.5mm and a stroke of 68.5mm, the engine operated with the same double-action charging pump low on the engine case as its larger predecessor. It immediately displayed good performance, which during the 1936 season was improved to 36hp at 6,000rpm. The new 350 was thus as good as or even slightly superior to the British Norton. It was to be ridden by Walfried Winkler, Siegfried Wünsche and Walter Hamelehle.

The structure of the machine's frame was largely the same as that of the improved 500 (ULD 500-II), the radiator was placed vertically (to avoid nose-heaviness) in the double cradle frame, which was given the rear-wheel suspension that had already proved itself in the 250.

Beginning with the Eilenriede, the motorcycle won all the national races in 1938, and Walfried Winkler became German Champion.

When it became necessary for the company to also become involved in the 350 class, the ULD 350, a scaled down version of the 500cc four-piston machine with double-action auxiliary pump low on the crankcase, was created in a very short time and was successfully ridden by Walfried Winkler, Heiner Fleischmann and Siegfried Wünsche.

Parallel to the factory 350s, in 1939 a small series of machines for private riders was built in Zschopau. The SS 350 was largely similar to the factory machine and it was received by DKW fans just as enthusiastically as the SS 250. Several examples of this model also survived the war and then gradually began reappearing at postwar races – until the ban on superchargers put an end to this. The photo shows an example owned by Dr. Krackowizer of Salzburg.

The engine and suspension were again reworked during the winter of 1938-39, while at the same time work began on the supercharged 350cc machine (US 350). But in 1939 Heiner Fleischmann was able to gain clear mastery over the British competition with the modified UL 350, the charging pump machine, and won the European championship in his class. (As Ewald Kluge was the European 250 champion, DKW two-strokes won both of the European championships held that year!)

Both machines, the ULD 350 and the US 350, were used experimentally during training for the Eilenriede race in April 1939; the new supercharged machine was ridden in turn by Winkler, Fleischmann and Petruschke. They turned in a number of fast lap times, roughly similar to those previously achieved by the 500 class.

During the race Fleischmann rode the improved ULD 350 and in his first start on a DKW he defeated the NSU, his previous brand. Riding the supercharged 350, Petruschke finished second, just behind Fleischmann (according to the racing division management's description, bad weather prevented the supercharged machine from being ridden to its full potential).

The next event in the 350 class was the Hamburg State Forest Race, where Fleischmann rode the supercharged machine, and he succeeded in recording times equivalent to those of the 500 class. Despite several record lap times, repeated sparkplug problems denied him victory (the Englishman Thomas won on a Velocette). Sparkplug problems were common during those years of rapid two-stroke development – the sparkplug manufacturers were often unable to keep pace with motorcycle development, which taxed the plugs to the utmost.

Unlike the SS 250, the SS 350's primary drive chain was not encapsulated in a light metal case. Drip lubrication supplied the primary chain.

DKW World Records

The success achieved by DKW motorcycles in road and track races often spurred the companies to pursue existing world records and world-record times.

As early as 1929, Baron König-Fachsenfeld (a well-known expert in streamlining and himself a former motorcycle racer) and Meyer of Stuttgart installed a DKW PRe racing engine (the 500cc deflector piston twin-cylinder) in a production DKW sports car with rear wheel drive with the assistance of Obering. Prüssing. The vehicle succeeded in setting twelve international records in the J Class at the French Monthiéry track. (The next year an attempt was made to repeat this success using a front wheel drive car equipped with the same engine, but mounted transversely. It was only partly successful, because in the turns, which were not banked, the inside cylinder facing failed to work properly.)

In 1932 Walfried Winkler broke the first four world records in the 250cc class on the concrete road in Tat, near Budapest.

Riders Geiss and Winkler wee able to establish new world records in the 175- and 250cc classes in 1934. That same year, on the Avus, two production RT 100 motorcycles made an assault on the existing 24-hour record under riders Geiss, Winkler. Müller and Klopfer. Both machines surpassed the existing best performances over 1500km, 1,000 miles and 24 hours.

In 1935 the record machines were fitted with streamlined partial fairings for the first time. The result was new records in the 175- and 250cc classes on the autobahn near Frankfurt/Main.

In 1937 there followed an ONS record week on the Frankfurt autobahn. Fully faired machines (created with the help of Baron König-Fachsenfeld) were used in this event. The fully enclosed bodies so negatively influenced the rider's sense of balance that full streamlining had to be dispensed with, but after the upper part of the fairing was removed, Ewald Kluge was immediately able to best the existing records. Then the arrival of gusty winds prevented a continuation of the record-breaking attempts, which in clam wind conditions would undoubtedly have produced far better results.

In addition to being entered in races, the DKW racing machines were also successfully used in record-setting attempts. In the photo left, the well-known German designer Richard Küchen, who was also active in Zschopau for a time, observes preparation of the 175- and 250cc reed valve machines, which underwent (admittedly minor) modifications in preparation for short distance records with Walfried Winkler as rider. *Right*: Walfried Winkler during pursuit of a record (with streamlined helmet and front fairing).

Partially-faired DKW record machine with 250cc reed valve engine. The standard radiator with its high drag was replaced by a special water hood to increase coolant volume. The power plant and most of the machine were faired.

Record attempts were held (and conducted successfully until they were cancelled due to adverse wind conditions) on the autobahn again in 1938. This full fairing was originally envisaged for the record machines. It was created in cooperation with the well-known streamlining expert Baron Koenig-Fachsenfeld.

Full encapsulation, however, affected the rider's sense of balance. The upper fairing was therefore partially cut away and the machine was then ridden as illustrated.

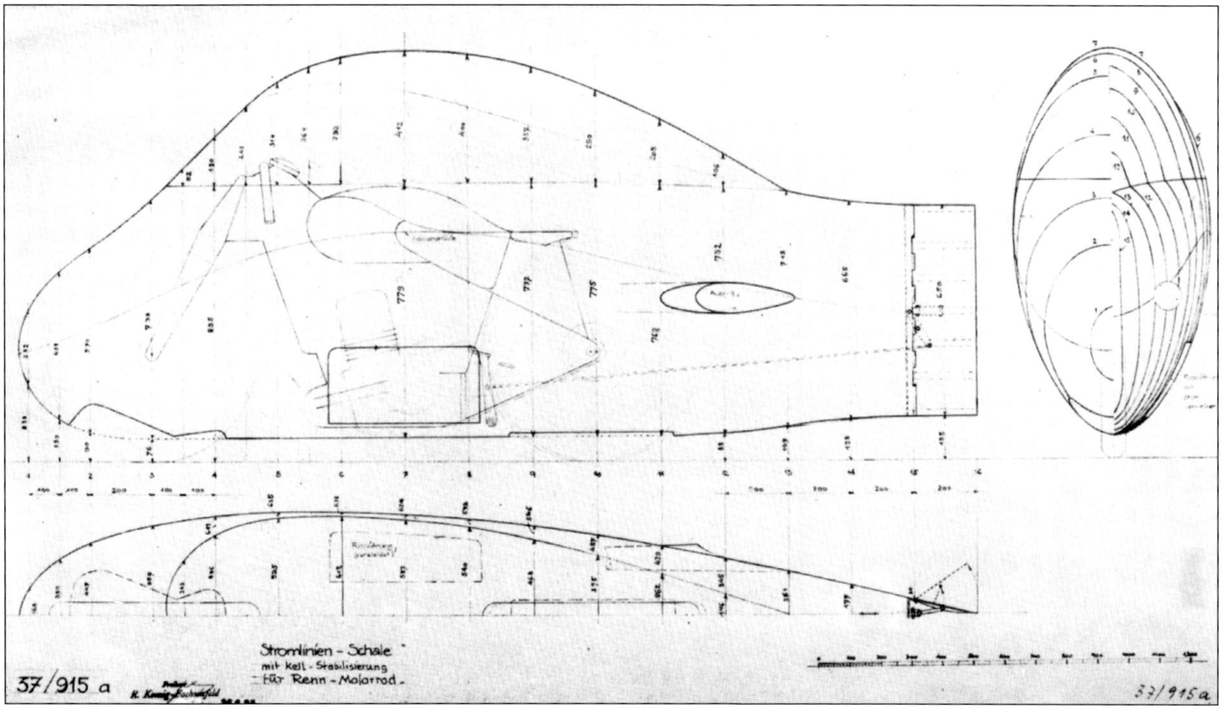

Preliminary studies by Koenig-Fachsenfeld on which the construction of the fairing for the DKW record machines was based.

Ewald Kluge and Walfried Winkler – with streamlined crash helmet extensions (à la Henne/BMW)

At the beginning of 1939, further drag measurements were carried out in the Zeppelin Airship Company's wind tunnel in Friedrichshafen (here with a 125cc double-piston reed valve machine – unfaired in the above photo). Admittedly there were no more record attempts – but during the first two years of the war special versions of the new supercharger engines for alcohol operation were completed in Zschopau and these were supposed to be used for record attempts. These, too, did not take place.

The well-known streamlining expert, Baron Koenig-Fachsenfeld, at record attempts by DKW machines, for which he had developed the full fairing.

DKW Racing Machines for Private Riders

It was previously mentioned that limited numbers of ARe 175 and ORe 250 deflector piston charging pump machines were sold to private buyers with almost the same equipment and performance as the factory motorcycles – probably, in Germany at least, the first "production racers."

Then, in 1935, so as to be able to offer private or up and coming riders a competitive racing machine at an affordable price, DKW launched the SS 250 series of models.

In the beginning, production parts were largely used to make the suspension and chassis – the drive train was mounted in the pressed component frame (with no rear wheel suspension) with the SB 500's pressed component parallelogram fork with enclosed tubes, large drum brakes in both wheels and the short SB tank. The drive train consisted of the first twin-piston engine (UL 250) with the piston charging pump, which increased the engine's conveyed volume, sitting at the front of the engine case, and the initially three-, later four-speed hand- and foot-shifted SB gearbox with primary gear drive, and wet clutch plus kickstarter. The radiator, still obliquely mounted like the cylinder, was a "balcony radiator" analogous to that of the 500cc production models, which had a cutout in the center to accommodate the forward frame element. The engine delivered 20hp at 4,800rpm.

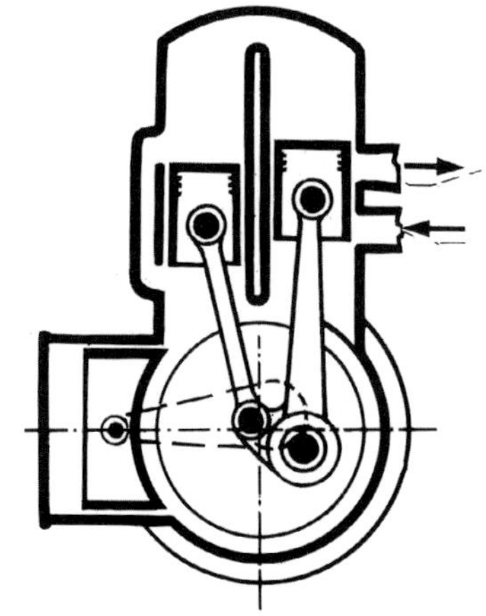

On the 250cc Super Sport machines (production racers for private owners, so to speak) the auxiliary pump, located on the front of the engine case and activated by two excenters, served to increase the case intake volume, as previously seen on deflector piston engines, only with considerably greater total volume. The rear (outlet) piston was responsible for controlling the intake of the two carburetors. In the early years the Super Sport machines could be licensed for use on roads (with headlight).

In 1936-37 the SS 250 was delivered with a double-cradle tubular frame (no rear wheel suspension) with the radiator mounted between the front tubes and separate cylinder head and engine cooling hood, the gearbox still in a case similar to that of the SB but now with foot-shifter only, a longer and narrower fuel tank, and no headlight. The front fork was initially still the SB version, but later it was replaced by the true racing fork.

From the end of 1937 the SS 250, with an engine now delivering 22hp at 4,800rpm, had a completely different appearance, even more similar to the factory machines: the engine with ribbed cooling hood on the cylinder head, carburetors slanted upward, the separate foot-shifted four-speed racing gearbox blocked onto the engine case, the double-cradle frame with the original high-grade racing fork and with the Benelli-design (welded) swing arm rear wheel suspension with the vertical guide cylinders in which rode the swing am end pieces. The 1938 model was largely similar to that of the previous year, except the carburetors had streamlined covers over the air intakes.

Finally, in 1938, the two carburetors, still positioned on the rear (outlet) cylinder, moved between the exhaust pipes, which were positioned somewhat further apart. The gorgeous Elektron alloy central rear brake hubs, like those used by racing machines, provided braking. In the course of the year, about 200 examples of the SS 250 were built and sold. In later years, after retiring from active racing, Arthur Geiss looked after the type's use in racing (in 1937 August Prüssing also added a special race organizer, the well-known and respected motor journalist Adolf Meurer (ADOMEU), to handle organizational matters and publicity for the factory riders; separation of the technical and organizational direction of a factory racing stable later became standard practice).

In addition to the SS 250, in 1939 about fifty examples of an SS 350 racing machine were built. It was largely similar to the UL 350 factory racer (see page 94). Some of the 250- and 350cc DKW racing machines at least survived the war years that followed, and then formed the basis for the rebirth of motorcycle racing in Germany after the war.

In 1935 the double-piston cylinder of the SS 250 (with small light metal head screwed on directly) sat on an SB engine case (initially with three-speed, later four-speed gearbox). The frame and front fork were similar to the components of the SB 500 production machine. Combined hand and foot shifting. In 1935, riding machines like this (but with battery instead of magneto ignition), at the International Six Day Race DKW factory racers won the Silver Vase for Germany for the first time.

From 1936 the SS 250, though still with the sheet metal frame and no rear wheel suspension, was only available in racing configuration (but still with the SB block case and kickstarter.

Beginning in 1936, the SS 250 had a four-speed gearbox.

SS 250 street version (with battery ignition system – coil box – and mufflers).

At the end of 1936 the SS 250 underwent significant changes; double-cradle frame and slender pressed steel fork, larger fuel tank, radiator between the front tubes, separate cylinder head and water hood (as on factory engines), carburetor angled up and to the rear. The engine delivered approximately 22hp at 4,800rpm.

The modified 1936 engine in the steel tube chassis.

In 1937 the SS 250 became even more similar to the factory machines (with their large tank and original racing fork).

Carburetor arrangement on the SS 250, early 1937.

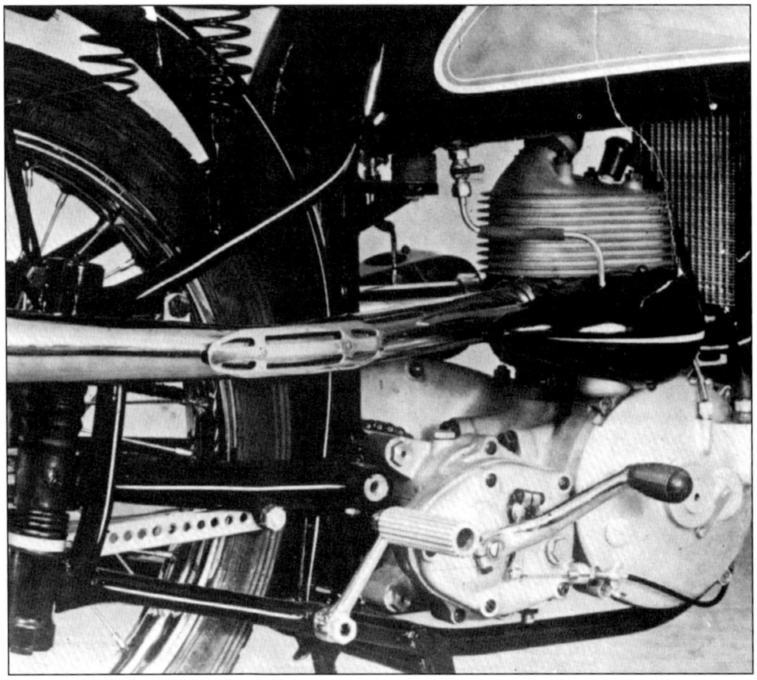

Left: Then, at the end of 1937, a completely new SS 250 arrived: chassis with rear wheel suspension, radiator and cylinder installed vertically (to shift the center of gravity further to the rear), ribbed water hood, separate four-speed racing gearbox without starter. *Right*: The SS 250 of 1938; essentially the previous year's model, streamlined covers over the carburetors.

The SS 250 of 1939 with the two carburetors now behind the cylinder between the exhaust pipes – a gorgeous motorcycle, the dream of many young riders with racing ambitions (and an important basis for the revival of racing sport in Germany after the war, for after all a considerable number of these machines was built).

DKW Off-Road Sport Machines

For many years the DKW machines entered in off-road sporting events and long-distance endurance races, including the six-day races, were standard machines from the SB, RT and NZ series, only carefully prepared (some with high exhaust systems, waterproof ignition systems, stone protection for the engine case and double Bowden cables). In 1937-38 the Auto Union DKW sales program even included an NZ 350 off-road machine, after the *Wehrmacht* and associated paramilitary units and organizations became numbered among the buyers of off-road-capable motorcycles, in addition to numerous private purchasers.

In 1935 a DKW three-man team made up of Ewald Kluge, Walfried Winkler and Arthur Geiss won the Silver Vase at the International Six-Day Race, which was held in Germany (although Winkler had to ride with a badly injured foot in the final days). It was the first time that the Silver Vase, which was almost as coveted as the International Trophy, was won by a German team. (As it had been the previous year in England, the Trophy was won by the BMW factory team.) Interestingly, the DKW machines used in the race (maintained by Wolf Doernhoeffer) were SS 250 racing motorcycles modified only slightly for this special purpose. They were powered by liquid-cooled twin piston charging pump engines, which withstood the difficult race without complaint.

In the endurance races of the prewar years, whose courses only partially ran through the real terrain that typified postwar courses, factory and private riders rode machines that differed only slightly from the production street versions, such as this SB 350 (1936).

Riding an (almost production standard) RT 3 PS (98cc), the DKW team of Herrmann, Klopfer and Walter finished the International Six Day Race in Wales with no penalty points.

Left: Ilse Thouret, successful endurance rider on DKW machines in the early Thirties, takes delivery of her SB 250. *Right*: This DKW factory rider team also rode standard but carefully prepared SB production machines in international endurance races: Kirchberg (later head of the experimental department in Nuremberg), Ischinger (later head of production in Ingolstadt and technical director in Nuremberg), and Keitel (later deputy head of the experimental department at Zündapp).

Left: In 1935 the Auto Union factory riders Walfried Winkler, Arthur Geiss and Ewald Kluge won the Silver Vase in the Six-Day Race on SS 250 charging pump machines modified for street use. *Right*: After the success at the 1935 Six Days, in 1936 the company entered not only the 250 but also the 500cc class with liquid-cooled racing machines – but it was a failure. Here H.P. Müller, who together with Ischinger and Kirchberg rode half-liter charging pump machines (and was the only one to finish with no penalty points).

This RT 125 factory machine was ridden in the 1938 Six Day Race, equipped with rear-wheel suspension. In 1939 a team from the Dutch DKW importer entered a team in the Six Days in Salzburg. In the author's possession, it survived the war and the postwar period in Chemnitz, Saxony.

Engineer Franz Ischinger built three different versions of the air-cooled loop scavenging engine with counter-running charging pump low on the crankcase in the Zschopau racing department for use by the factory off-road team: there was a 175cc version with vertical grey cast iron cylinder (center photo), a 250 (bottom photo) with the engine installed tilted slightly forward with out-canned light metal cylinder (what is probably the only surviving example is in the Augustusburg museum) and finally a 350 with twin-cylinder engine and double-acting crankcase charging pump (engine case with pump from the earlier PRe deflector piston engines), cast light metal cylinder block from the SB 500 production engine, out-canned and scaled down to 350cc. All three models had a separate (Hurth) four-speed gearbox, tubular frame with swing arm rear wheel suspension of the factory racing machines. The trapezoid fork and rear brake hubs also came from the racing machines.

(Incidentally, Winkler's injury was the reason why the board of Auto Union forbade factory riders from further participation in off-road races and similar events, so as not to expose its top riders, who were indispensible for road racing, to additional risk.)

The next year modified DKW racing machines again took part in the six-day race in Germany – including 500cc twin-cylinder (four piston) motorcycles ridden by H.P. Müller, Ischinger and Kirchberg – but this time luck was not on the side of the DKW men and their "estranged" racers (BMW's Trophy team also began using supercharger machines in 1935.)

Racing engineer Ischinger, who was responsible for off-road racing until his departure to Horch, also built special off-road machines. They were designated ORS 175- and 250cc machines with a vertical, air-cooled flat piston engine with loop scavenging, with a counter-running charging pump low on the engine case (in the style of the earlier ORe racing machines). Its light metal cylinder from the 250 was equipped with a shrunken cylinder liner, and the separate drive train (with special gear ratio) came from Hurth of Munich. The engine and gearbox were installed in a special tubular frame, which had a trapeze racing fork at the front, improved ground clearance and rear wheel suspension of the racing machines. Probably the last surviving example of the beautiful ORS 250, of which only a handful were made, is preserved in the Two Stroke Museum in Augustusburg (East Germany).

Ischinger also conceived a basically similar machine (of which just two were made) for the 350 class. It also had an air-cooled twin-cylinder engine with double-action charging pump (this was adopted, complete with engine case, from the earlier PRe engines, while the cylinder block was a resleeved light metal casting of the production SB 500 cylinder) installed in a chassis that was almost the same as that of the ORS 250, also with a Hurth gearbox. Engineer Ischinger personally rode this machine in the 1939 Six Day Race (which was not completed) in Salzburg.

For the rpm and power bands of engines destined for use in off-road sport, it was obviously possible to also equip loop scavenge engine with the additional gearbox charging pump and thus achieve increased performance. Not surprisingly such a possibility was considered at the time when the switch was being made from deflector piston to twin-piston engines in racing machines (for this period coincided with the introduction of loop scavenging into regular production). Tests revealed, however, that in the higher rpm ranges at which racing engines operated, increasing the crank chamber's conveyed volume adversely affected the scavenge flow during gas exchange in the cylinder, consequently the decision – not wrong, as the future showed – was made in favor of the double-piston design for racing engines.

The Racing Department of the DKW Factory in Zschopau

The racing department in the DKW factory was – until its disbandment when the war broke out in 1939 – completely independent of the production organization (only design was under the factory's chief designer). From modest beginnings (an appendage of the experimental department), it ultimately became a "factory within a factory."

The tasks of the racing department were:

1. Design of racing and off-road sports machines
2. Manufacture of individual parts
3. Testing and experimentation
4. Transport
5. Participation in races (field service)

The racing design bureau consisted of:

1 designer as department head
4 designers for engine, gearbox and suspension

The racing department's personnel consisted of:

1 senior engineer (management)
1 experimental engineer
1 test bench engineer with
3 engine stand fitters for engine development
1 technician with
1 typist for materials procurement and deadline monitoring
1 foreman with
34 men for the mechanical workshop
1 foreman with
20 men and
1 marker
1 inspector
1 storekeeper
1 assistant for chassis assembly
1 foreman with
8 men for engine and gearbox assembly
1 assistant foreman
3 plumbers
3 welders for plumbing work
1 experimental rider for the racing department and
2 riders for the off-road sport department
20 apprentices.

The field service was subdivided into the technical and organizational areas. Here, too, technical direction was in the hands of the senior engineer in charge of the department. For big races he was accompanied and assisted by the test bench engineer, particularly in training for time keeping, the creation of synoptic tables over the progress of the training and race, as well as the supervision of modifications to the machine during training.

The field service's technical personnel consisted of:

1 foreman or senior fitter
1 mechanic
1 ignition specialist

As well, there were:

7 factory riders
2 truck drivers for the racing service vehicle.

The senior engineer also looked after the off-road sport department when it was in the field.

In 1939 the racing and off-road sports department occupied a space of approximately 835m². As this proved inadequate, an expansion to 2000 square meters – with a simultaneous expansion of the pool of machine tools – was planned for 1940. This, too, did not happen.

In the years from 1937 to 1939 the racing department on average made:

20-25 racing machines for the factory riders
50-75 racing sport machines for training new riders
20-25 off-road sport machines for the factory riders

And approximately fifty off-road machines for *Wehrmacht* and official agencies. It was also responsible for repairs after each event, twenty to thirty per year.

The racing machines were transported to the races in a five-ton MAN truck, which covered between 30,000 and 40,000 kilometers per year.

Summary of an Era

After the Second World War (during which he was placed in charge of Auto Union's DKW factory in Zschopau), Obering. Prüssing (1967†) summarized the state of DKW racing engine development in a "look back and view forward" – at a time when the future in Germany was completely uncertain. More than thirty years later, it is interesting to read his thoughts:

"The racing engines made in the DKW factory were all building blocks in the creation of a high-performance two-stroke engine. Without the examples that already existed for four-stroke engines, we had to find our own

Left: Prüssing's two-stroke auxiliary engine for gliders (which he built in Berlin before joining DKW) in a glider training aircraft by Wolf Hirth. *Right*: Prüssing as head of the DKW racing department in the boxes – Wünsche must come in to refuel at once!

way, and we were therefore forced to proceed step by step during the long years of racing two-stroke development at DKW.

Efforts to develop the normal three-port single-piston two-stroke engine into a high-performance engine failed on account of the high scavenging losses caused by this type of gas exchange and its symmetrical control diagram. For this reason we succeeded in developing to their limits, not least because of unbearably high fuel consumption, the deflector piston ARe, ORe and PRe racing engines equipped with counter-running crankcase charging pump. The addition of the charging pump resulted in an improvement in charge in the higher rpm ranges, but in the lower rpm ranges fuel consumption was too high because of the fresh charge that escaped through the outlet.

Loop scavenging bestowed advantages on normal three-port two-stroke engines without charging capabilities thanks to more favorable thermal conditions, better performance in the low rpm range and reduced fuel consumption. Experiments in combining loop scavenging with additional charging pistons, however, produced less than satisfactory results, because the gas speed in the cylinder at higher rpm was obviously too great and led to detonation phenomena not seen in deflector piston charging pump engines.

Experiments were made with a control piston or poppet valve to control the intake and outlet in the cylinder working area. Once again the results were below expectations, especially as the engines were more complicated and the mechanical design costs were disproportionate to the results achieved.

On the other hand, because of its asymmetrical control diagram, the U-cylinder engine with Zoller-designed articulated connecting rod brought with it the possibility of charging or even overcharging, and because of this and the considerably greater displacement performance resulting from the uniflow scavenging, the DKW two-stroke racing engines were superior to the competition at least until 1938. The potential of the double-piston engine, however, was limited by the cylinder spacing, the combustion chamber shape and the axial offset of the engine.

The opposed piston design offered better prospects of creating a high-performance two-stroke engine with supercharging, but designing the crank drive caused problems, whether two crank shafts working on a common output shaft via gears were used, or rocker arms and additional connecting rods, because of the inertia forces of the oscillating components which limited revolutions. Experiments in this direction (with rocker arms and additional connecting rods) took place in the DKW

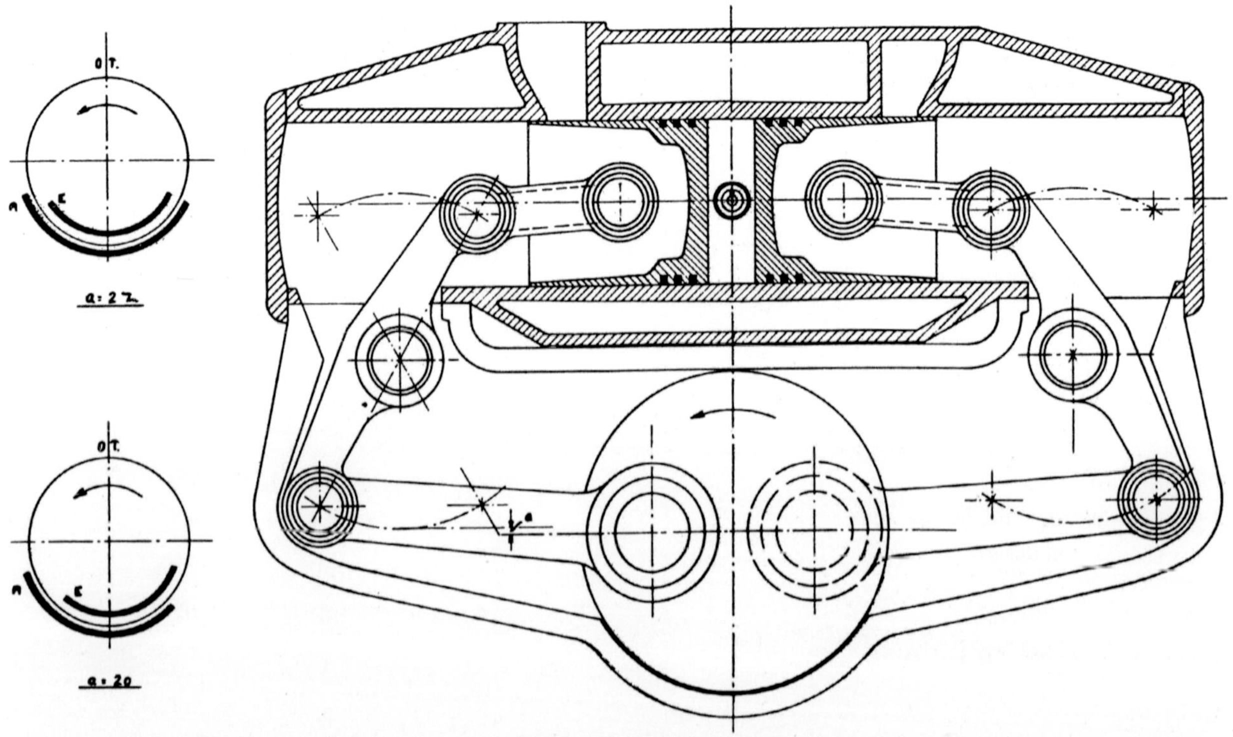

Schematic of the opposed piston engine with rocker arm crankshaft drive designed by Richard Küchen. Following unsuccessful experiments at Zündapp, he later also built the engine at DKW in Zschopau (the two diagrams on the left show how an asymmetry of the control diagram was achieved through different offsets). The experiments at DKW were also terminated without success. The idea of the opposed piston design was later revived – but with a different arrangement of the crankshaft drive.

factory but were unsuccessful and had to be abandoned – even though this design may be justified for slower-running engines.

The well-known opposed piston engine designed by Junkers must also be eliminated from consideration for a racing two-stroke engine because of its excessive mechanical complexity and the undesirable high inertia forces. Control pistons oscillating in the cylinder head, on the other hand, lead to thermal difficulties in the cylinder head, especially in air-cooled engines.

Despite what has been said, however, the possibilities of the normal double-piston design to not appear to have been exhausted. Only the path of working with mixture scavenging must be abandoned. For even with double pistons, it is impossible to avoid part of the fresh charge delivered to the cylinder by the charging system escaping through the outlet port unused. An effort must therefore be made to work towards making the mixture preparation take place inside the cylinder rather than outside. The inject system will result in difficulties in the beginning, for pumps for the small quantities needed are very expensive to manufacture, even though the injection must not take place with the extremely high pressures seen in diesel engines. The pumps currently available do not appear suitable for the perspective task at hand.

Injection development will be made more difficult by the unmistakable tendency in racing engines of dividing the class piston displacement into small cylinder units, as the following examples of existing racing engines show:

500cc four-cylinder	Gilera/Italy
	Ariel/England
	AJS/England
250cc four-cylinder	Benelli/Italy
Double U-cylinder	DKW 250cc
	DKW 350cc
Triple U-cylinder	DKW 500cc

As a result, the injected quantities per cylinder become even smaller, but the creation of suitable pumps will be an urgent and surely solvable task – unless an injection method is developed that is free of high-precision pumps.

Two paths to this end are possible:

1. Injection of a complete fuel-air mixture produced outside the cylinder;
2. Introduction of the fuel during the scavenge process in the scavenge port. Here longer mixture preparation times are available.

Another possibility would be to control the injection electromagnetically, as used successfully by Moto Guzzi and several aero-engines. In this case too, however, its use in two-stroke engines would be made more difficult by the doubled number of injections in the time unit.

If the injection problem is solved satisfactorily, however, double-piston and opposed-piston two-strokes will be able to operate more economically, as they will be scavenged with pure air and it will be possible to largely prevent fuel loss through the mixing of fresh charge and burnt gas. High-performance two-stroke engines of this type will inevitably be more complex than before, as overcharging will only be possible with a supercharger and the switch to separate lubrication will be necessary, quite apart from the complexity of the double piston or opposed piston design.

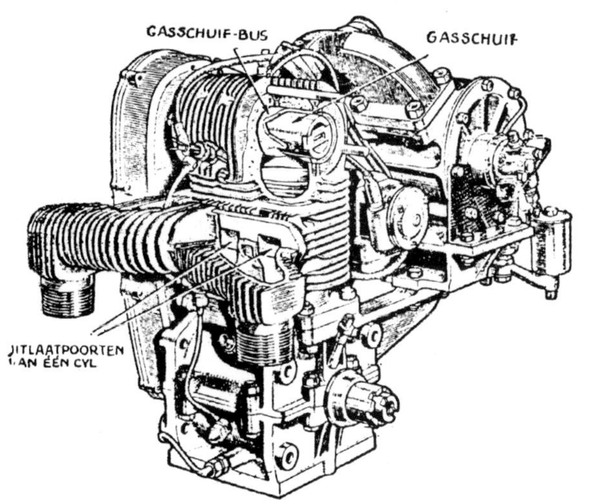

In his "Balance," Prüssing also spoke of this as a possible future development of a high-performance two-stroke: single piston engine, in which the piston controls the scavenge slits (not shown in the drawing), while the outlet was to be controlled by a conical rotary valve (Aspin rotary valve).

Despite what is said above, attention should also be paid to continued test results with slider valve control in the cylinder head, as in the Cross or Aspin designs, in which the Aspin cone sleeve valve appears to offer better prospects for use in the two-stroke engine. It is not known what advances were made by the two English designs during the war years.

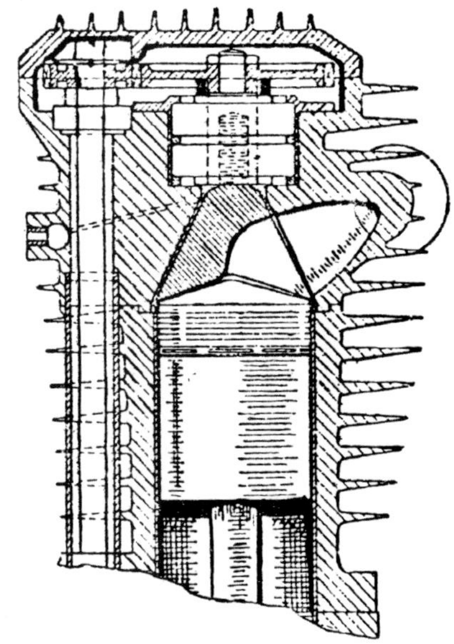

Partial cutaway drawing of an English two-stroke engine development: it is a supercharger-boosted twin-cylinder in which the fresh charge was fed into the cylinder head by a rotary roller slide valve, while the pistons controlled the outlet slots – almost impossible to realize because of the thermal piston loads (see Prüssing's Balance).

Only with respect to superchargers – in any case necessary for future high-performance two-stroke engines – does the previous development work done by DKW also appear to be the correct path for the future."

Much of what August Prüssing wrote at that time was done on the basis of the current state of technology and with the proviso that there was no outside interference in technical development. For apart from the fact that no one could foresee the development of electronics and half-liter technology – when racing engine development was shelved by DKW, the people in Zschopau still knew nothing about the unsuspected possibilities of making gas dynamics usable for the operating process in the two-stroke engine. No one was thinking about the possibility of a ban on superchargers for racing engines (which most thought, when it came into effect in 1951, was the end of the racing two-stroke) either.

All in all: when the lights went out in the DKW racing department, it was the end of an era in two-stroke development which the men of DKW had helped shape.

The Second Leg: DKW Automobiles

The Rear Wheel Drive Vehicles from Spandau

As briefly described in his biography, Rasmussen's interest in building automobiles was apparent during the early years of engine production in Zschopau: apart from the experiment with his own tandem two-seater which, using the first of Ruppe's stationary engine, was created in the "Kaisersaal" in Zschopau in 1919-20, his spontaneous interest in Dr. Slaby's SB electric car (an its subsequent temporary fitting with the 175cc DKW two-speed motorcycle gearbox) also sprang from this tendency.

But if a small auto concept – and even if only projected for the lowest performance class – was to be the basis for noteworthy series production, then a multi-cylinder engine was necessary for the required performance. As, in Rasmussen's opinion, only a two-stroke would do, the series of DKW single-cylinder engines would have to be augmented by a twin-cylinder design. Rasmussen wanted one anyway in order to expand his motorcycle production program, and when it was ready for quantity production in 1927, first with a displacement of 500 and later 600 cubic centimeters, it also filled the requirement for the construction of a proper small car. Rasmussen's engagement in Berlin and Spandau (first by joining Dr. Slaby's company and then by taking over the operation and moving it to Spandau, where there was more room to expand) was definitely tied to the realization of his automobile-making plans. When, on the other hand, he secured Dr. Slaby's continued partnership, making him technical director of the Spandau branch plant, it showed the direction he envisaged for the coming DKW car: with a self-supporting, faux-leather-covered plywood body with wooden frame.

The first DKW automobile developed by Dr. Slaby according to Rasmussen's concept appeared in May 1928. Designated the P 15, it was available as an open two-

Thirty men demonstrate the strength of the load-bearing plywood body.

This twin-cylinder liquid-cooled engine with flange-mounted three-speed transmission was installed in the Spandau DKW car. The engine was developed from the motorcycle power plant. Generator with ignition distributor in front powered directly by the crankshaft.

The DKW P 15 car, developed in Spandau, with 600cc twin-cylinder engine, rear wheel drive and load-bearing faux-leather-covered plywood body. The car seen here is a two-seat roadster (also available as a convertible with two folding seats in the rear). Year of manufacture 1928-29.

Cutaway view of the DKW Roadster (convertible) revealing its structure and arrangement of assemblies.

seater (roadster) or two-seat convertible. The latter was capable of carrying two extra people in the rear (whose folding roof formed the backrests). This was a body style then in use by other makers of small cars, Hanomag for example.

The liquid-cooled 600cc two-stroke twin (with deflector pistons) was installed in the conventional place in front under the hood, with the crankshaft installed longitudinally. Power was transmitted to the three-speed transmission (made by Prometheus of Berlin, in which Rasmussen had an interest) by a single disc clutch, and from there via a Cardan shaft to the (Prometheus) differential in the rigid rear axle. The wheels and axles were suspended (as on earlier Slaby designs) on leaf springs.

In the second year (1929), three- and four-seat convertible sedans (with fixed door frames) were added, and in 1930 they were joined by a shapely two-seat sports car painted in the colors of Saxony (white and green). It had a 600cc 18hp engine and Bugatti rear end (with the driver, who had a more powerful charging pump engine from the Zschopau racing department, centrally seated in the car, which weighed just over 500 kg, he could certainly be seen at sporting events.)

In Zschopau, meanwhile, a larger two-stroke automobile engine had been created. It came from engineer Paffrath, who was well known for his other work (in the motorcycle and engine fields). Rasmussen had taken over his design (and his associate Gehle). It was a four-cylinder 90° V engine with deflector pistons. A double-action crankcase-independent charging pump was envisaged for each bank of cylinders, alternately delivering a fresh charge to the working cylinders in one or the other side. The vertically divided cylinder/crankcase (Paffrath had been awarded a patent for this configuration) was not used as a pre-compression space, consequently the engine initially used splash lubrication (see photo page 118) and later pump pressure lubrication (see photo above) instead of mixture lubrication.

The two-seat convertible. Year of manufacture 1928-29.

The first DKW automobile brochure from Zschopau, 1929.

This 1929 convertible was a true three-seater (third seat crosswise in back).

Here the 600cc DKW has already molted into the four-seat convertible (more accurately: convertible sedan). Year of manufacture 1929-30.

The PS 600 Sport was built in 1930 and 1931. This DKW sports car had an 18hp engine and attractive lines (after opening the long hood, one interested person asked the ironic question: where is the engine? A DKW man replied: "Just reach in, where it's hot is the engine!") With a price tag of 2,500 Reichsmarks, it was cheaper than the three-seat convertible.

After production of the SB single-seater both with electric drive and (experimentally) a DKW engine stopped (see page 19), a larger electric car was built there. It was conceived primarily as a "Droschke" (taxi) but also as a delivery vehicle. It was powered by a 4.6hp electric motor (installed under the floor in the middle of the vehicle), which was connected to the differential rear axle by a Cardan shaft. The 120 Ah battery was located under the hood.

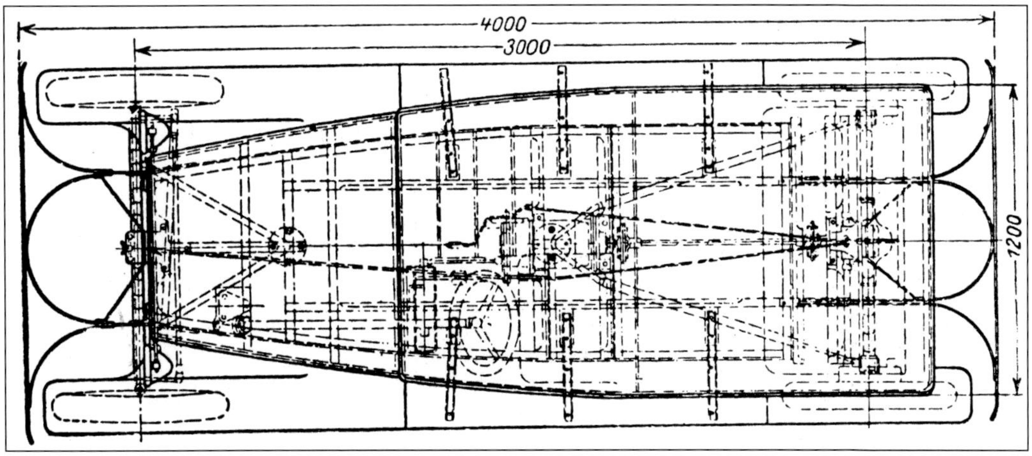

Structural details show that this electric car was the direct forerunner of first "true" DKW automobile (P 15) brought out in 1928: the load-bearing car box (without chassis) was made of plywood with wooden stiffeners. It was covered with thin copper sheet. Transverse leaf springs sprung the rigid axles against the load-bearing body. Weight with batteries 900 kg. Speed 40kph, radius of action 100km.

Equipped with the twin-cylinder motorcycle engine with charging pump, the green and white DKW sports car was often victorious in its class. Here it is being driven by the Berlin racing driver Simons.

In April 1930 Baron Koenig-Fachsenfeld, well-known as a racing car driver and later an expert in streamlining, set 12 new international performance records driving a production DKW sports car powered by a 500cc charging pump engine (over 100, 200, 500 and 1,000 miles, 200, 500, 1000 and 2000 kilometers, plus 3, 6, 12 and 24 hours) on the track in Monthiéry, France.

Refueling stop during the record setting drives on the track in Monthiéry, France. On the hood is Obering. Prüssing, who had provided the car's engine, and behind him Baron Koenig-Fachsenfeld.

The DKW engine almost disappeared beneath the 40-liter fuel tank of the DKW record car, which achieved average speeds of between 104 and 110kph.

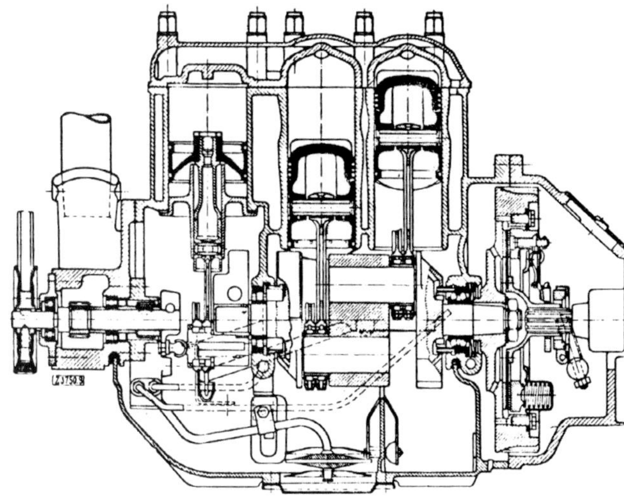

Cross-section of a cylinder bank of the DKW four-cylinder two-stroke engine with double-action charging pump in front.

This engine, which beginning in 1929 appeared in a variety of displacements and remained in production until the early months of the war, was displayed in advertisements under the signum 4+8 (as a four-cylinder two-stroke, equivalent to an eight-cylinder four-stroke). It was built in a number of versions, initially with a bore-stroke of 60x68mm and 780cc, 68x68mm and 980cc (output 20 and 25hp at 3,200/3,500rpm) and from 1935 with a bore-stoke of 70x68mm and 32hp at 3,800rpm from a displacement of 1054cc. The latter variant initially found itself in the "Schwebeklasse" (floating class) (which got its name from the rigid rear axle with high-mounted transverse spring, the "floating axle," which from then on was used in all DKW cars, including the front wheel drive car made exclusively in Zwickau) and later the "Sonderklasse" (special class). Instead of a wooden body, the latter had steel body similar to that of the Wanderer W 24 on a chassis frame. In 1932 the three-speed transmission was replaced by a four-speed unit (later delivered by Hurth of Munich) with selectable freewheel.

The freewheel, which was later also installed in the DKW front wheel drive cars, was displayed in the company's advertising, not without justification, because of the fuel savings it allowed. In fact, however, its purpose was to avoid the two-stroke's annoying sputtering when coasting downhill – and as the braking effect of two-

Four-cylinder 4 = 8 sedan with 25hp engine, year of manufacture 1929-30.

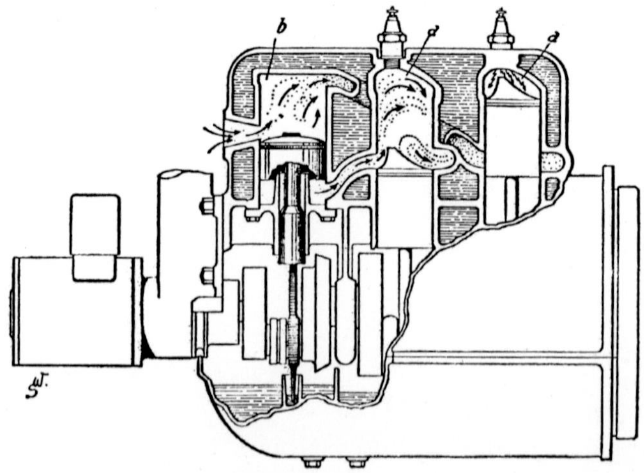

Functional diagram of the DKW four-cylinder engine (with deflector pistons and pressure-free crankcase).

stroke engines was systemically limited anyway, a virtue could be so to speak made of necessity.

In Zschopau the four-cylinder engine (which could not be converted to loop scavenging because of the position of the double-action charging pump) remained (because of its fuel consumption and its mechanical running noise) a problem child to the end, when a lengthened exhaust manifold made it thermally more sound and a downdraft carburetor more cultivated. Its chosen replacement was the three-cylinder in-line engine, which was to have powered the F 9 front wheel drive car scheduled to enter production in 1940.

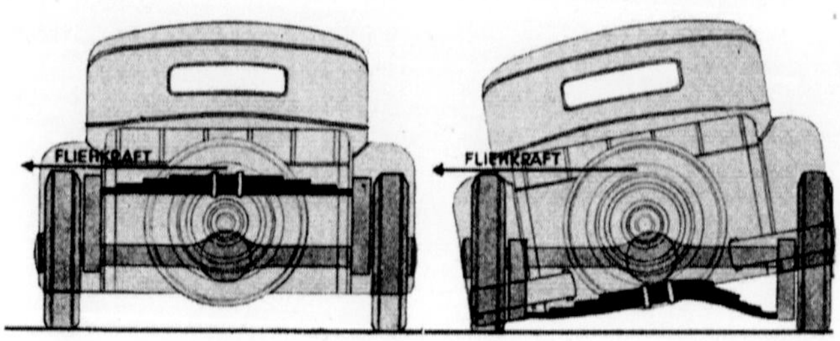

"As the springs in the "floating axle" act on the car's center of gravity (left), the body does not roll in turns (right) – improved driving safety, greater driving comfort." (Original DKW sound track 1929)

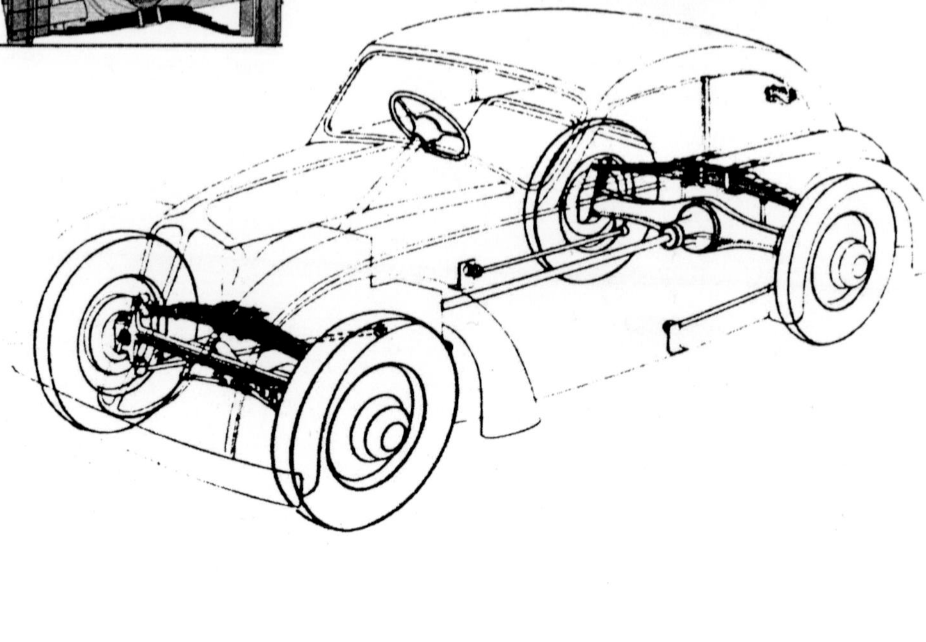

See-through drawing of the Schwebeklasse, which reveals the arrangement of the rigid rear axle with high-mounted leaf springs ("floating axle").

DKW four-cylinder model (V 800 or V 1000), built in 1930-32, now in the Transportation Museum in Dresden. In the beginning, the leather covering tended to separate during the car's life (as may be seen here). Later, however, the Spandau factory rectified this problem.

By 1932 the four-cylinder car was called the Sonderklasse – in 1932-34 the model shown in the photo was designated Sonderklasse 1001.

With respect to its roomy, streamlined body, the DKW Schwebeklasse, first presented in 1934 and then in 1935 offered with a more powerful 30hp engine, was an avant-garde experiment that was surely too far ahead of its time. Although performance, roominess and road handling were very good (in large part due to the floating axle used here for the first time), it was not popular with buyers.

Convertible sedan version of the 1934-37 Schwebeklasse.

The Schwebeklasse factory cars, ready for the 2000-km drive through Germany in 1934 (in the center is Zentzytzki of Auto Union's advertising department, who arrived at the finish line with a lad of five hours).

Built from 1937 to 1940, the (third) Sonderklasse with the 32hp four-cylinder engine, but now with all-steel body and chassis frame. The chassis and body design were similar to those of the Wanderer W 24.

In 1931 (and later) the Berlin racing car driver Gerhard Macher (who had previously driven the DKW 600cc sports car with success), entered the Monoposto (here on the Avus) built for him in Spandau. The car was equipped with two Zoller double-piston engines and a Zoller supercharger. Wearing the hat is Dr. Slaby.

Look beneath the hood of the DKW 1.5-liter racing car: the engine compartment is truly filled, with the supercharger sitting between the two coupled Zoller double-piston engines each with four pistons.

The Front Wheel Drive Cars from Zwickau

There are no surviving documents that reveal when Rasmussen made the decision to build a parallel model series of small cars with front wheel drive, which he envisaged would be produced in the Audi factory in Zwickau.

It was certain that it was necessary to find a new use for the Zwickau factory, whose sales of large automobiles were steadily shrinking, if the company was to continue to exist at all. It was also certain that Rasmussen was convinced that, in the economic conditions prevailing in Germany, production of a new automobile could only be justified if they succeeded in offering a small car that was less expensive to buy and operate than those of its competitors. Contemporaries also remember that Rasmussen himself undertook the first provisional studies and "try-outs" in his factory in Zschopau to determine the minimum weight that the body of a small two-seater should have – and in his calculations he found that the dimensions he was seeking were not that far off those used by Dr. Slaby in the first DKW two-seater he designed in Spandau in 1928.

It is no longer possible to determine if those who seem to remember that there was contact with Munich motorcycle and two-stroke designer Gockerell (also written as Cockerell) are correct. This seems quite probable, because in 1926 in Munich (after his Megola motorcycle with a 640cc five-cylinder rotary engine in the front wheel and a series of well-made small motorcycles with [largely liquid-cooled] two-stroke engines were produced there) Gockerell tested prototypes of automobiles with front wheel drive, including one with a twin-cylinder and one with a six-cylinder two-stroke inline engine. Also suggestive of contact between Rasmussen and Gockerell (who perhaps could have brought about the decision in favor of front wheel drive) is the fact that one of the Stiebling brothers who worked for DKW (and later for Framo in Hainichen) had also worked in Gockerell's design bureau in Munich, and perhaps it was he who made contact between the Munich designer and Rasmussen.

In any case, Rasmussen gave his Zwickau AUDI factory a precisely outlined order to develop a small car with front wheel drive. This is revealed by a documentation made by one of only two surviving designers (out of 24) then active in the AUDI factory. The following is an extract from that account:

"In October 1930 Herr Rasmussen came to the design bureau with factory manager Schuh and expressed the desire that we design and build a prototype of a small car as quickly as possible, using a DKW two-stroke motorcycle drive train made by the Zschopau motor works. Herr Rasmussen explained that he intended to build a cheap, but capable car that would appeal to the general population and sell well.

The design was to incorporate:

350cc, possibly 500cc motorcycle engine,
front wheel drive with Tracta joints, wheels mounted on transverse springs front and rear,
Spandau-made screw steering,
narrow chassis frame,
low center of gravity.

He requested the soonest possible delivery date and gave us five to six weeks to complete the design work. Three prototype vehicles were to be built simultaneously, and at least one vehicle was to be running in six weeks. We were only able to meet this target by issuing the workshop interim drawings, in order to reduce the drawing work to a minimum. All formality was avoided in assigning tasks to the workshop. The blueprints came directly from the design bureau to the foreman in prototype construction. There was thus also no regular work scheduling.

Until the DKW front wheel drive car, the AUDI factory had mainly built large, powerful automobiles and a few trucks up to 3 tons. But with no experience in the area of the task they had been assigned, the designers had their hands full creating something fundamentally new.

The first prototype car was running just before the specified six-week period ran out, and in Herr Rasmussen's presence the car's handling characteristics and speed were tested on Audi's experimental track, with all of the participants driving the vehicle. There was unanimous approval of its outstanding handling and good performance. Fully fueled with no occupants, with a three-seat open body, the car weighed 450 kg. Maximum speed was measured at 85 kilometers per hour.

The chassis of the DKW F 1: individual wheel mounting on upper and lower leaf springs, additional control and damping springs in the rear, screw steering in front with Tracta joints (which were later replaced by DKW's own wide angle joints designed by Engineer Jung). Despite the cross-members, the frame girder was not sufficiently rigid and was later replaced by a closed box girder, and ultimately by a wide T-girder frame (also see photo on page 124).

After these test drives, Herr Rasmussen immediately made the decision to put the vehicle into production and to take it to the automobile show in spring 1931."

From the beginning, therefore, the DKW "*Frontwagen*" (patented name meaning front wheel drive car) made in Zwickau differed in two fundamental details from the Spandau models: they had front wheel drive, and while (apart from the sheet steel bodies of the two- and four-seat full convertibles and two-seat sports cars) they had a synthetic-leather-covered plywood body, it was not self-supporting. Instead it was mounted on a chassis frame (which was changed several times in the course of development).

DKW automobiles did have one thing in common until the end, however: the two-stroke engine.

DKW F 1 front wheel drive car here with the steel roadster body. This version was only built in small numbers.

The majority of F 1 roadsters were built with a much less elegant faux-leather-covered wooden body. The second generation cars had doors and a trunk cover, however.

Until the introduction of loop scavenging on DKW 600 and 700cc front wheel drive automobile engines (1933), these engines too were delivered with deflector pistons. The Dynastart system was still the first of its kind, the "Blech-Luma" made in Stuttgart (the unstable sheet metal was later replaced by a cast aluminum housing). The simple Hardy disc is still on drive shaft inside the transmission output.

The often successful DKW-Front-Monoposto. On the left, Ove Rasmussen at an ice race (grips on the tires!).

Wheel mounting (on leaf springs top and bottom) and drive train of the F 1's front wheels – Hardy flexible joint discs inside, Tracta wide-angle CV joints outside.

Front wheel swivel bearing and joint arrangement on the F 1 – note the grease cups.

Above: After the successful record attempts by Baron Koenig-Fachsenfeld in the DKW rear wheel drive sports car on the Monthiéry track in 1930, at the instigation of a "Herr M. of Stuttgart," in 1931 renewed attempts were made to set records with a 500cc Monoposto. They were halted (after a short-distance best time was recorded), because in the unbanked turns the unanticipated centrifugal effect caused the cylinder on the inside of the turn to be starved of fuel.

Below: Look under the hood of the front wheel drive record car of 1931, revealing the front wheel drive train with 500cc PRe twin-cylinder racing engine. The motorcycle racing carburetor, flange-mounted to the transverse cylinder block, proved unsuitable because of centrifugal effect in the unbanked turns at Monthiéry and prevented the setting of new records. Flywheel magneto ignition (photo right).

Convertible sedan version of the DKW Meisterklasse 701 Type F 2, year of manufacture 1932-33. 700cc, 22hp.

Partial cutaway of the DKW front wheel drive car's drive train with loop scavenging. On the right side of the engine case is the lever for engaging and releasing the freewheel. The new rubber-cushioned medial joint had replaced the previous Hardy discs. In the drawing is the twin-cylinder engine's crankshaft, mounted on six roller bearings. 600cc (Reichsklasse) with bore-stroke of 74x68mm and 18hp at 3,500rpm, 700cc (Meisterklasse) with bore-stroke of 76x76mm and 20hp at 3,500rpm.

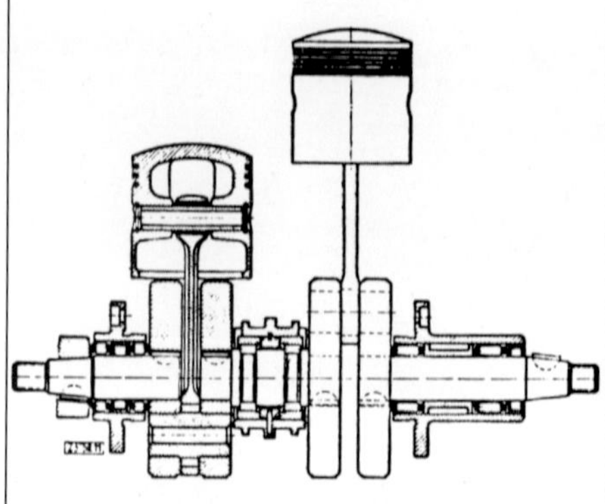

Crank drive of the DKW 600cc twin-cylinder engine.

Convertible sedan version of the DKW Meisterklasse Type F 4 year of manufacture 1934-35.

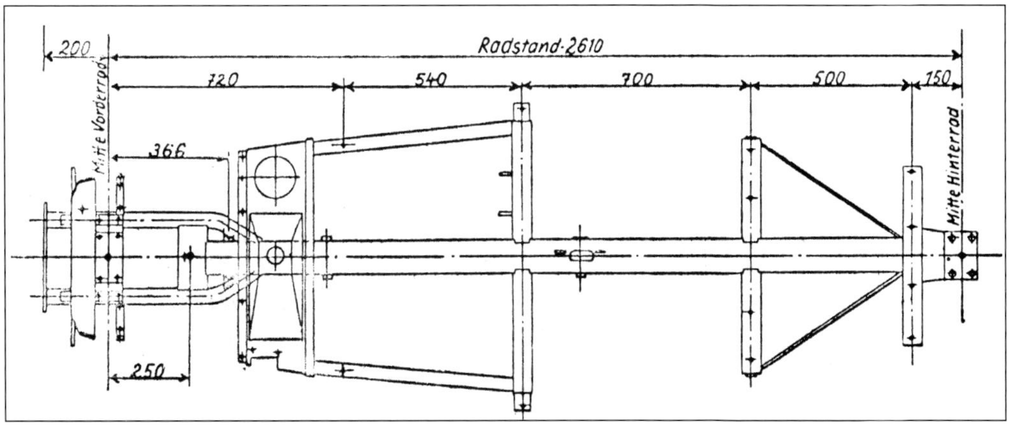

The F 5 and F 7 models had – with minor variations – this frame with square central member.

DKW Meisterklasse convertible sedan Type F 5, 700cc, year of manufacture 1935-36.

DKW F 5 K – Luxus Sport 700 front wheel drive car, open two-seater with steel body, year of manufacture 1936-37.

DKW Reichsklasse Type F 5 600cc convertible sedan, year of manufacture 1936.

DKW Reichsklasse Type F 7 600cc sedan, year of manufacture 1937-38. 600cc, 18hp.

DKW Meisterklasse F 8 700cc 20hp sedan (recognizable by its vertical radiator grill rods), year of manufacture 1939-42.

On the left of the photo is the DKW Meisterklasse Type F 8-700 Cabrio 2 (two seats), and at right a 1939 DKW Front Luxus Type F 8 two-seat convertible.

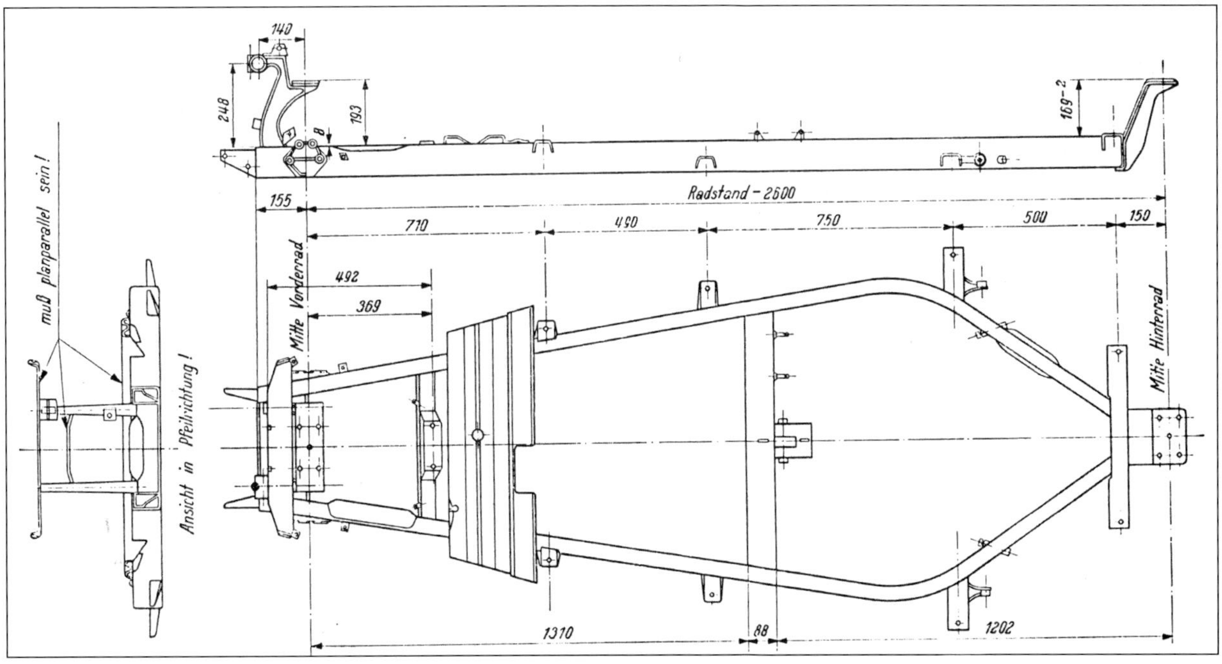

Dimensional drawing of the box frame of the DKW Reichs- and Meisterklasse F 8.

DKW Integrated Engines

The first products made by the DKW factory in Zschopau were engines. The very first was a toy motor, but in 1919 a 5hp stationary engine (which also powered Rasmussen's first experimental car) was unveiled at the Leipzig Fair. Unfortunately no technical documents or personal memories of the engine survive. That year the company also delivered the first auxiliary bicycle engines for installation by dealers or private buyers.

Even after DKW began selling complete two-wheel vehicles in 1921, the engine sector remained important part of the company's program. For these engines (at first without a gearbox or with just reduction gears to the lay shaft in the engine case) were sold to many companies that used them to power their own two- or three-wheeled vehicles.

And even after many manufacturers had stopped producing them, from the Twenties until production at Zschopau stopped in 1945 there were numerous basic types (air-cooled single-cylinder models with displacements of 100, 200, 300 and 461 cubic centimeters, plus the air-cooled twin-cylinder TL500 and the liquid-cooled twin-cylinder models ZW 600 and ZW 1100). These basic types came in a multitude of variants, resulting from the special requirements of the customers. These

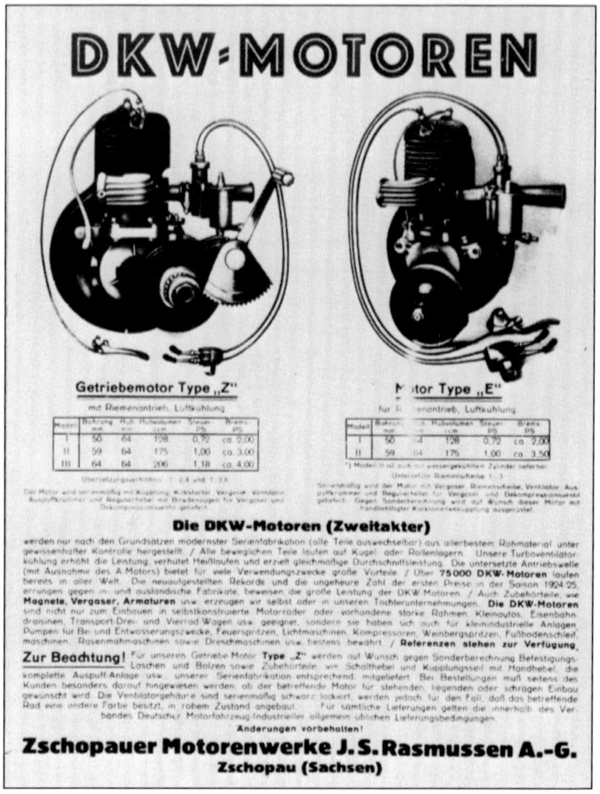

Modell	Bohrung mm	Hub mm	Hubvolumen ccm	Steuer-PS	Brems-PS
I	50	64	128	0,72	ca. 2,00
II	59	64	175	1,00	ca. 3,00
III	64	64	206	1,18	ca. 4,00

Modell	Bohrung mm	Hub mm	Hubvolumen ccm	Steuer-PS	Brems-PS
I	50	64	128	0,72	ca. 2,00
II	59	64	175	1,00	ca. 3,50

Left: DKW engine advertisement from the mid 1920s. Right: DKW Type E engine with speed-reducing gearbox and fan forced cooling, delivered to manufacturers for installation in vehicles. It was also available with liquid cooling.

DKW Type A integrated engine (without speed-reducing gearbox) with cooling fan.

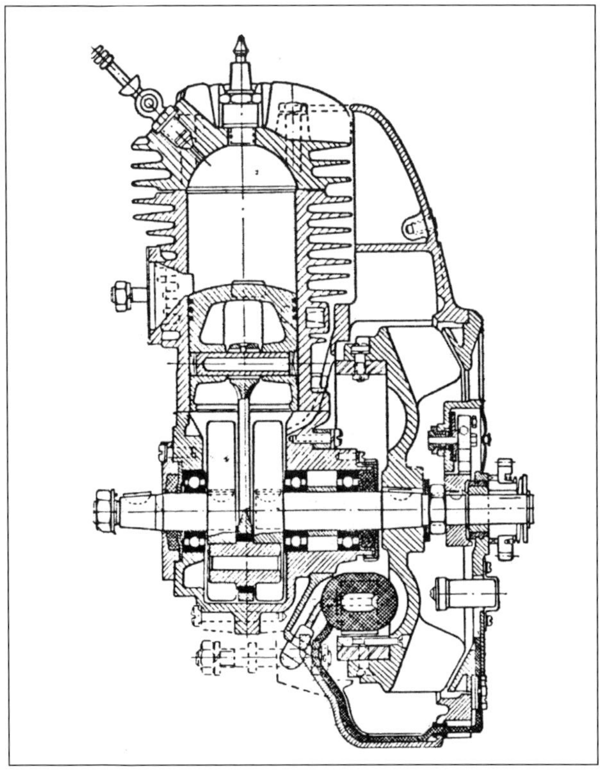

Sectional drawing of the DKW Type A engine with cooling fan.

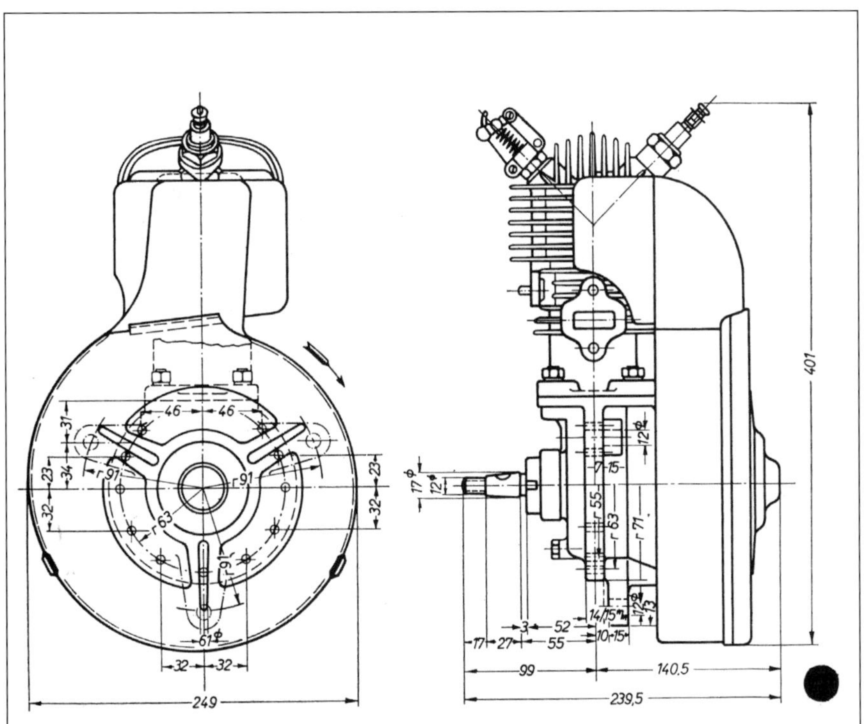

Type A engine installation drawing.

Elcamo outboard motor.

DKW 600cc twin-cylinder engine with liquid cooling and flywheel magneto ignition for use as an aero-engine.

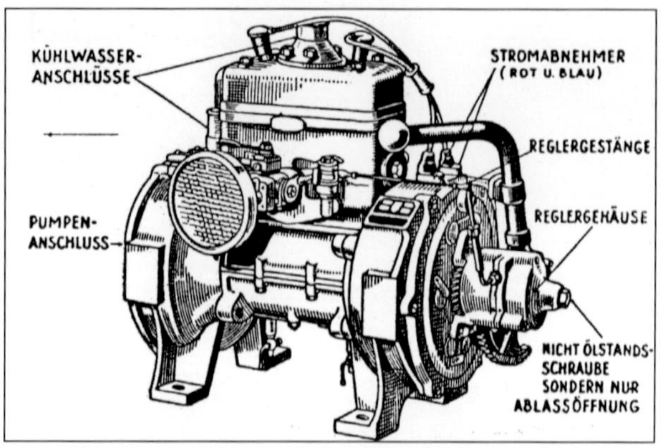

DKW ZW 600 twin-cylinder engine, liquid-cooled, with speed governor for powering pumps, generators and fire-fighting equipment.

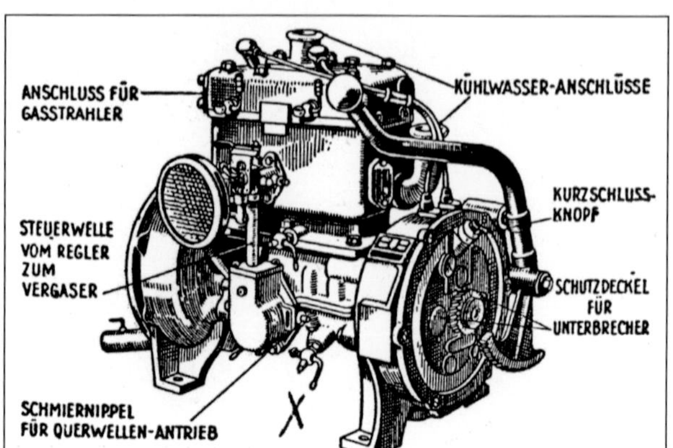

DKW ZW 600 twin-cylinder engine, liquid-cooled, with speed governor for powering pumps, generators and fire-fighting equipment.

A DKW Boxer two-stroke engine made in the 1920s. There were air- and liquid-cooled engine versions, with and without reduction gearing (1:2.4). This engine, which was also offered for use in aircraft, was available with a displacement of 350cc with a bore of 59mm and stroke of 64mm, 412cc with a bore and stoke of 64mm, and 500cc with a bore and stroke of 68mm. The air-cooled variants produced 8, 10 and 13hp at 3,800rpm, the liquid-cooled versions 11, 14 and 18hp.

DKW Type 0 Special 300 integration engine with speed governor, reduction gearing and clutch for installation in harvesters.

DKW engine in a harvester (these harvesting machines were the forerunners of later combine harvesters).

Tree and hop sprayer with DKW engine.

1925 Kramer motorized mowing machine with DKW engine.

Left: Stationary electrical power unit – generator powered by a DKW fan-cooled engine. *Right*: High-pressure circulating pump powered by a DKW engine (Schumann Equipment, Leipzig).

special orders became even more important when, during the 1930s, several very enterprising competitors (such as Fichtel & Sachs) also established themselves in this not uninteresting market. By the end of the 1930s there were more than 500 such variants in DKW's catalogue – some of which differed only in length and the gradient of the cone on the output shaft.

In 1921 Flader of Jöhstadt, a maker of fire-fighting equipment, first built a small fire pump with a DKW engine, the same one used in the Lomos. That was a pioneering feat at that time, for apart from the usual hand pumps there were only large and expensive fire pumps with steam and gas engines. From these beginnings, Flader later became one of the most important recipients of DKW engines. In the years before and during the Second World War the most important was the 1100cc twin-cylinder that powered the portable pumps so vital to the air defense organization.

Prior to this, the agricultural, forestry and winemaking industries had developed into a second field for the use of engines. Small and light, yet powerful, single-cylinder two-stroke engines (air-cooled, the majority with fan cooling) were used to power grass mowers, harvesters, crop sprayers, cultivators and many other types of agricultural equipment. One of DKW's most important products was the Type O Special 300, which powered sheaf-binding harvesters (and take some of the load off the draft animals). This engine (or a smaller one from the DKW engine series) was also used in team-pulled mowers, allowing them to be easily pulled by a pair of

Egon Scheuch of Erfurt developed the "Scheuch single-axle tractor" to take the place of draught animals. The DKW O Special 300 engine (see page 133) could be easily removed and used to power other agricultural machinery. The photo shows DKW employees during an information meeting with Scheuch (in middle). The white-haired gentleman next to him was the head of the DKW field service, Ing. Bachem, who as the young owner of a garage in Bad Godesberg had taught the German crown prince to ride a motorcycle – and after the Second World War taught the crown prince's oldest son to fly. Behind the wheel is DKW's head of training, Ing. Doernhoeffer, behind him (4th from right) his then assistant, the author of this book.

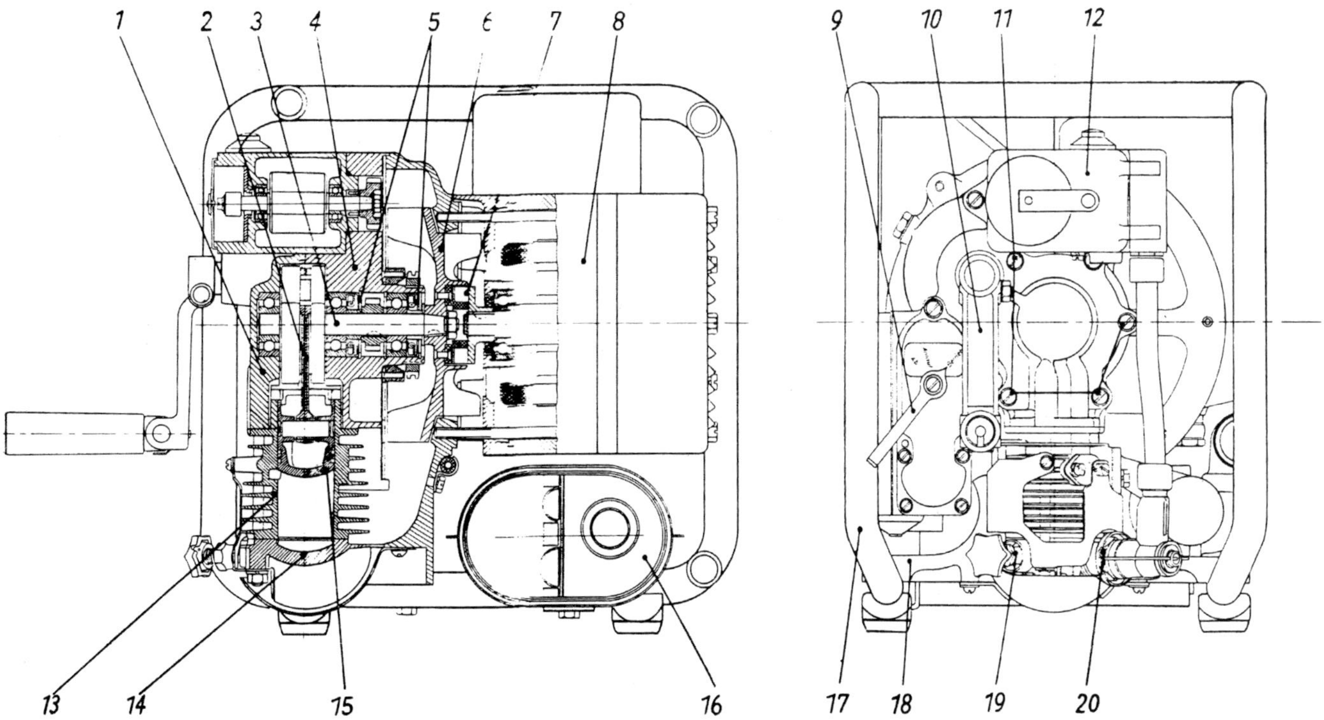

KL 32, the engine that powered the 400 Watt generator used in Wehrmacht machine units.
1 = Crankcase, 2 = connecting rod, 3 = crankshaft, 4 = rear crankcase section, 5 = shaft seal, 6 = flywheel, 7 = clutch, 8 = generator, 9 = throttle lever, 10 = starting crank, 11 = crankcase bolts, 12 = magneto ignition, 13 = cylinder, 14 = cylinder cover, 15 = piston, 16 = exhaust muffler, 17 = supporting structure, 18 = engine mount, 19 = bleeder valve, 20 = spark plug.

oxen. Fully motorized cultivators needed no animals at all, as the engine also propelled the device, and this kept the still-fragile plants from being trod on by the animals.

DKW engines were also used to power construction machinery, compressors and generators. In addition, they served to motorize small vehicles, both for use on the road (for example, in the "Blitzkarre," the first Borgward vehicle of all) and in the country (rotary cultivators).

Over time, a sort of sales division developed between the three main suppliers of engines (DKW, Sachs and Ilo), especially in the boom years after 1933" DKW (Auto Union) mainly provided engines for electric motors and fire pumps, Ilo for delivery and transport vehicles, Fichtel & Sachs for agricultural and construction machinery.

By 1932 DKW had developed engines (with extensive accessories) for the "Small Loading Machine C" (100cc) and for the army's "Loading Machine D" (460cc). These were delivered in significant numbers for many years. Later came the small 400-Watt electrical system with the DKW KL 32 engine. An interesting development by the Zschopau factory did not reach fruition: a small 15cc engine for powering the generator of a so-called "Tourist" or "Coupler Device." As there were no miniature magneto ignitions at that time, the engine used glow plug ignition (it had to be heated with a blowtorch). The tiny engine delivered 0.3hp at 4,800rpm – thus closing the circle to the first toy engine ("The Boy's Desire").

Before the war DKW (like Ilo) built twin-cylinder aero-engines that passed official acceptance tests by the DLV. Single-cylinder liquid-cooled DKW engines were also used in outboard motors, including those manufactured by Elkamo/Erfrenschlag.

The extensive engine production by the Framo factory in Frankenberg, later Hainichen, which was established by Rasmussen (and remained in his possession after the formation of Auto Union) should not go unmentioned. Framo had a multifaceted production program and for years was one of DKW's suppliers (including carburetors, armatures and motorcycle saddles). More and more, however, it shifted its emphasis to the production of transport vehicles.

This production branch began with a three-wheel vehicle, development of which began in Zschopau, using parts from the Lomos. Other such vehicles with three

DKW, later Framo, three-wheel delivery vehicle, based on the Lomos armchair motorcycle.

DKW-Framo three-wheel transporter (from the short period during which DKW vehicles had to be sold under the brand name DGW ["The Big Marvel"].

The same transporter with enclosed superstructure: horizontally mounted engine that turned with the front fork, three-speed gearbox with kickstarter converted into hand starter.

1932 Framo motor tricycle (with DKW three-speed block engine with cooling fan that turned with the front wheel).

and four wheels followed. They included a small car (like the original Stromer, a three-wheel car, or the four-wheel Piccolo), and it is largely unknown that, very early on, Framo developed and tested a special all-terrain vehicle, so to speak a predecessor of the Jeep and its later European successors (see photo page 139).

The last model of a small transport developed and built by Framo, however, had a 500cc four-piston two-stroke engine with liquid-cooled engine (designed by Ing. Petersen, formerly of the racing design bureau Zschopau), instead of the DKW TL 500 air-cooled 500cc twin-cylinder.

Framo three-wheel delivery vehicle, available with loading bed and enclosed superstructure and choice of one- or two-cylinder DKW engine with fan cooling. Encapsulated front wheel chain drive. Four-speed gearbox with reverse. Central tube frame. Year of manufacture 1933-34.

Framo Stromer, original three-wheel automobile with 200cc DKW engine and central tube frame.

Framo small automobile (four-wheel version) based on the Stromer, but with a 500cc twin-cylinder engine. Prototype only.

Rasmussen and Framo proposed this "people's car" (Volkswagen) to the German government in the mid-1930s. The design was rejected, however.

Framo's last attempt to produce an automobile: the Piccolo four-wheel, four-seater with 200cc air-cooled DKW engine.

Interesting prototype of a three-seat all-terrain vehicle by Framo, with liquid-cooled DKW three-cylinder engine (ZW 600), four-speed transmission with reverse gear and two-stage reduction gearing (total of eight gears). Narrow-track rear axle with no differential; rear wheel drive chain/chain.

DKW as the Basis of Auto Union

The Auto Union A.G. was created on 29 June 1932: on that day the results of lengthy negotiations reached their legal conclusion. Chemnitz was chosen as the seat of the new company, and its first year of business began retroactively on 1 November 1931.

The initiative for the founding of the new company was largely that of the State Bank of Saxony and, on the industrial side, of Jörgen Skafte Rasmussen. His engine works in Zschopau formed the incorporating company in the merger and thus the basis and backbone of Auto Union, which, may be seen as an "emergency association" of the Audi factory in Zwickau (already in Rasmussen's possession), the Zschopau engine works with its subsidiaries and auxiliary operations, the Horch factory in Zwickau and the automobile department of the Wanderer factory in Chemnitz, resulting from the economic crisis then gripping Germany.

As a result of the merger, all of the automobile manufacturers in the Free State of Saxony were united in Auto Union. It had been under consideration for a long time to also include the truck factories in Saxony in the merger, however this idea was later abandoned.

The entire corporate administration of Auto Union initially had to be housed in the administration office spaces of the DKW factory, which were entirely inadequate. As previously mentioned, DKW's administration building was a structure of unusual design situated on the public road from Zschopau to Marienberg, and which, from the reception and boardrooms at ground level extended seven stories down to the narrow floor of the Dischau Valley, was filled with the DKW factory buildings. Not until 1935 did Auto Union acquire the Presto Company's idle bicycle factory on Scheffel-Strasse (later Bernd-Rosemeyer-Strasse) in Chemnitz. After major renovations and expansion, in June 1936 it became the new administrative headquarters. The rest of the property was used to house the customer service and spare parts departments with the spare parts depots and factory repair departments of the DKW and Wanderer marques.

The technical and sales administrations of the individual main factories initially remained where they were, but the influence of the central administration departments grew steadily. The company also established a central design bureau (ZKB) and a likewise centralized experimental department (ZVA) in a new building complex on Kauffahrtei-Strasse near the main administration building. Projects reaching further into the future were assigned to it under the leadership of the technical director William Werner.

Background to the Merger

The actual cause for the merger of the Saxon automobile makers was the grave economic situation in all of Germany in the early-1930s, a consequence of the world economic crisis and the political situation. The collapse of Nordwolle in Bremen and the closing of the Danat Bank in 1931 had led to radical measures by the banks and stock exchange and currency control. Despite drastic measures, the deflationary efforts by Brüning's first cabinet (price controls, high bank rates, pay cuts) had no success, and when Brüning's second cabinet stepped down in June 1932, there were already six million unemployed on the street, being wooed by extreme political organizations. Civil war loomed, there was a state of emergency in Prussia, emergency decree followed emergency decree. Hindenburg, Hitler and Thälmann ran for the position of Reich President.

The rapidly deteriorating situation had placed the State Bank of Saxony in a desperate situation. It was heavily invested in the Zschopau engine works, when slumping sales put it into liquidation difficulties (though not in immediate danger). Much more serious, however, were its ties to the Horch Company in Zwickau, which was hopelessly in debt.

The situation of this, the largest automobile maker in Saxony, was desperate. If no way out was found, it was feared that the state bank would be unable to withstand the looming bankruptcy – and that would have meant that others in debt to the state bank would be sucked into the maelstrom of the economic collapse, surely including Rasmussen's engine works in Zschopau.

In the early summer of 1931, therefore, the state bank approached Rasmussen with the proposal of shutting down the Horch factory "until the arrival of better days" and placing the Zschopau engine maker in charge of maintaining the Horch factories and supplying Horch customers with spare parts.

State bank president Degenhardt, Jörgen Skafte Rasmussen and Dr. Richard Bruhn (a member of the Zschopau Engine Works' board of directors delegated by the state bank) met to discuss the plan, however serious doubts arose. Rasmussen and Dr. Bruhn feared that such a step would mean the end of Horch – with unforeseeable consequences for the hard-pressed automobile industry, not least for the staff of the Zwickau factory. The mining and industrial city of Zwickau already had a crushing number of unemployed, and adding the factory's 2,000 men to the rolls would be unbearable.

And so, in the end, it was decided to initially postpone shutting down the factory and instead to seek other ways out of the looming danger. These considerations and efforts ultimately resulted in the merger of Horch, Audi and the Zschopau Engine Works (including the purchase of the Wanderer automobile division) to form Auto Union.

Horch and AUDI – Creations of August Horch

The Horch-Werke AG, Saxony's oldest automobile maker, was established by August Horch, who was born in Winningen an der Mosel in 1868. As a young man, he went on the road as a trained blacksmith (like his father) and then acquired basic training as an engineer at the Technikum in Mittweida, Saxony (which Rasmussen later also attended).

He was taken with the new "motor cars," and in 1896 he obtained a position with the company of Benz & Cie. in Mannheim, where he experienced the developmental beginnings of automobile construction. Benz had constructed his first drivable motor vehicle there ten years earlier, and with Horch's assistance a much-improved motorcar with a 2¾hp engine, two-speed transmission and rubber tires was built in 1896. But all of this was happening much too slowly for Horch – he had his own far-reaching plans. In 1899, therefore, he left Benz and set up his own company, August Horch & Cie., in Cologne-Ehrenfeld with his partner Herz, who had also left Benz. The first Horch motorcar was completed in 1900. It had a four-cylinder engine (with light metal case), shaft drive, spur gear differential and other innovations and was offered in two versions (with 5- and 10hp engines).

The production facility in Cologne soon became too small, however, and in 1903 the company moved to Zwickau, which offered more suitable fabrication opportunities. The production program encompassed two- and four-cylinder cars, which soon helped the Horch marque to earn a solid reputation. In 1904 the firm was turned into a joint stock company under the name Horch-Werke AG Zwickau. There was a new four-cylinder Horch car in 1903, a 2.6-liter model was added in 1904, and in 1905 a 40hp car with new and advanced design features.

August Horch's involvement with automobiles was not limited to his activities as a designer and manufacturer – he was also an enthusiastic and successful racing driver. In the years 1905-1909, Horch cars – some driven by

Horch himself – achieved considerable success in difficult endurance competitions, the Herkomer and Prinz-Heinrich races. Of course, participation in these races benefited development of the company's production vehicles.

But it was Horch's successful involvement in motor sports that led to differences in opinion with his colleagues on the board, who thought that Horch's development and racing costs were too high. The differences ultimately became so grave that there was an open rupture at a board of directors meeting – in 1909 August Horch angrily parted ways his company.

But that was not to be the end of his involvement in the automobile industry. With the help of good friends, powerful textile industrialists, before 1909 was over the new August Horch Automobil-Werke GmbH was established in a shutdown factory not far from the original Horch plant.

Soon afterwards a legal battle developed over the name Horch – August Horch lost and was forced to remove his name from the company title. It was replaced by Audi – the Latin translation of the German word Horch (English hark). As Horch recalled in his memoirs, it was the son of one of his partners (Fikentscher) who suggested the name, after he happened to hear Horch and others discussing a new name for the company. In 1910 the company Audi-Automobilwerke GmbH was entered in the Zwickau commercial register.

Even under another name, the new company was a competitor that Horch could not take for granted. In the beginning it concentrated on making its proven cars, but then it expanded its program and in 1911 unveiled smaller models with 6- and 8hp engines designed to attract a new class of buyers.

At Audi, on the other hand, the new 10/25 car designed by Horch, more modern and powerful than the cars made by his previous company, was ready in 1910. And of course August Horch again became involved in racing. In 1911 a team of three Audi cars, with Horch as one of the drivers, entered the International Austrian Alpine Race – all three cars finished with no penalty points. This success was followed by further victories in the Alpine races in 1912-1914, and when the First World War broke out the Audi program included dive cars plus two truck and delivery van models.

After the war, during which Audi and Horch had been burdened with armaments contracts, Audi continued its tradition with a 14/50 four-cylinder car, then built the Model 18/70 PS (with six-cylinder in-line engine), which in turn was followed by the Imperator with a five-liter, eight-cylinder engine. Production of this car continued even when (after Rasmussen took over the majority of the company's shares) production of the Dresden and Zwickau models, equipped with Rasmussen's (Rickenbacker) six- and eight-cylinder engines, began. Audi had become a joint stock company during the war, and when an increase in share capital became necessary in 1928, the State Bank of Saxony, which was involved in Audi, urged Rasmussen to purchase the newly issued common stock (a package of one-million) and thus acquire a majority interest in the company. Rasmussen also took over as chairman of the board, with Dr. Hahn as his deputy – August Horch also continued as a member of the board. At that time Heinrich Schuh and Kurt Arzt were also members of the board (heads of engineering and sales, respectively). Both men retained their positions when Auto Union was founded.

Even after Rasmussen had gained considerable influence in Audi, the company initially continued building large automobiles, even the Imperator alongside the Rickenbacker models. It is no wonder that the company kept losing money (even though its staff was drastically reduced, in 1931 to about 140 men). Even the production of an Audi car with a Peugot engine, in cooperation with the DKW factory in Spandau, went ahead briefly. Rasmussen saw it as a parallel to the DKW cars with the four-cylinder V two-stroke engine for those who were interested in getting into the one-liter displacement class but did not want a two-stroke. The Audi factory only became healthy when production of the DKW-Front began there.

Had Rasmussen not taken over Audi then – against the advice of Dr. Hahn – then the marque would probably have disappeared from the market and from memory for all time.

The situation in the nearby Horch plants was even worse than that of Audi, however. Soon after the First World War, Dr. Moritz Strauss, owner of the Argus Engine Works, had become the majority shareholder and had taken over as chairman of the board of directors and moved the administration to Berlin. After the departure of its founder, Horch made cars and trucks before and during the war and succeeded in maintaining the reputation for quality it had earned. The attempt to break into the domain of Opel, NSU and Wanderer with smaller cars had been abandoned, and after the war it returned to its own field of large vehicles. After the 10/50 luxury car (with overhead-valve four-cylinder engine), in 1926 came the eight-cylinder with two overhead camshafts designed by Baurat Daimler (the son of Gottfried Daimler). It was the first German eight-cylinder, but after much publicity it was replaced by a single-cam design, which became a great success. Horch was even able to pay an 8% dividend for the business year 1927-28.

The business report for the second year following, however, showed a different, less favorable picture of the company's economic situation. While on 1 November 1929 a profit carried forward was shown, by 31 October 1930 a loss of just under five-million was accrued.

In those years of crisis, there was no longer a market for the high-quality products of the Horch plant with the famous eight-cylinder inline engine for sedans and convertibles and an eight-cylinder V engine for convertibles. And so the financial situation arose which ultimately led to the founding of Auto Union.

The Wanderer Automobiles

The Wanderer-Werke AG in Chemnitz-Schönau had been founded by Richard Jänicke and Johann Baptist Winklhofer in 1885. Initially the production program included high-grade machine tools and typewriters (Continental brand) plus bicycles. The production of motorcycles was added in 1902 and the building of automobiles in 1911. Its first car was the Wanderer Puppchen, a two-seater that became a bestseller. The car (with the seats in a tandem arrangement) had an 1150cc four-cylinder engine that produced 12hp and had magneto ignition and a three-speed transmission with reverse gear. The Puppchen had a top speed of 70 kph.

After the war Wanderer continued its tradition in all branches of production, including automobiles. Development of the prewar small car continued, resulting in 6/18, 5/20 and 6/24hp versions, and with four forward gears it was capable of 90 kph. The popular W 235 with 6/30hp from a displacement of 1.55 liters followed in 1926, and the two-liter W 240 with 8/40hp in 1928. That year the production of automobiles was moved to the new Siegmar factory near Chemnitz. There followed a 10/50 six-cylinder model (W 250 with 2.5 liter displacement in sedan and convertible versions), but in 1930 there was a return to a 6/30 four-cylinder with improved design and more attractive form.

The production of motorcycles was abandoned in 1929. Drawings and completed production equipment for a single-cylinder shaft-drive model (which still had inherent teething troubles) was sold to the Czech armaments factory owned by F. Janecek, where it later formed the basis of the very well-known Jawa motorcycles (the shaft drive model was soon abandoned).

At that time the company reached a deal with Dr. Porsche for the design of a new engine (which was then taken over by Auto Union).

Diversity of production was a factor that put Wanderer ahead of the two Zwickau automobile makers: it was less affected by economic fluctuations and crises and was justifiably proud of the more secure position it had achieved in the automobile sector. It was therefore no easy task to convince the proud company with its general manager Stuhlmacher (and later Klee) of the necessity of concentrating the Saxon automobile industry and inducing it to lease part of its newly-built factory in Siegmar, which had begun producing automobiles, to Auto Union and sell the production facilities and trademark rights (insofar as they remained restricted to sales of Wanderer automobiles) to the new firm.

Rasmussen's Group of Companies

Rasmussen's industrial holdings were not limited to the Zschopau Engine Works with its subsidiaries in Scharfenstein, Annaberg and elsewhere. A description of the group of companies from 1934 (see page 31) gives some idea of the wide range of ideas guided by Rasmussen – which also, however, held serious risks. But it also shows the geographically scattered nature of Rasmussen's holdings and influence. The structure of his group also ranged from feeder operations for the main branch of automobile production, to the production of refrigerators, to series production of light sporting aircraft with DKW engines in the Erla Iron and Aircraft Works, which commenced in 1933.

Even though the Rasmussen group with its twelve companies, which employed approximately 15,000 people, had not yet undergone its final rounding out when the period of economic crisis began, it was obvious that the motor vehicle industry was the focal point of the group.

Even in the midst of the crisis in 1930, the Zschopau Engine Works was not facing bankruptcy, but when production start-up in Zwickau of the front wheel drive car, which was vital to the survival of the Audi factory, was delayed, DKW motorcycles piled up in the factory courtyard and in temporary premises in the Erz Mountains, and the prolonged dealer changes accepted as payment caused its debt to the State Bank to reach serious levels, the liquidity of the Rasmussen group was stretched to the utmost: the last balance sheet before the founding of Auto Union (31/12/1930) showed a loss of almost 1.8 million against a balance sheet total of just under 22 million, and its bank debts were 2.277 million. In this situation the State Bank of Saxony succeeded in having Dr. Bruhn installed as a member of the Zschopau Engine Works' board of directors to carry out sales reorganization tasks. He and Rasmussen then worked out and ultimately implemented the state bank's concept for a fusion.

The question of the scope of the fusion first had to be cleared up. From the very beginning it was clear that the production program should be fundamentally limited to private automobiles (and motorcycles) and that it should be geographically restricted to the Free State of Saxony (the body works in Spandau was a necessary structural exception).

As pure automobile producers, the two Zwickau companies presented no problems in this respect, and the division according to equipment and production program for the facilities making Wanderer automobiles had been clearly spelled out in the preliminary negotiations.

Only the Rasmussen group was polymorphic and also diversely interwoven. A fundamental simplification was required, which admittedly was not easy, for some of the group's companies were buyers of DKW products (such as the Erla Aircraft Works, for example), some were subcontractors (like Scharfenstein and Brand-Erbisdorf), and some were both – like the Framo factory in Hainichen, which was managed by the eldest Rasmussen son Hans.

For the process of rationalization and the merger to succeed, it was vitally important that Rasmussen did not refuse to accept a radical concentration. He also agreed that the parent factory in Zschopau, the body works in Spandau and the light metal foundry in Annaberg (Erz Mountains) would be carved out for the DKW program (automobiles, motorcycles, integrated engines). There was also the Luma-Werk in Stuttgart, which Rasmussen had taken over from its previous owner Friedrich Münz, where special electrical systems were produced for the DKW production program (until this was switched to the former Schüttoff Motorcycle Works factory on Rössler-Strasse in Chemnitz).

All the remaining parts of Rasmussen's industrial holdings that did not directly and exclusively serve the planned Auto Union program, were sorted out and placed under the administration of "Industry Management and Trust Ltd.," which was founded for this purpose and headed by Rasmussen's son Dr. Ove Rasmussen, head of the Zöblitz Metal Works.

When all of the other conditions for the merger were finally created, there remained two problems. One was the need to obtain a government guarantee from the Free State of Saxony for the vital millions in operating credit from the state bank, which required the approval of the state parliament (*Landtag*). This could only be hoped for if the National-Socialists (who at that time had not yet come to power) abandoned their obstructionist policies in the *Landtag*. Gauleiter Mutschmann received the necessary instructions from Munich, and the NSDAP parliamentary group did not sabotage the approval by the state parliament.

That left the second problem: the Free State of Saxony made approval of state backing contingent on the federal government's participation in the rehabilitation of the Saxon motor vehicle industry through an abatement of tax (the companies involved in the proposed merger had considerable tax arrears that were enforceable at any time). This it succeeded in obtaining after tough negotiations. The way was thus finally clear the establishment of Auto Union AG, and incorporation took place on 29 June 1932.

Dr. Richard Bruhn, J.S. Rasmussen and Baron von Oertzen were named members of the board, with Dr. Carl Hahn and Ing. William Werner as deputy board members.

To what extent this body with its staff in the factories would succeed, without a change in the economic situation in Germany, at first remained to be seen.

Auto Union AG headquarters on Bernd-Rosemeyer-Strasse in Chemnitz (converted building of the former Presto-Werke, which produced automobiles and bicycles).

DKW and Auto Union until the End in Saxony

In 1931-32 there was no doubt as to the necessity of a merger of the four Saxon vehicle makers as a condition for their continued existence. It was clear to leading economists, however, that in the absence of generous support measures by the other German *Länder* (states) and the federal government, new ways would also have to be found within the rest of the German motor vehicle industry to divide the work. But even under the roof of the new Auto Union, in the economic conditions in 1932 the stated goals could only be reached if it was possible to concentrate the participating forces to a few persons and bring about a relationship of close trust between the leading bank (the State Bank of Saxony) and one of the leading technicians, who had a name, experience and creative initiative and who was also capable of handling an operation as complex as the new group of companies.

This person was Rasmussen, in whose vision and initiative even the state bank placed its complete trust.

In the past, two-stroke engines and small front wheel drive cars had taken market tendencies into consideration. The two-stroke engine also appeared to have a promising future – because of its structural simplicity, but also because many technicians had ignored it and instead dedicated their efforts to further refining the four-stroke engine. When the Saxon companies were combined to form Auto Union, Rasmussen's willing cooperation was something it could not do without. Quite consciously, the program set up and put into practice by him had to be given priority and made the backbone of the new company.

When Auto Union was created, DKW's technological ideology led the group and was the most active. Horch's conservative promotion of the large automobile had resulted in a certain torpor, and it was incapable of surviving on its own program alone – the same was true of Audi (where production of the DKW front wheel drive car had already become a saving straw). Wanderer, on the other hand, was in the process of abandoning its outmoded automobile designs and replacing them with a model designed by Prof. Porsche.

It thus appeared that the DKW program would be able to quickly take control in Auto Union and become its main foundation. This in fact did happen – DKW was responsible for more than 50% of sales and the greatest part of the profits earned.

Nevertheless, the economic turnabout that began when the National Socialists took power in the spring of 1943 was, overall, decisive to Auto Union's survival and upward trend. For without the new government's measures to promote motorization (no matter what the reason), the increases in sales and production that began in all of Auto Union's factories (like the rest of the German motor vehicle industry) in 1933 would not have been possible.

Rasmussen's withdrawal (voluntarily at first) from his technical leadership position – as a result of serious differences of opinion with fellow board member Dr. Bruhn – was tragic, and his summary dismissal that followed was shameful for those who initiated it. But the DKW legacy that he left behind was stable enough to remain the most important factor in the Auto Union group during the remaining years of peace.

After Rasmussen's departure, William Werner (who was awarded a doctorate of engineering by the Technical University of Dresden in 1941) took over technical management of the board. Dr. Bruhn remained chairman (von Oertzen had been forced, for political reasons, to take a post out of the country), and Dr. Hahn (who left Auto Union temporarily to take a leadership position in a company outside the auto industry but soon returned) oversaw sales as a deputy member of the board.

View of the DKW plant in Zschopau – in the center of the photo the administration building on the valley slope.

Aerial photo of the Audi factory in Zwickau, owned by Rasmussen.

There is no question that it was he, who in the face of other unmistakable trends, held up the DKW banner with incomparable élan in and outside the company and who repeatedly motivated his coworkers and the dealers and carried them along with his DKW enthusiasm.

The (unusually) small circle of board members worked together extremely well, with little friction, and was an important factor in the straightforward development of the complex group of companies. William Werner, with his great experience in manufacturing technology and business organization, had a clearly defined area of responsibility. Dr. Bruhn and Dr. Hahn, very different by nature, augmented him very well and, despite their differences in character, experience and temperament, always took the path of fruitful synthesis: the thoughtful Dr. Bruhn, averse to any sort of adventure, and his younger temperamental colleague Dr. Hahn, full of imagination and inventiveness, created an atmosphere of "creative unrest" (as one of their closest colleagues once put it), which found its justification in the glorious rise of the company.

Even after Rasmussen's departure, there was never any question as to whether the company would retain the two-stroke program and continue on "dual tracks." Even after the merger and the reorganization of the board of directors, all of the factories initially continued with their previous programs without competing with one another. The former rivalry between Horch and Audi had already been robbed of its sharpness when the Audi factory began producing DKW front wheel drive automobiles. This took up so much of its capacity that in 1938 production of the big Audi cars (with Horch six-cylinder engine and modified Wanderer chassis) was moved to the Horch factory. Assembly of the Audi front wheel drive cars with 2- and later 2.3hp Wanderer engines had earlier been moved to Horch, in 1934. In the DKW sector, in 1932 there was a stationary and integrated engine program that fully met the market's requirements – despite not insignificant competition. The now thirteen main types required no fundamental changes in the period until 1939: one- and two-cylinders, air or liquid cooled, left- or right-handed, stationary or suitable for installation in vehicles, they covered a significant part of the requirements in agriculture and forestry, in the trades and industry as well as firefighting and were also used to power three- and four-wheeled vehicles.

DKW motorcycles – from the world's largest motorcycle factory, which the Zschopau plant had been since 1928 and remained until the war – already formed a cohesive type program when the merger took place that, apart from constant technical development, only underwent some streamlining until 1939.

The DKW automobile program was still in flux in 1932. The DKW front wheel drive car was no miniaturized mid-size car – it was an independent development based on motorcycle technology. The entire concept of the small vehicle, with its front wheel drive and wooden body, was meant to catch the swelling wave of mass motorization, indeed its advantages were designed to spur it even further. Thanks to their popularity, the Reichs- and Meisterklasse cars (with 600- and 700cc twin-cylinder two-stroke engines), available as sedans and convertibles, with two- and four-seat metal bodies from the Saxon bodymakers, soon accounted for the bulk of Auto Union automobile production. They remained basically unchanged into the Second World War. In 1939 the daily output of DKW front wheel drive cars was 230, motorcycles more than 250.

The attempt to also exploit the two-stroke's advantages in a larger, more powerful car (an expansion of the program that appeared necessary) had little initial success. This was in part due to use of the four-cylinder V two-stroke engine designed by Paffrath and Gehle, with its two double-action, crankcase-independent charging pumps. The engine, which had a displacement of 800 and later 1000cc, was expensive to produce, its reliability was poor and fuel consumption high. The rear wheel drive car (made in the Spandau factory) was itself a problem. A development of the four-cylinder models, the Schwebeklasse, which appeared in 1934, failed to attract a sufficient number of buyers despite its load-bearing body and spacious and aerodynamically advanced but rather plump form. And when the "new" Sonderklasse (before the Schwebeklasse, there had twice been a type with this name, but with a wooden body), with a steel body similar to that of the Wanderer W 24 (on a modified DKW-

DKW automobiles built in the Audi factory in Zwickau.

The Horch factory in Zwickau.

Front F 8 chassis) came out in 1937-38, problems with the engine remained (after the third engine change customers received a Wanderer W 24 for a slight additional charge).

A body similar to that of the Sonderklasse was also chosen for the DKW F 9, a three-cylinder car from the Central Design Bureau (ZKB) in Chemnitz. The car was supposed to have been presented at the automobile show in Berlin in 1940 as a more expensive but suitable alternative to the "threatening" Volkswagen. Perhaps, if built in sufficient quantities, it might replace the twin-cylinder front wheel drive car one day. After the distributors stored the pressing tools in western Germany, the body, with minor changes, was used on the first postwar DKW car (Type F 89). Made from existing drawings, it was also used on the F 9 made by the state-owned IFA after the war, first in the former Audi factory in Zwickau and later in the former BMW plant in Eisenach.

But metal was not the only material considered to replace the faux leather covered Spandau wooden body of the DKW front wheel drive car: an entirely new replacement, something that "continued the tradition of the unconventional in the DKW line" – a plastic body.

Experiments in this direction were already far advanced when war broke out and they were continued in the first years of the war. In cooperation with Dynamit-AG of Troisdorf, layers of phenolic resin with paper inserts were used. Driving and fall (catapult) tests were satisfactory and resulted in the ordering of a 15,000 ton press, which was put together in a new building at the Spandau factory.

In any event, in the last year of peace Auto Union presented a gapless program – from light 125cc DKW motorcycles to large 500cc sport machines with twin-cylinder engines and rear wheel suspension, from popular DKW front wheel drive cars to mid-size Wanderer automobiles, and finally the large luxury cars made in the Horch factory. New developments for the coming years were standing ready in all of the Auto Union factories. The distribution organization, lead by the sales directors for the individual categories located in the main administration in Chemnitz, could fall back on the field services of the various companies, most of which had been in place before the merger, and a proven network of dealers who were bound to Auto Union by contract (with terms for discounts, exclusion of competition, customer service, etc.). There had only been wholesalers with subagents for DKW motorcycles until 1930. The exceptions were the Auto Union branch dealers, largely independent sales establishments, most of which already existed at the time of the merger. The conscious support of independent dealers paid off after the war when the new Auto Union was created.

At the end of 1934 Auto Union AG already had more than 1,000 automobile and about 3,000 motorcycle dealers. By mid-1939 these figures had risen to about 1,700 car and 5,000 motorcycle dealers, with DKW dealers far in the majority in the automobile sector.

It is interesting that in its fist year in business, Auto Union (1931-32) exported 1,428 DKW motorcycles and 480 cars of all four brands. The number of motorcycles exported almost doubled in 1934-35, but car exports increased tenfold. And in 1936-37 the number of motorcycles exported rose by 93% compared to the previous year. In the last peacetime business year (1938-39), including the first two months of the war, 14,142 DKW motorcycles, 2,895 DKW engines and 15,581 automobiles (all four brands) were sold abroad.

Foreign sales of DKW motorcycles were boosted by their many racing successes. Australia was a prime example: thanks to bad experiences with motorcycles, which were equipped with English Villiers twin-cylinder two-stroke engines, it was almost impossible to buy a two-stroke. That is until they sent Ewald Kluge there with a 250cc reed valve DKW. In 1937 he won four events and set a new track record against English four-stroke machines. The ice was broken and in the years that followed this important market was secured for DKW.

The following glowing words appeared in the Auto Union business report in 1937 (in addition to motorcycle racing, the company was also heavily involved in automobile racing, not least in Grand-Prix):

> "As before, the company is strongly committed to motor vehicle sport. It is a fact that in recent years Auto Union has been more involved in motor vehicle sport than any other company in the world. It is the only one that is simultaneously involved in big international car races, motorcycle racing and

Wanderer automobile factory in Chemnitz-Siegmar.

Auto Union A.G. factory in Spandau.

international endurance and off-road races. It regards this involvement in sport not only as a national obligation, but also as proof of the company's technical ability, a source of new design knowledge and an international demonstration of German knowhow and German craftsmanship that cannot be overestimated."

The following tables provide an interesting impression of the development in Auto Union from its creation until the beginning of the war in September 1939:

Auto Union AG Work Force

31/10	Total	Workers	%	Clerical Staff	%
1932	4,359	3,461	79.3	898	20.7
1933	7,371	6,281	85.2	1,090	14.8
1934	12,256	10,781	87.9	1,475	12.1
1935	16,503	14,024	85	2,479	15
1936	20,154	17,272	85.7	2,882	14.3
1937	21,530	18,351	85.4	3,179	14.6
1938	22,673	19,145	84.9	3,528	15.1

New Car Registrations in Germany

Year	Total	Auto Union	%	DKW	Wanderer	Horch	Audi
1932	39,529	6,459	16.3	9.3	4.1	2.5	0.4
1933	82,048	16,465	20.1	12.6	5.2	1.5	0.8
1934	130,938	28,590	21.8	15.9	3.9	1.2	0.8
1935	180,113	38,154	21.2	15.7	4.0	1.1	0.4
1936	213,117	50,962	23.9	18.8	3.8	0.9	0.4
1937	216,538	54,765	25.3	19.5	4.5	0.9	0.4
1938	222,778	52,172	25.3	17.9	4.4	1.0	0.1
1939 (until 31 July 1939)	125,237	28,788	23.0	16.6	4.9	1.0	0.5

DKW Motorcycle Registrations in Germany

Year	Total	DKW
1933	50,108	10,956 = 21.9%
1934	78,179	24,523 = 31.4%
1935	102,831	36,847 = 35.9%
1936	125,131	43,581 = 34.6%
1937	141,796	48,210 = 33.9%
1938	150,562	44,637 = 29.3%
1939 (until 31/7)	119,019	36,457 = 30.6%

In the first years of the war the prevailing problem was the assignment of new tasks to the production facilities, a process that developed slowly at first. There was still a considerable quantity of stockpiled production materials (as a result of the strained materials situation before the war), with which series production could be maintained, at least in the beginning. DKW front wheel drive cars were in great demand – because of their wooden bodies they were not requisitioned by the military. During the 1940-41 business year no fewer than 33,646 DKW engines, 20,254 DKW motorcycles and 5,411 cars of all four brands (production of which then dropped off rapidly) were delivered. The following year approximately 7,000 motorcycles left the Zschopau factory for civilian use and export. And when the production lines in the other DKW factories had long since stopped moving, in 1942 another 1,500 DKW front wheel drive cars were delivered by the Audi factory.

Despite this "peacetime production in war," initially there was still sufficient startup material for the peace that was expected shortly (a sign of the optimism of those years). Initially – for soon all of the factories became fully involved in war production and the regular "scrap drives" soon caused the carefully husbanded reserves to dwindle away (including the DKW racing department's extensive parts warehouse).

Naturally the production of motor vehicles played a major role in the war production by the Auto Union factories (in addition to other production). At Zschopau it was motorcycles (initially the NZ 350, later the RT 125 as well) and engines for a wide variety of aggregates used by all three branches of the military – in addition to the complete KL 100, KL 101 and KL 32 small machine units, the final years of the war especially the 1100cc twin-cylinder engine for portable pumps.

Then came the catastrophic year 1944 – both for industry in Saxony and Auto Union. No longer was the phrase heard: "Saxony – the air raid shelter of the Reich." In 1943 and early 1944, the Spandau factory with its large stockpiles of wood suffered severe bomb damage. Then on 9 September 1944 it was the turn of the Wanderer factory in Siegmar (in which tank engines were made), in October the Horch and Audi factories in Zwickau, including their subsidiaries, were heavily bombed, and on 5 March 1945 Chemnitz was devastated by two night raids. The workshops on Kauffahrteistrasse and the electric works on Rösslerstrasse suffered heavy damage – the main administration building was left intact however. The Zschopau factory sustained little damage.

By the beginning of May it was clear that the Russians would be marching into Chemnitz. And after a plan discussed by the board at the beginning of the year to take a small administration apparatus to the south of Germany was not implemented, with the end of the war now in sight, on 6 May 1945 the board of directors headed for Zwickau, which was already occupied by the Americans. It authorized three representatives (Dr. Schüler, Ludwig Hensel and Walter Schmolla), who in cooperation with the newly established communist worker's council, were to lead the company for the time being.

A few days later the Russians occupied Chemnitz. The administration building on Bernd-Rosemeyer-Strasse was repurposed into a hospital for patients suffering from venereal diseases, and the new board worked with what was left of the administration in the former rooms of the spare parts division in the back lot.

All of the production facilities were completely dismantled – in Chemnitz no different than in Zschopau and Zwickau. The personnel who accompanied the trains reported that the machines, exposed to the elements and improperly packed and transported, were abandoned by the thousands near Brest-Litovsk.

Many employees from the technical offices were forced to work in Russia: from Zschopau, apart from the factory manager Otto Hoffmann, chief designer Weber and ten of his staff. The majority of the factory managers and other employees in management positions were arrested by the occupying power – most never returned from the camps.

The old Auto Union, however, the biggest industrial group in the Free State of Saxony, received a deathblow in 1945. The provisional board of directors tried to preserve the tradition of the company in a new time – but its efforts were in vain. Auto Union was replaced by the "Vehicle Construction Industry" (IFA). On 1 July 1948 the state government of Saxony informed the board that the assets of Auto Union AG had been expropriated. On 17 August 1949 the company was removed from the Chemnitz commercial register.

They Rode DKW Motorcycles to Victory

Facing Page:
Top row: Siegfried Wünsche from Dresden, who joined the Zschopau factory team in 1933. He became a successful motorcycle racer on DKW machines before the Second World War, then in Ingolstadt he was again part of the DKW factory team.

Walfried Winkler, born in Chemnitz, was a DKW racer in the early days, beginning with the Reichsfahrt Model. He later rode the 175 and 250 charging pump machines and then the 250 double-piston machine with reed and rotary intake valves. In 1938-39 he raced the new 350cc factory racer and then, after the war, a DKW racing machine he made himself, with rotary supercharger. All in all, he was the most successful DKW rider ever.

Ewald Kluge, also of Dresden, became known internationally, even before he won the English TT riding the 250cc DKW rotary valve machine. He was one of the most popular and dependable DKW motorcycle racers before and after the war.

Bottom row: Bernhard Petruschke, the Berliner on the DKW factory team, who rode the 175 and 250 double-piston machines, was always in the leading group of DKW riders and was a masterful rider.

Heiner Fleischmann from Amberg – riding the 350 double-piston DKW, he was superior wherever he raced for the Zschopau factory.

Walter Hamelehle, whose DKW career (after success racing other types of motorcycle) began with the new 350 in 1938-39.

This page:
Top: Wilhelm Herz of Lampertheim was a leader on the team riding the 500cc double-piston DKW motorcycle.

Center: Kurt Mansfeld, the daredevil – on the 500 DKW one of the most dashing riders in the International Extra Class. He always knew how to push his machine to its limits.

Bottom: Karl Bodmer, a cool, dependable rider, who was always in the top group on the 500cc double-piston DKW.

Top: Toni Bauhofer, previously a leading rider in the half-liter class on the five-cylinder Megola and later as a BMW factory rider, continued his success after Prüssing brought him to DKW and of course gave him the 500 to ride.

Bottom: Toni Bauhofer on the DKW double-piston 500. On this motorcycle he won the Eilenriede championship in 1932 and 1934.

Opposite page:
Top: Start of the half-liter class race at the Eilenriede race; the first three starting numbers belonged to DKW factory team riders.

Bottom: Toni Bauhofer especially liked the Eilenriede course – here he rides toward his third championship at the gates of Hanover.

Hans Winkler of Munich (who preferred the 500cc DKW) and Arthur Geiss of Pforzheim (a lightweight, he was predestined for the small DKW racing machines and enjoyed a successful racing career). The pair were good friends.

Arthur Geiss accepts the victory laurels at a race in Hungary.

Arthur Geiss at full speed on one of the first 175 reed valve machines.

When an accident forced him to retire from racing, Geiss (wearing hat) looked after the ever-growing number of private racers using DKW motorcycles.

Seven times German champion – one of the most likeable and coolest motorcycle racers on the 500cc DKW: Otto Ley from Nuremberg.

Opposite page:
Top: Sepp Klein of Frankfurt (No.24) and Xaver Gmelch of Munich with the first 500 class liquid-cooled, twin-cylinder, deflector piston racing machines in 1929. Geiss' machine is experimentally fitted with Gazda sprung handlebars.

Bottom left: Heiner Fleischmann on the DKW 350cc double-piston machine.
Bottom right: Fleischmann after a victory on the Solitude (while still with NSU). Behind him is Edmund Bühler, who was then a well-known private racer and after the war became a motorcycle importer in Stuttgart.

Racing director August Prüssing in conversation with Otto Ley, seen here with one of the first double-piston twin-cylinder machines.

24
IV-1344
23
27

26

Dem Sieger

H.P. Müller from Bielefeld – one of the most versatile and successful, and in the opinion of many the best German motorcycle racers ever. He became German champion on a 600cc Victoria motorcycle-sidecar in 1932. In 1936, by then with DKW/Auto Union, he repeated his success, becoming runner-up champion on DKW motorcycles. From 1937 to 1939 he drove Auto Union racing cars and won the French Grand Prize in 1939. After the war he again became German champion (1947), this time on a DKW 250 made in Ingolstadt. These are just several highlights from his endless list of successes.

Obering. August Prüssing, head of DKW's racing department, in conversation with motorcycle racer Toni Bauhofer of Munich.

H.P. Müller, for a change on a 1939 DKW SS 250, the racing motorcycle for private owners.

Ewald Kluge during his successful prewar period as Auto Union's leading rider on one of the first 250cc reed valve DKWs (recognizable by the exposed flywheel).

Ewald Kluge and Bernhard Petruschke – first and second in the 250 Class at the 1938 Grand Prize Race in Geneva.

Ewald Kluge's unique triumph: on the 250cc reed valve machine at the TT on the Isle of Man in 1938.

Above:
Left: Walfried Winkler chats with Bernd Rosemeyer, lead driver of the Auto Union racing car, just prior to the start of a world record attempt on the Frankfurt autobahn. Between the two is Haase, the tireless mechanic who looked after DKW racing motorcycles.
Right: Walfried Winkler on the partially faired 175cc DKW racing motorcycle during an attempt on a record.

Walfried Winkler, who in 1938-39 crowned his successful prewar period as a motorcycle racer on the DKW 350cc double-piston machine.

Walfried Winkler on a DKW 350 on the Grossglockner high Alpine road.

Left: After the war Walfried Winkler, worked tirelessly to build a 250 four-piston machine with rotary supercharger using original and newly made parts. He then rode it in West Germany until machines with superchargers were banned from competition (1951). Then he went to work for Victoria in Nuremberg as head of the off-road racing department and later joined Porsche. *Right*: August Prüssing, head of DKW's racing department, in conversation with Englishman Stanley Woods during the Tourist Trophy Races on the Isle of Man.

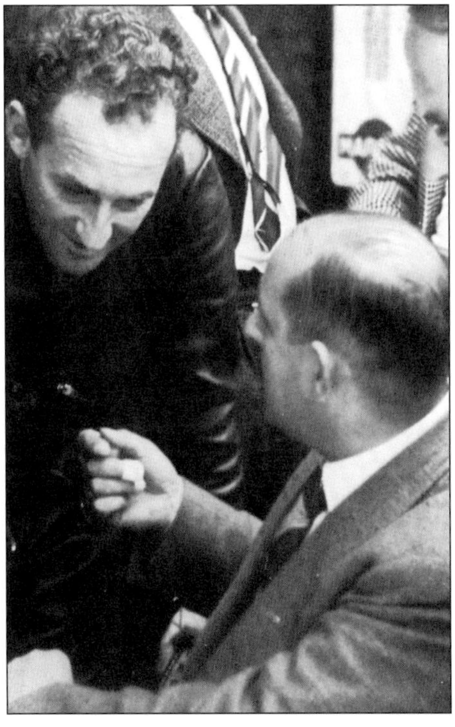

Walter Hamelehle during a pit stop (at the Sachsenring races) on the DKW 350 racer ...

... and here he blazes past on the brawny double-piston two-stroke.

Two reed valve machines during refueling – not with a 1:25 mixture like the other DKW two-strokes, but with 1:50 (because the engines were equipped with an oil pump that supplied the crank drive, which in these engines was not washed over with a fresh charge).

The victorious 1936 DKW team on the Solitude racetrack. From left: Fleischmann, Winkler, Müller, Prüssing, Ley, Kahrmann, Schumann, Böhm (then still svelte), Babl, Bock and Geiss.

Bernhard Petruschke on one of the last 250cc reed valve motorcycles.

Toni Babl with his Swiss co-rider Julius Beer in 1936 at the starting line of the 600 team race.

After Babl's death, Beer rode in the sidecar of Hans Schumann, who rode the motorcycle-sidecar combination in the 1000 class.

Karmann and Eder in a typical cornering position on the DKW 600 combination.

Babl and Beer on the DKW 600 combination on the Solitude racetrack in 1936.

Karl Hofmann, who rode the sensational three-cylinder DKW designed by Ing. Wolf to victory in the 350 class.

Karl Hofmann with the later DKW 350 built under the direction of Helmut Görg.

Siegfried Wünsche on the DKW 250 during the 1953 Tourist Trophy Race (where he was unable to repeat Ewald Kluge's prewar success, but nevertheless performed well against strong foreign competition).

DKW factory rider August Hobl of Ingolstadt. His accomplishments included victories on the last 125cc machines built without superchargers (see pages 224-225).

DKW Heirs All over the World

In the turmoil of the early postwar years the fate of the DKW brand must have appeared all the more uncertain when the residence of the manufacturer and of Auto Union lay within the Soviet-occupied zone, where all industrial firms were placed under sequester or confiscated, with the most important being completely dismantled. It was therefore no surprise that attempts – authorized and unauthorized – were made to follow on what the DKW brand had meant for decades.

And while in Ingolstadt and Dusseldorf a new Auto Union and under its roof DKW motorcycles and DKW front wheel drive automobiles with DKW two-stroke engines were awakened to new life, the former Auto Union companies in Zschopau, Zwickau and Chemnitz and the other Saxon (and the few outside Saxony) of the former automobile industry were combined to form the nationally-owned IFA (Industrial Administration Vehicle Production). Piece by piece, the empty halls were laboriously refilled with machine tools (initially recovered from the rubble and repaired), and a modest production program was begun – the construction of motor vehicles was all the more difficult, as important suppliers were located in the west of divided Germany. Consequently new manufacturing plants also had to be created for these vital production components. Despite all difficulties, however, the Zschopau factory again began producing motorcycles, beginning, as might be expected, with the RT 125. This was followed by the newly designed 150- and 250cc two-stroke single-cylinder models, as well as a 350cc two-stroke boxer model – under the new brand name MZ (Zschopau Motorcycle Factory). Within a few years production levels reached prewar levels.

Production of the 700cc Master Class began in the IFA's Chemnitz factory (a former Wanderer operation) and in the Audi factory in Zwickau, later also in the BMW factory in Eisenach, followed several years later by the F 9 three-cylinder model. And while the Master Class was replaced by a new development (with a plastic body), the Trabant with a 600cc twin-cylinder two-stroke engine with rotary intake valves, in Eisenach the F 9 was developed into the Wartburg – still powered by a three-cylinder two-stroke engine. The Trabant and the Wartburg were both designed with front wheel drive.

Several years later Dr. Werner and Dr. Müller, who after the war initially moved to Oldenburg and there established and built up the North-German Central Depot, found themselves in Rotterdam again, along with other former Auto Union workers from the technical side of the company. There, in a newly established and spotlessly clean factory, they made Mopeds (and the associated engines, which by the way also had rotary intake valves) with the Italian-sounding name Berini. In fact this new brand name was created from the first letters of the three associates: Bernhard, Richard and Nikolaus. The Dutch company (Pluvier) developed well, and a new, larger and highly modern factory was built in northern Holland (H.P. Müller, the famous DKW racing rider and brother-in-law of the company head Dr. Gerd Müller, was technical director there). Then came the first great decline of the Moped market and the end of production of two-wheeled vehicles in Holland.

The ban on superchargers for Germans (who were initially excluded from international sport) issued by the FIM after the war did not take effect until 1951. They therefore had the opportunity to compete in races in Germany even with prewar machines equipped with superchargers or (as two-strokes) charging pumps. Many of the prewar racing machines had been lost due to events during and after the war, but some were recovered or rebuilt from parts. The photos illustrate several examples from that period – veteran DKW racing machines that once again enlivened the racing scene until their days ended in 1951.

Prototype of a 60cc small motorcycle built by the nationally owned IFA for the first postwar Leipzig fair (note that the motorcycle still wears the DKW-AUTO UNION emblem). The engine was equipped with an auxiliary charging pump. Front and rear wheel suspension based on the Phänomen design. Shaft drive! The motorcycle never entered production.

But DKW motorcycles also began appearing elsewhere here and there – not only private road machines that were returned to service (it was estimated that there were 100,000 in West Germany alone!) – but also new beginnings with "recreated" new DKW models. The RT 125, in particular, could be found round the world: in America, in England, in Poland, in the USSR and in Japan, new motorcycle brands and models appeared on the market that could not deny that their inspiration had first seen the light of day in Zschopau.

While (see above) the motorcycles with displacements greater than 125cc produced by MZ in Zschopau were original designs and not a direct revival or development of the NZ models from the final war years, the Czechs presented their new Jawa models, which looked like they came directly from the drawing board of Hermann Weber.

There was a good reason why – in addition to the BMW copies – an entire series of two-stroke models based on DKW designs appeared in the Soviet Union: not only was a cadre of DKW technicians taken to Russia for several years to help establish a modern motorcycle

250cc four-piston supercharger machine made by Walfried Winkler from existing and newly made parts after his return from Russian internment in the Soviet occupation zone. With this machine he competed successfully in races in West Germany until the ban on superchargers took effect.

Two views of the incredibly fast racing engine created by Carl Döring and Erich Wolf from an RT 125. It had a counter-running auxiliary pump in the crankcase.

This engine was created after additional charging devices were banned from racing sport in 1951. It had a reversed Puch twin-piston cylinder, but without an auxiliary piston charging pump.

Another experiment by Döring of Wiesbaden: twin-piston Puch cylinder with exhaust at the back of the RT 125 engine and a counter-running auxiliary pump on the crankcase.

After the war K.H. Meller, a private rider from Hamburg, built an opposed-piston racing engine based on a DKW SS 250 or 350 – but that was surely too difficult a task for a private citizen.

Karl Lottes, a well-known private rider of DKW motorcycles before the war, built a new racing machine using one of the last 250cc four-piston DKW racing engines. The supercharger and drive had to be procured elsewhere, and a chain-driven Bosch racing magneto was installed in place of the original flywheel ignition.

Another experiment under pressure of the supercharger ban (also by Lottes): the charging pump of the SS 250 engine was amputated and a rotary intake valve took its place. The carburetor was originally high, on the cylinder, and a small cap closed the intake openings.

H.P. Müller, one of the most and successful German motorcycle racers (who had already been chosen to drive the Auto Union racing car, invested endless effort (and much time and money) in the construction of a supercharger machine from an SS 250. (The supercharger came from a prewar NSU machine.)

In addition to the 250cc supercharged machine he built in Chemnitz from existing and newly manufactured parts (see page 171), when Walfried Winkler moved to West Germany he also brought with him a complete 125cc twin-piston record engine (see page 98). Near Victoria in Nuremberg, he installed the engine in a chassis complete with fairing. Planned attempts to break the world record never took place.

industry – not only did the Soviet design bureau in Chemnitz design developments of the NZ 350 (with telescopic fork and rear-wheel suspension), including a 350 twin-cylinder, it also built and tested prototypes in its own experimental workshop (in the former Bark engine factory in Oberkunewald). These eventually went into production as the ISH and other Soviet motorcycle models.

Incidentally, the same design bureau produced a 250cc machine, the forerunner and inspiration for the 350cc boxer machine with shaft drive later built in Zschopau. This engine concept was based on development work carried out in Zschopau late in the war, whose goal was to create an ultra short stroke boxer engine for use as an aircraft engine starter. The highlight of the work in the Soviet development facility, however, was a racing machine (designed and built with 250- and 350cc engines) with opposed piston supercharged engine and shaft drive from the transversely mounted engine to the rear wheel. While nothing of this machine remained in Germany, one of the racing machines based on this design and built by Kuhnke and Braunschweig has survived. In any case it has strong similarities to the original concept – see the photos on page 180.

The Only DKW Six-Cylinder

In closing, another design is worthy of mention, because, though in another sense, it must likewise be considered part of the DKW gene pool. Its father was Dipl.Ing. Müller, who halfway through the war had replaced Dr. Venediger as head of development at the DKW factory in Zschopau and after the war established his own design bureau in Andernach. After numerous two-stroke engine designs entered production outside Germany (including the Swedish 750cc three-cylinder SAAB engine), his bureau created a six-cylinder two-stroke engine with a V configuration by skillfully combining two three-cylinders à la DKW F 9. Testing revealed astonishingly good values, not only with respect to power and torque delivery, but also fuel consumption, weight and external dimensions: with a bore of 62.5mm and a stroke of 70mm (with a resulting total displacement of 1280cc) with a compression of 9.5 produced 83hp at just 5,000rpm, had its maximum torque of 14.5mkg at 3,400rpm – and it was amazingly light, just 84kg, which gave it a power/weight ratio of exactly 1kg/hp. With a consumption of 8.6 liters (of normal gasoline) at 100kph and 11.2 liters at 140kph, the lively power plant's fuel consumption (with a 1:25 mixture) was no greater than that of comparable four-stroke engines (see photos page 181).

Because of its characteristics, the engine – initially created in the Müller bureau more for "fun" – would probably have become the engine for the Auto Union Munga as well as for the developed version of the F 102 from Ingolstadt. Unfortunately, the changes in ownership rules, which generally put an end to the two-stroke engine, prevented plans of this nature from being realized. And Dipl.-Ing. Müller's untimely death also prevented other plans for this true DKW engine from reaching fruition.

Incidentally, a few examples of the planned rear-wheel hub engine were built in Andernach after the war – before this interesting design was sold to England.

The DKW RT 125 was copied all over the world. One day in 1945-46 a railroad car arrived at the BSA factory in England containing all the RT 125 manufacturing documents from Zschopau, part of the booty from occupied Germany. The company subsequently produced 125- and 175cc versions of the motorcycle as the Bantam (with the "English" reverse arrangement of kickstarter and foot shift lever).

Copies of the RT 125 turned up everywhere after the war: in America (see below), in Poland, in the Soviet Union – and also in Japan, where it was built in several factories at the same time.

The American copy of the DKW RT 125: the Hummer by Harley-Davidson.

Under cover of Wehrmacht repair contracts, the Czechs pursued development of their prewar two-stroke machines (made under license from DKW) during the war, and when the war was over the 250cc single-cylinder Jawa was ready as was the OGAR with a 350 twin-cylinder engine (which later also powered Jawas). A postwar DKW from Zschopau would probably have looked very similar – and the carburetor cover was exactly the same as the one produced by the DKW people in Ingolstadt after 1950.

At the Cologne IMFA in 1980, Yamaha proudly revealed the model of the "first Yamaha." The machine was an exact copy of the DKW RT 125 with the Jurisch rear-wheel suspension – probably because the sample they had was equipped with it. Yamaha later issued an advertising pamphlet in which the Japanese expressed their gratitude for "this outstanding model," a noble gesture rarely made in this industry.

The Russians fancied the motorcycles from DKW at an early stage: for several years this E 300 (the original was built in Zschopau in 1929) was built under license in considerable numbers by the Promet factory in Leningrad – 60,000 in just the first year! The Russians produced four-color instructional manuals, which German troops made use of during the war. The Germans had nothing like it, not even in Zschopau!

A Soviet ISH – a developed version of the DKW NZ 350 with telescopic fork and rear wheel swing arm (15hp at 4,500rpm, four-speed gearbox).

Soviet copy of the RT 125 – but with telescopic fork and rear wheel swing arm.

Another Russian RT 125 on display.

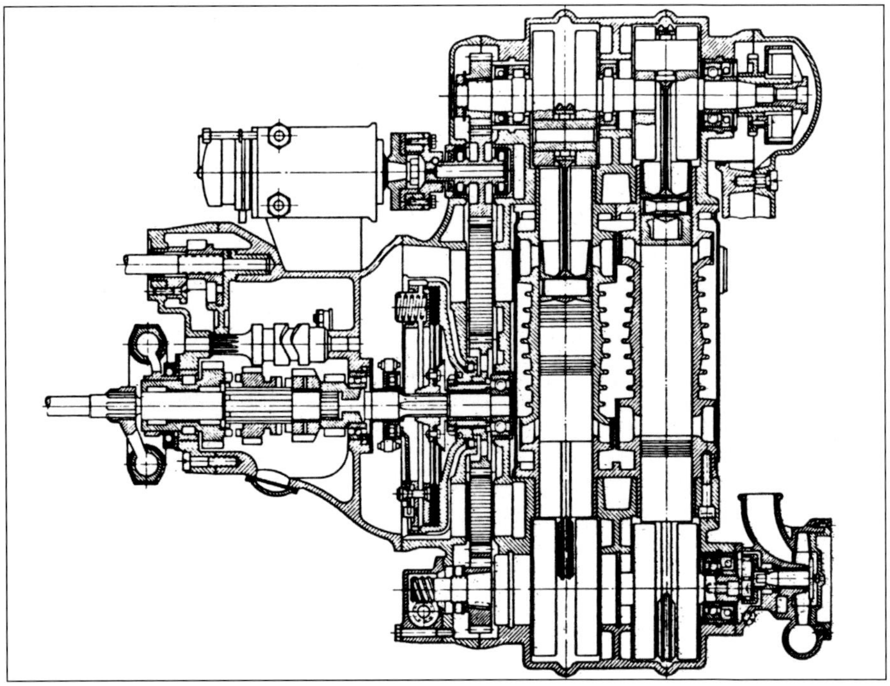

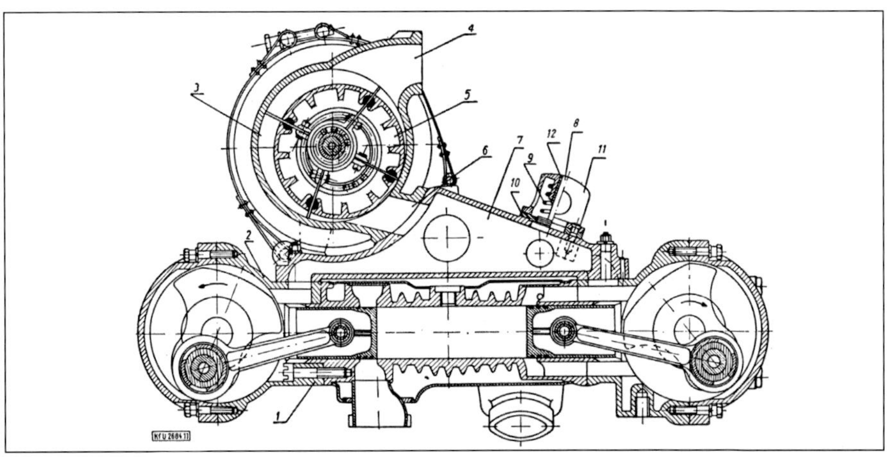

This interesting engine was developed immediately after the war by DKW specialists forced to work in a Soviet factory in the Chemnitz area. Several examples of the engine (250- and 350cc) were completed and tested. It was a four-piston opposed-piston engine with charging or over-charging by the rotary supercharger developed in Zschopau and the two twin-cylinder crankshafts coupled by spur gears.

The two sectional drawings show the innards of the twin-piston engine very clearly. One can see the 180° offset of the two shafts, through which the two pairs of pistons found themselves in the dead points alternately, and one can also see that the rotary supercharger delivered the fresh charge to the cylinder – with one case for one, the other for the other cylinder – via the two crank chambers and scavenge slots. As a result, the exhaust piston was sprayed with cooling fresh charge, at least from below – the exhaust piston was the thorny issue, as with every other opposed-piston two-stroke.

The drawings also reveal the secondary drive (water pump, tachometer, supercharger and standing magneto) as well as the starter, which worked via freewheel, and the drive train (with reduced rpm via dry clutch, shifting claw four-speed gearbox and driveshaft to the rear wheel). The GS 250 had 45hp, the GS 350 55hp, each at 7,000rpm – tremendous figures for its day.

Complete view of the opposed-piston racing machine with the transversely mounted engine. More work undoubtedly had to be done to the chassis.

In 1949-50 Kuhnke of Brunswick, who had raced his own DKW before the war, had a racing engine built based on the design of the Chemnitz opposed piston engine. He did not want it transversely mounted nor did he want shaft drive, and in order for the very long power plant to fit in the frame of a DKW SS it had to be positioned at an incline and the bottom front of the twin-tube frame cut away. The machine was fast – but Kuhnke was still struggling with the unavoidable teething troubles of this delicate object when, in 1951, the ban on superchargers made further work pointless. The Kuhnke engine used four exhaust pipes – the sparkplugs were located on the underside of the cylinder (!). This unique motorcycle is now part of the collection of the Two Wheel Museum in Neckarsulm.

After the war the nationally owned IFA resumed the production of motorcycles in Zschopau, initially with a slightly modified RT 125 (telescopic fork and rear wheel suspension).

When the Zschopau company was renamed the Motorradwerk Zschopau (Zschopau Motorcycle Factory) (MZ), new motorcycle models with 125-, 150- and 175cc engines were developed there and manufactured in considerable numbers. Special models allowed MZ to play a sometimes dominating, technically leading role in international racing and off-road sport competition for many years.

Front and side views of the six-cylinder engine by Müller-Andernach (see text on page 175).

The crankshaft of the six-cylinder V engine: two connecting rods per crank pin, between them spacers, which with piston rings kept the crank chambers (as pre-compression spaces) separated.

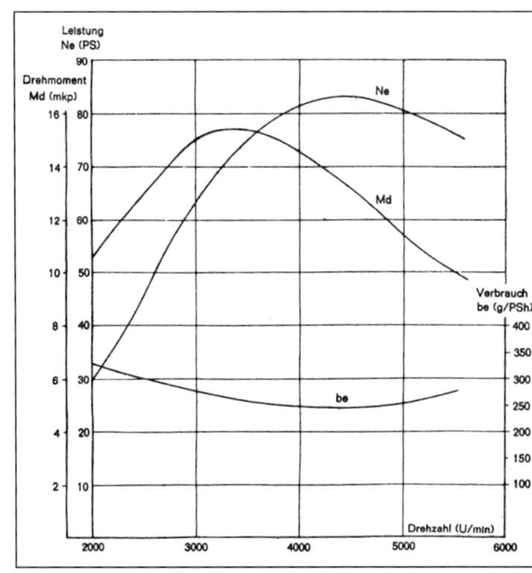

Performance and consumption diagram of the Müller six-cylinder two-stroke engine.

One of the two (identical) cylinder blocks. The cylinder heads are cast with the cylinders in one piece (in grey cast iron), a common light metal cooling hood covers the water spaces. The sparkplugs are seated centrally.

For the Second Time: No Auto Union without DKW

In June 1945, just one month after the surrender, talks were held in the Auto Union branch office in Munich in which Dr. Bruhn looked for possibilities for a new beginning for Auto Union.

A resumption of automobile or motorcycle production was out of the question at that time, for with one exception (a factory in Spandau that was ill-suited to the production of automobiles) all of the production facilities of the former Saxon group of companies were in the zone occupied by the Soviets. The four Auto Union branch offices in the western occupation zone (Munich, Nuremberg, Hanover and Freiburg/Breisgau) were also unsuitable for a resumption of automobile production because of their inadequate spatial possibilities.

Auto Union did, however, have one advantage over the other automobile factories in western Germany: because of their front wheel drive, the DKW vehicles had not been used by the *Wehrmacht*. Therefore in West Germany alone there were still more than 65,000 Reichs- and Meisterklasse cars, and there was also a significant number of these vehicles in other countries. Dr. Bruhn's circle in Munich included Dipl.-Ing. Schittenheim, who had been responsible for the group's entire spare parts organization in Chemnitz – he was the man needed to organize the supplying of spare parts for the "surviving" DKW cars. There was also Erhard Burghalter, former head of the Auto Union branch office in Stettin (who was supposed to organize distribution) and finally Oswald Heckel, former general representative of Auto Union in Bulgaria, who brought with him years of experience in dealing with dealers. The circle was completed by Dr. Hahn, who had also found a temporary home in Bavaria and who now participated in the planning that ultimately lead to the establishment of the company Central Depot for Auto Union Spare Parts GmbH, in his familiar agile way.

Ingolstadt was selected as the seat of the new company. Former military structures offered sufficient space for warehouses and offices, and the city promised its support. The company also succeeded in obtaining credit from the Bavarian State Bank in Munich, which enabled work to begin.

At about the same time, following the Ingolstadt example a Central Depot for Auto Union Spare Parts GmbH was also established in Oldenburg for the British occupation zone. Its founder was Dr. William Werner, the former chief technical officer, and Dr. Gerd Müller, head of the Auto Union board of management services in Chemnitz. The duplication appeared necessary, because at that time the occupation authorities still kept their zones strictly separated, even economically.

Despite this, Dr. Bruhn wanted to unite the two companies under one roof, and he therefore initiated negotiations in Oldenburg. When he visited his birthplace in Fleckeby, he was denounced and arrested by the English. He was not released until 1947, without ever having learned the reason for his imprisonment. He was, however, forbidden to work, which was not lifted until early 1948.

The arrest of Dr. Bruhn was a serious setback for the Ingolstadt group. Dr. Hahn was of the opinion that without Dr. Bruhn and his connections, the establishment of the new company was doomed to fail, and he initially pursued his own plans. The other participants in the establishment continued the work that had been started in the area of spare parts supply and also steadily expanded their circle of coworkers with a view towards a possible, though surely also initially modest, production of vehicles.

In Ingolstadt as in Oldenburg (and also in Bude, where the central depot's offices were located), all considerations and plans continued to be based on the DKW complex. But apart from the fact that many of the

Dr. Carl Hahn (†) deputy board member of the AUTO UNION AG in Chemnitz and head of distribution for the AUTO UNION GmbH in Ingolstadt/Düsseldorf.

Dr. Richard Bruhn (†), chairman of the AUTO UNION AG in Chemnitz and responsible for the overall management of the AUTO UNION GmbH in Ingolstadt/Düsseldorf.

executives in their old homes were not sold on the technical peculiarities of the DKW program, those who gradually came, especially to Ingolstadt – workers and specialists from the other Auto Union brands – predominated, all happy at the chance now offered them by the former Cinderella of the company. Of course they were also later joined by DKW specialists – but significant elements that had been closely associated with the DKW two-strokes in their Saxon homeland were absent. Some remained in the Soviet occupation zone – out of familial or other reasons, or in the hope that production would somehow also be resumed in their former places of work – or they had been imprisoned by the occupying power or new rulers. A great number of DKW specialists, on the other hand, had found new careers in the vehicle industry in western Germany

The former technical director of the Horch factory, Fritz Zerbst, joined the Ingolstadt group in 1946, as well as Geite from the Horch development department, who later became head of DKW sporting operations with Auto Union, Jakob or Horch, and the Horch body designer Kurt Schwenk (who later successfully resumed the work on a plastic body begun before the war). From the former sales department for DKW stationary engines, engineer Klinke was one of the early additions. But especially vital to the future destiny, especially of DKW motorcycles, was that engineer Franz Ischinger, once head of the Zschopau off-road sporting section and later involved in racing car development at Auto Union in Zwickau with Dr. von Eberan, had also found his way to Ingolstadt.

In August 1947, a group of former employees visited Dr. Bruhn in his "exile" in Fleckeby to ask him to actively help in the formation of a new Auto Union. Dr. Bruhn agreed and in 1948, after successful denazification, went to work with the goal of reactivating Auto Union and winning back reputation and significance for the company. In agreement with the Ingolstadt Central Depot, which was supposed to have retained its independence indefinitely, Dr. Bruhn initially formed a "working group" of former leading employees – now Dr. Hahn again placed himself at the group's disposal. He succeeded in securing millions in bank credit and also convinced the old dealers, who trusted in the success of the project, to commit to changing depots in order to secure the additional needed credit from the Bavarian State Bank.

The New Auto Union GmbH

In September 1949, all obstacles of a legal and financial nature were finally overcome, and the new company was founded in Ingolstadt as Auto Union GmbH. Dr. Bruhn assumed overall control of sales including exports, Dr. Hahn became head of distribution and Director Zerbst was placed in charge of the entire technical field. Director Günther (formerly of the Horch works) was chosen to be acting manager.

The reason why they simply couldn't continue the old Auto Union limited stock company (although the government in the Soviet zone had shut it down as a company) and instead had to establish a new Auto Union (limited liability company), was that the occupying powers had confiscated all German state-owned companies. This included any company with more than 50% of its assets owned by the state. Because of the company's ownership, there was a danger that the western assets of the old Auto Union AG might also fall under this law, thus making the establishment of the limited liability company necessary. The limited stock company transferred the trademark and production rights and its branch offices to the new limited liability company.

In the years that followed, Auto Union GmbH became involved in a wide variety of businesses. In 1978, after selling all of its industry assets and becoming a furniture company, the name Auto Union was transferred to VW.

In Ingolstadt, however, planning and preparation for the start of production had already commenced even before the official founding of the Auto Union GmbH. The first program – apart from the procurement and distribution of original spare parts for older production DKW automobiles – consisted of the manufacture of the RT 125 motorcycle and a new delivery van with the proven DKW 700cc front-mounted engine (type designation F 89 L).

One of the first ads by the new AUTO UNION of Ingolstadt. It declares that "DKW is back!" and goes onto say, "The new RT – better than ever."

Designer Schwenk had prepared drawings and production documents for the new delivery vehicle (fast truck), production of the RT 125 W (as it was officially called) was based on a prewar machine provided by a DKW dealer in Regensburg.

The production of motorcycles (and the initial preparations for this) was the responsibility of Engineer Ischinger, who first had to convert an old grain silo in Ingolstadt into a multi-story factory building by installing windows and making other modifications. Initially the factory was responsible for manufacturing the engine and final assembly of the RT 125 (and, until the erection of a new and larger facility near the original, also of the larger motorcycle models that came later), while the first frames were procured from the Hoffmann Company in Lintorf, where for a time the Vespa scooter was built under license and later other motorcycle types including

Engineer Nikolaus Dörner, design.

Engineer Franz Ischinger, production.

Engineer Herbert Kirchberg, experimentation.

The converted granary, in which the postwar production of motorcycles in Ingolstadt began.

The later new-construction, in which all DKW motorcycles were made until 1958.

the well-known *Gouverneur* with a 250- or 300cc four-stroke Boxer engine (competition for BMW!).

Production of the delivery vehicle took place elsewhere – like all of Auto Union's production and administration offices, scattered over the entire metropolitan area. That is why, when talk turned to the Auto Union in Ingolstadt, the phrase "united smelting works" was commonly heard.

The DKW Automobile Plant in Düsseldorf

The previously mentioned working group under Bruhn devoted a significant portion of its planning work to the revival of automobile production. Here too there was no question that it could only be a DKW model – and it was equally clear that, especially as the production of motorcycles and delivery vehicles had to be steadily increased, that there was no possibility of it happening in Ingolstadt. After a number of inspection trips by members of the management team, the choice finally fell on Works II of the Rheinmetall-Borsig-AG in Düsseldorf. Its central location, proximity of important suppliers and not least the considerable reservoir of labor there were decisive factors. A lease-purchase agreement was signed on 13 March 1950, averting the threatened dismantling and destruction of the former armaments plant, and the company also secured the financing needed to rebuild the factory, 80% of which had been destroyed. Based on the contract, in 1954 ownership of the plant, which at first had only been leased, was transferred to Auto Union GmbH.

After the new Ingolstadt models – delivery van and motorcycle – were displayed at the Hanover Spring Fair in 1949 and received a very positive reception from the dealers, before the end of the year the facilities in Ingolstadt delivered the first 500 RT 125 W motorcycles and approximately 500 F 89 L delivery vans. In 1950 these figures rose to 24,000 motorcycles and just under 7,000 delivery vans.

And while the rebuilding effort was still in full swing, in 1950 the Auto Union factory in Düsseldorf rolled out 1,380 DKW F 89 P automobiles, the "new" Meisterklasse (which initially was supposed to be called the F 10, a continuation of the old Auto Union type series). Its power

DKW motorcycle assembly line in Ingolstadt.

Production of DKW delivery vans in Ingolstadt.

Production of transmissions for DKW vehicles in the Berlin factory of the Auto Union GmbH. Some of the electrical systems for DKW motorcycles and automobiles from Ingolstadt and Düsseldorf were also made there (previously in the Auto Union's electrical works in Chemnitz).

plant was the modified 700cc front-mounted power unit, now installed forward of the front axle with the engine. The former wooden body was forgotten and the car had a shapely steel body on the twin-profile steel frame (similar to that of the former F 8). The body was manufactured with the tools (stored in West Germany) that were to have been used for the production startup of the DKW F 9 three-cylinder model in 1940.

And so when the year 1950 ended, the DKW brand had risen from the ashes like a Phoenix. DKW two-stroke engines, DKW motorcycles and DKW front wheel drive vehicles, again ideally suited to the economic circumstances of the day, had made possible the rebuilding of Auto Union and again made possible the creation of thousands of jobs.

Partial view of the Auto Union factory in Düsseldorf.

Production of DKW cars begins in the Düsseldorf factory.

DKW Automobiles and Motorcycles from Ingolstadt and Düsseldorf

Production of motorcycles in Ingolstadt began in 1949 with the RT 125 W, which was largely the same as the original from Zschopau, including the pressed steel fork with rubber band suspension. The changes included the seat suspension, and a small tool kit was contained in a recess in the tank. With 5hp at 5,000rpm and the three-speed gearbox with foot shifter, the drive train was also the same as that of the original model.

The somewhat bulkier casing cover on the clutch side of this RT 125 and the absence of foot-shifter and clutch hand lever indicate that this machine was equipped with an automatically shifting Kreis gearbox (a combination of centrifugal clutch and freewheel). This version was not built in quantity, however.

The engine-gearbox unit of the RT 125 from both sides – identical to the Zschopau original in all respects.

Tool kit in the larger 9.5-liter fuel tank of the RT 125 W.

The front fork's rubber band suspension. This is the version developed by Conti for Zschopau. It replaced the Neiman rubber-band suspension.

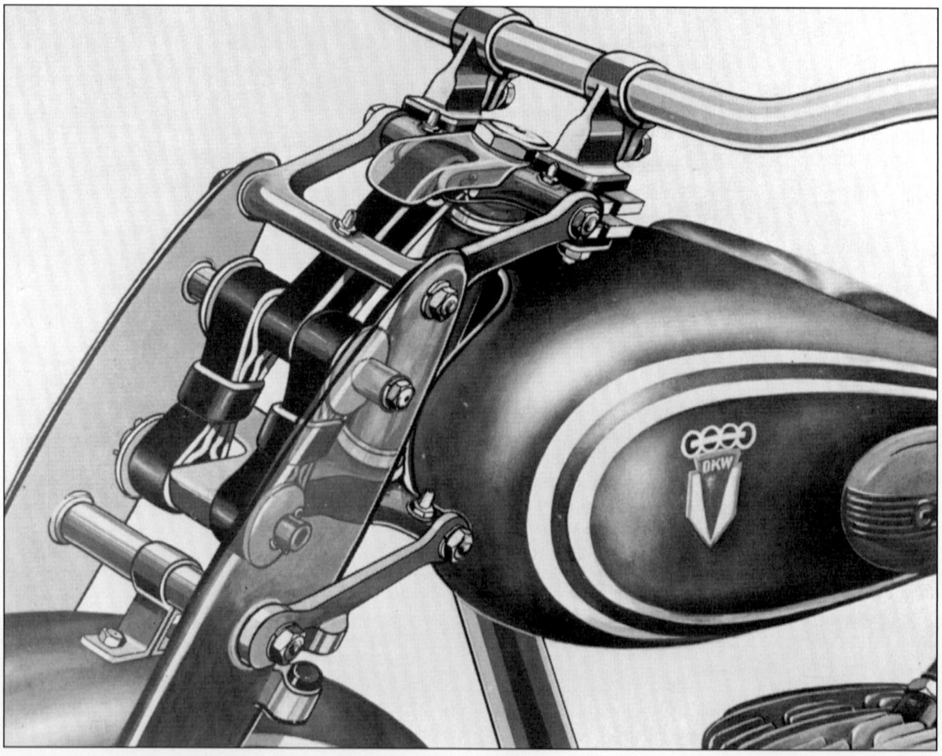

Unlike the Zschopau model, the Ingolstadt frame (initially built by Hoffmann in Lintorf) had dropouts for the rear axle (like racing bicycles) to simplify removal of the wheel.

By 1950 the RT 125 was being built with a telescopic front fork and rear wheel suspension. Cutaway of one of the fork tubes.

The rear wheel suspension was a short-stroke telescopic shock absorber with broad pick-ups for the axle sockets. The seat now had a rubber suspension. Engine power increased to 6.4hp at 5,600rpm. The maximum speed was now over 90kph (1956 model seen here).

The 100,000th DKW motorcycle left the Ingolstadt production line in 1953.

In 1951 the DKW motorcycle program was expanded by adding the RT 175 and RT 200 models, both with telescopic front forks and vertical shock absorber on the rear wheel. The gearbox was initially three-speed, later four-speed. The carburetor was still exposed and bolted directly to the cylinder. New rear brake hubs (simulated full hub brakes).

New more powerful engines with shapely carburetor cover, large air quieting space and carburetor mounted further back (lengthened, vibrationally-tuned intake pipe).

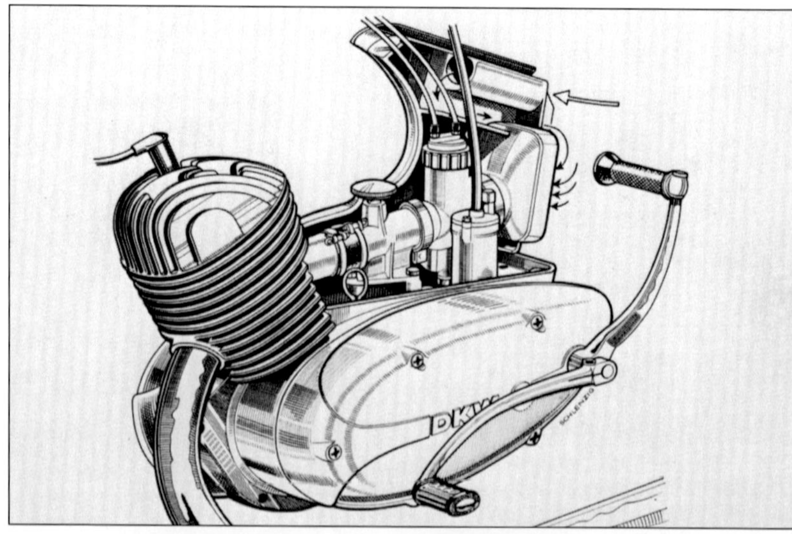

New progressively working, pneumatically damped telescopic front fork for the developed RT 175 and RT 200 models. New (real) aluminum hubs with drum brakes front and rear.

Instructive exploded drawing of the more powerful engines (now also supplemented by a 250cc version). Below the original RT 125 foot shifter, modified for the four-speed gearbox.

The DKW motorcycle program underwent a further expansion in late 1951 – early 1952, when production of the completely newly designed RT 250 began. With a bore-stroke of 70x64, the engine initially produced 12hp at 4,500rpm, which made possible a top speed of 105kph. Initially equipped with a three-speed gearbox bit later a four-speed unit, the RT 250 was capable of supporting a sidecar. Initially the suspension was similar to that of the RT 175 and 200.

In the beginning the RT 250 also had drum brakes (with ribbed steel jacket) front ...

... and rear. The chain was completely encapsulated. Short stroke vertical shock absorber.

As DKW's quarter-liter machine, the RT 250/2 was equipped with the encapsulated carburetor, new light metal full-hub brakes and longer stroke rear shock absorber like the smaller models.

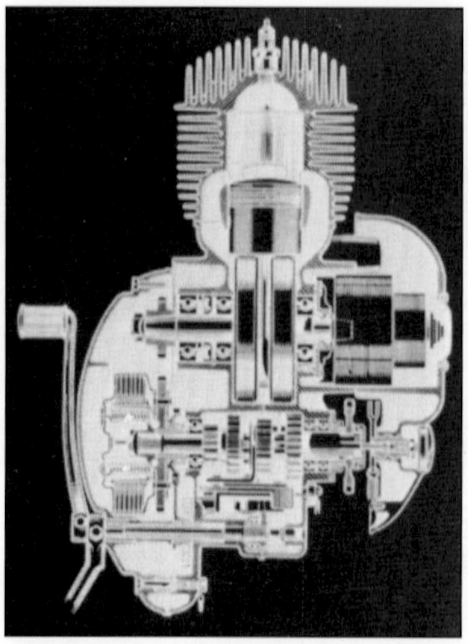

Cutaway view of the engine gearbox unit of the DKW RT 250/2 with four-speed gearbox.

In 1954 the RT 250 produced 15hp and was capable of 115kph. Improved telescopic front fork with shock absorbers.

Above left: The vertical shock absorber ultimately had a spring deflection of 85mm. *Right*: Cutaway drawing of the telescopic rear wheel shock absorber and the light metal full-hub brake.

In addition to "porcupine cylinders," in 1954 the RT 175 and 200 models also had a new suspension with swing arms and shock absorbers in the rear – model designations 175 S and 200 S. The chain, which previously was only shielded, now ran in a light metal chain box with continuous lubrication. The motorcycles also had larger fuel tanks.

RT 250 S – with adjustable swing arms and shock absorbers and 15hp (maximum speed solo 116kph).

Shock absorber with drive chain – the casing on the DKW VS 175.

By 1955 more DKW RT 175 motorcycles were being sold than any other – the RT 175 VS was introduced in 1956 and enjoyed similar success. It had a telescopic swing fork with shock absorbers in front and a redesigned headlight fairing plus fitted cockpit.

In 1955 the RT 250 was also switched to the new VS suspension (with front swing fork). The caster could be changed for use with a sidecar.

Left: The swing fork front wheel suspension of the DKW models VS 175, 200 and 250.

The new "cockpit" of the DKW VS models with integrated headlight fairing (handlebar fittings as once used on the Block models in Zschopau, see page 41).

The RT 350 appeared in 1954 as the flagship of the DKW motorcycle program. Its engine produced 18hp at 4,500-5,000rpm and it had a top speed of 120kph. It initially had vertical telescopic shock absorbers in the rear.

The following year the RT 350, DKW's big twin-cylinder machine, was given the porcupine cylinder with cooling fins and the suspension with the rear-wheel swing arm. Engine performance was unchanged, but its stability was increased and vibration behavior improved.

This twin-carburetor version of the RT 350 was not produced by the factory – instead it was a skillful conversion by the motorcycle's owner. The motorcycle is still running satisfactorily, although it has since been converted back to one carburetor.

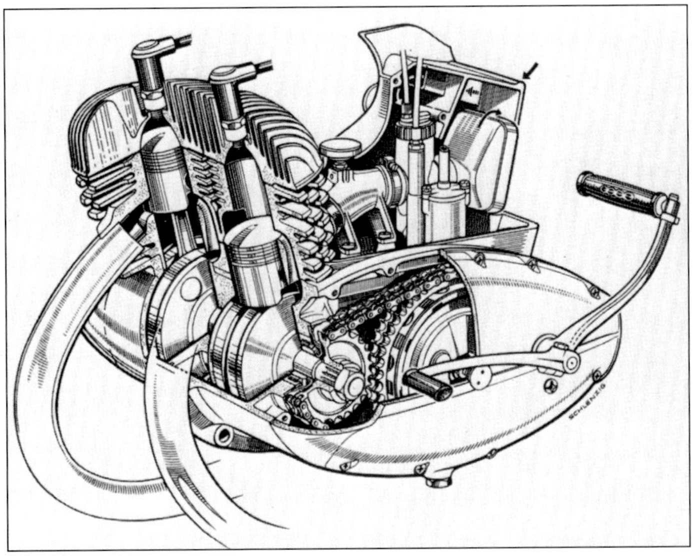

Above: Sectional drawing of the engine/gearbox unit of the RT 350's twin-cylinder engine: bore 62mm, stroke 58mm, short period performance 18.5hp at 5,000rpm, compression 6.5, maximum speed 120kph. The primary drive with endless Duplex roller chain, four-speed gearbox with dog clutch and kickstarter.

Right: The attractive engine unit of DKW's "big" twin-cylinder (of which there was no longer a version with front swing-fork). The RT 350 S was the last DKW motorcycle made in Ingolstadt – the tradition was then continued in Nuremberg.

Below: When the decline in interest in motorcycles began to become apparent, this prototype was created in Ingolstadt – in the belief that something different than the usual had to be offered the customer. The motorcycle never went into production, but it probably led to the moped model that was briefly manufactured by the Nuremberg Two-Wheel Union (see page 247).

DKW entered the scooter business in 1953 with the Hobby-Roller. It was an interesting design with a 75cc, 3hp engine.

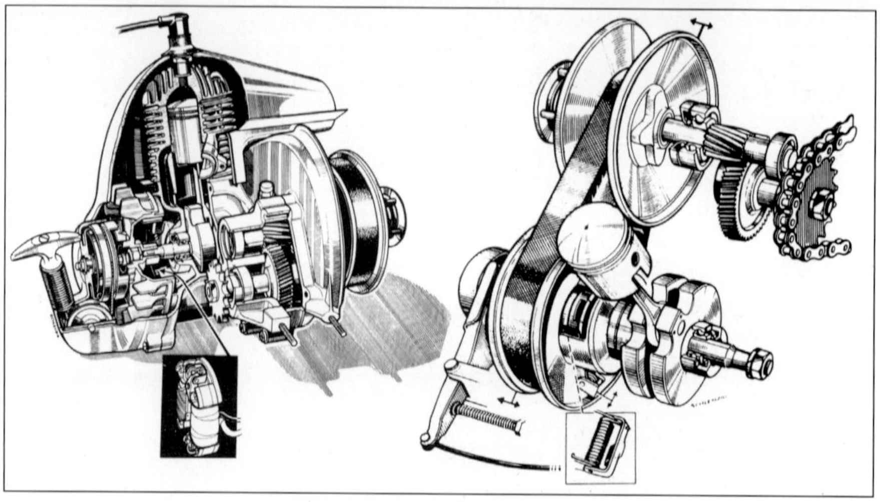

The fan-cooled Hobby engine with flywheel magneto ignition and hand starter. Uher-type infinitely variable belt drive.

The belt drive with the synchronous self-adjusting V-belt pulleys (infinitely variable reduction change, automatic operation under the influence of centrifugal or spring force independent of engine speed and load, also acted as starting clutch). Driving V-belt pulley ran at crankshaft revolutions, the driven pulley was supported by gear on the reduction shaft, from there chain drive to the rear wheel.

Engine, gearbox and rear wheel swing arm arrangement in the DKW Hobby-Roller. The swing arm was sprung with a progressively working rubber element working under pressure.

The production of mopeds was begun in Ingolstadt in 1956 after the Hummel (Bumblebee), a 50cc vehicle, was developed: 1.35hp at 4,400rpm, twist-grip-shifted three-speed gearbox, pedal kickstarter, rubber-sprung short swing arm fork in front, damped shock absorbers rear, pressed steel frame with integral tank, fully-encapsulated chain.

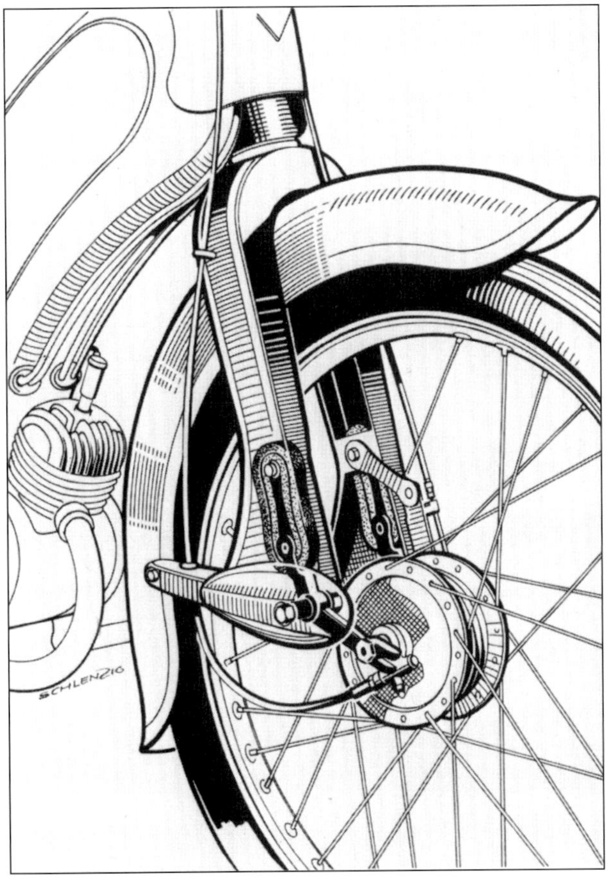

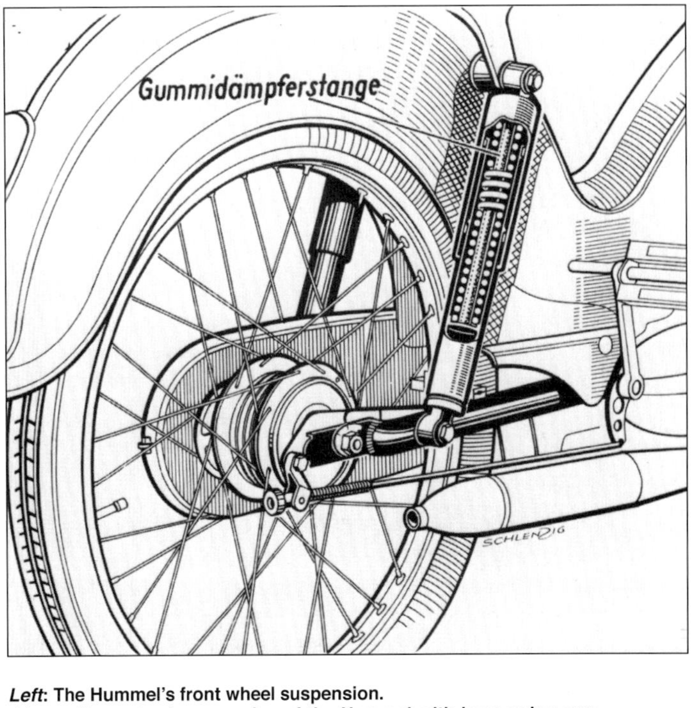

Left: The Hummel's front wheel suspension.
Above: Rear wheel suspension of the Hummel with long swing arm and shock absorbers (rubber-damped).

In 1949 DKW began making the F 89 L, a ¾ ton fast truck of completely new design. It was powered by the 700cc twin-cylinder engine from the prewar years with a three-speed transmission and differential in a common block. It was, however, so mounted on the tubular frame's two side members that the main weight of the power plant block was forward of the front axle, which resulted in more favorable conditions for front wheel drive. Independent suspension, with the front wheels mounted on wishbones and transverse leaf springs, the rear wheels on crank arms on a transverse torsion spring element. Telescopic shock absorbers, hydraulic duplex brakes.

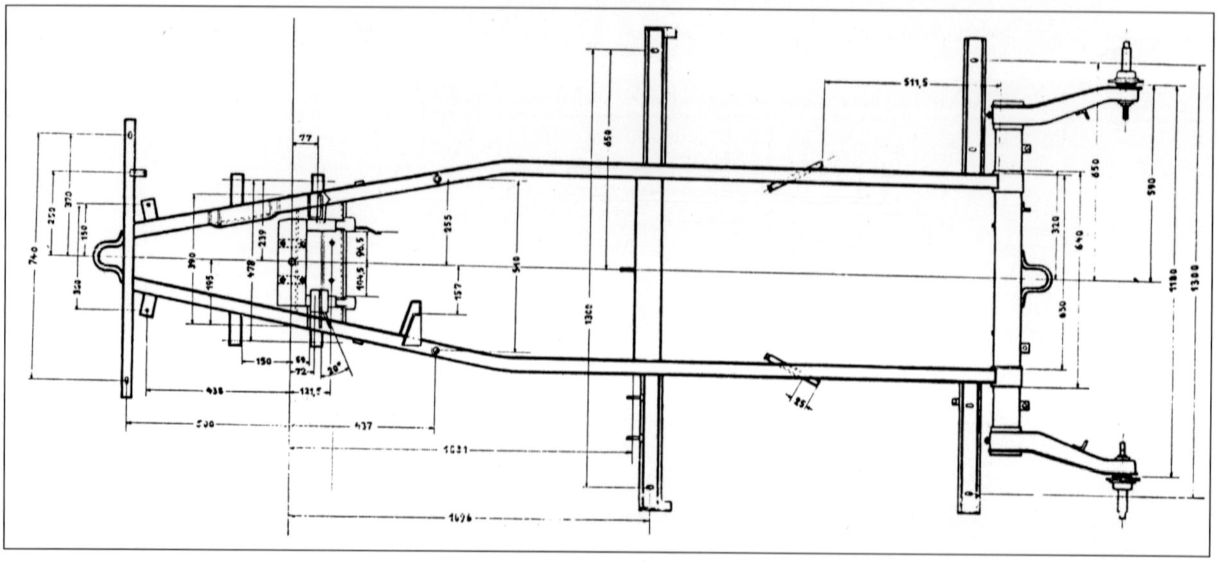

The chassis of the ¾ ton fast truck with 700cc engine.

Just ten months later, production of the new Meisterklasse Type 89 P began in the Düsseldorf factory. It also had the 700cc twin-cylinder engine with three-speed transmission and differential with a new Dynastart system – made in the Auto Union factory in Spandau – mounted forward of the front axle in a modified F 8 chassis. Independent suspension, including telescopic shock absorbers, similar to that of the fast truck (see drawing). Floating axle (rigid axle with high-mounted cross spring and telescopic shock absorbers) in the rear. Hydraulic Duplex brake system. Four-seat sedan with steel body (similar to that projected for the F 9). The engine, equipped with a light metal cylinder head, Solex downdraft carburetor and new exhaust system, produced 23hp at 4,500rpm. Top speed was 100kph.

See-through drawing of the new Meisterklasse.

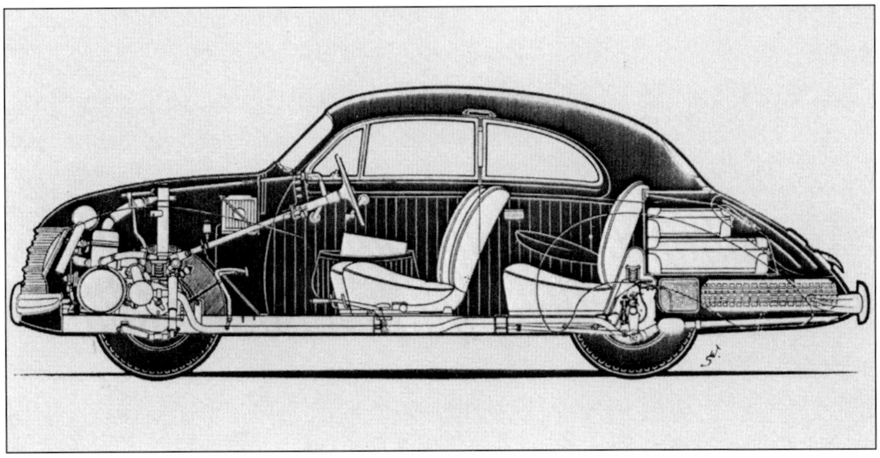

Interior layout of the new Meisterklasse.

Built from 1951 to 1954, the F 89 U (Universal) station wagon initially had a body of mixed construction. Later vehicles had an all-steel body. The power plant and suspension were the same as those of the Meisterklasse.

Front wheel attachment (triangular wishbone at bottom), suspension (transverse leaf spring above) and telescopic shock absorber of the new Meisterklasse.

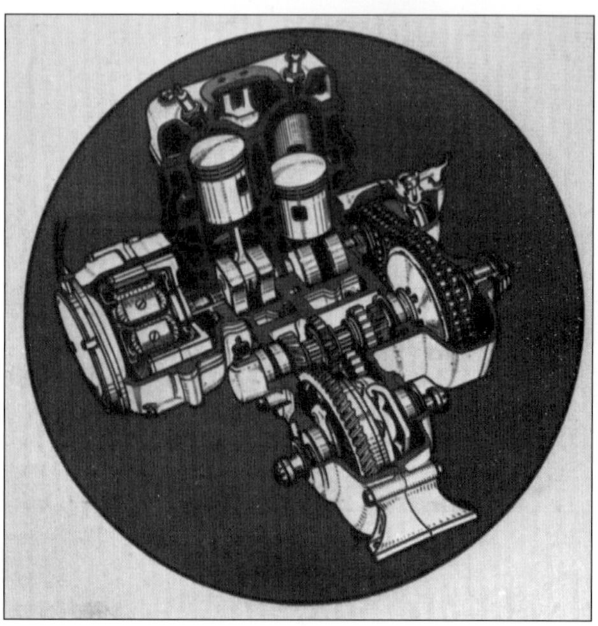

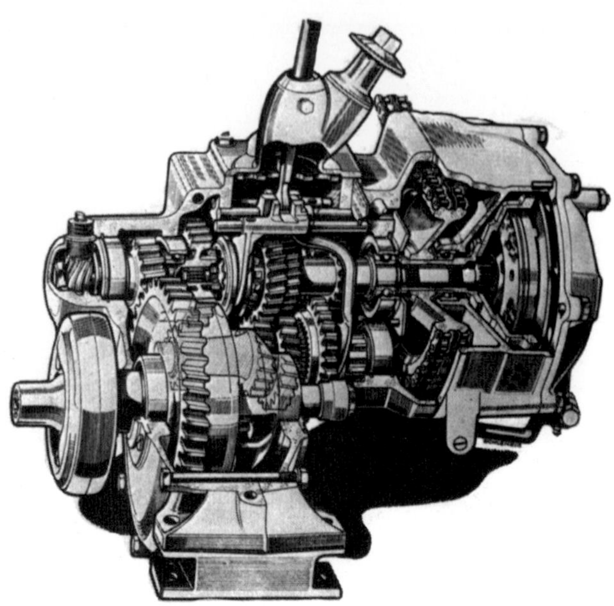

At the beginning of 1953 the three-speed transmission with multi-plate oil-bath clutch (left) designed before the war was replaced by a four-speed unit. The clutch (dry single disc clutch) was in a housing separate from the primary chain drive (right).

Based on the Meisterklasse, this two-seat luxury coupe with Hebmüller body was sold in 1951-52.

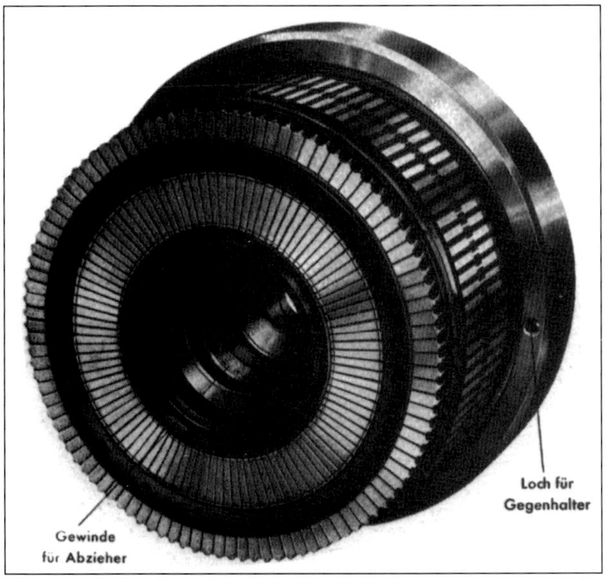

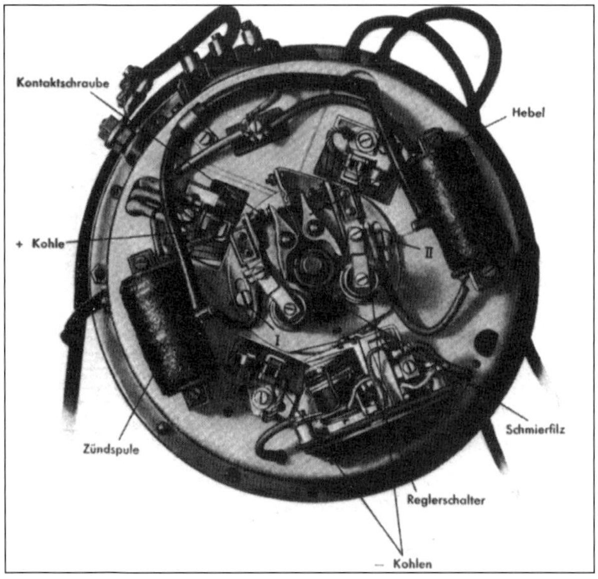

The new DKW Dynastart system (180 Watt) with internal drum armature and forward flat trajectory collector. Some of these systems were made in the Spandau factory, while others were delivered by SIBA (like the motorcycle systems).

Production of the Sonderklasse (Special Class), which was to replace the Meisterklasse, began in Düsseldorf in 1953. It had a three-cylinder engine and an all-steel body almost identical to that of the Meisterklasse on the identical chassis. Power train (three-, later four-speed transmission, with freewheel), engine mounted forward of the front axle but lengthwise. Engine performance (71x76mm bore/stroke) 34hp at 4,000rpm. Maximum speed 120kph.

Left: See-through drawing of the DKW Sonderklasse Type F 91, 1953-1955. *Right*: The Sonderklasse's three-cylinder two-stroke engine; ignition with three ignition coils and triple interrupter in extension of the crankshaft. Solex downdraft carburetor. Thermosiphon cooling. Mixture lubrication 1:25.

The Type F 93, the "Big DKW 3 = 6," appeared in 1955. Compared to the Sonderklasse it was 10 cm wider and had a new radiator grille. Its engine delivered 38hp at 4,200rpm and maximum speed was 115kph. The following F 94 differed only slightly but had an engine that produced 40hp.

Like all previous DKW models, both the fast truck and the 3 = 6 retained the torsion-resistant frame – at a time when (for cost reasons) the load-bearing body dominated the field of automobile construction.

The Monza, a sports version of the "Big DKW 3 = 6," was made from 1956 to 1958. A two-seat plastic body was mounted on the chassis of the normal 3 = 6. Quoted engine power was 44hp, the maximum speed 135kph. The total number delivered was just a little over 100.

With the relocation of automobile production from Düsseldorf to the new plant in Ingolstadt, in 1959 the newly designed DKW Junior entered production. The Junior was built there until 1962, the Junior de Luxe until 1963. Originally designed with a 660cc twin-cylinder engine (and so displayed at the Frankfurt Automobile Show in 1957), the car ultimately received a three-cylinder 750cc engine (68x68mm bore/stroke – later increased to 800cc in the de Luxe by increasing the bore to 70.5mm), 34hp at 4,300rpm, four-speed front drive, steel frame.

The Auto Union 1000 was delivered from 1958 to 1963. It had a larger 980cc three-cylinder engine (74x76mm bore/stroke) and 44hp at 4,500rpm but otherwise was the same as the "Big DKW 3 = 6."

The Auto Union 1000 Sp was offered as a two-seat roadster (left) and a 2/2 coupe (below). Both models had the same lines. Powered by a 980cc engine that delivered 55hp at 4,500rpm, the 1000 was capable of reaching 140kph.

Externally the Junior de Luxe differed little from the standard Junior.

See-through drawing of the Auto Union DKW Junior.

The F 11 and F 12 (see photo) models were manufactured in the new Ingolstadt plant from 1963 to 1965, replacing the Junior models. The F 11 had the Junior's 800cc engine, while the F 12 initially came with the 900cc three-cylinder which delivered 40hp. In 1964 the engine's output was increased to 45hp by raising the compression and it was installed in the F 12 roadster. In 1965 the engine was also installed in the F 12 sedan. The F 11 was based on the body shell of the F 12 (as a simply-equipped basic model) and the mechanics of the Junior de Luxe.

The self-stabilizing torsion crank axle with slit axle tube, the rear axle installed in the Junior.

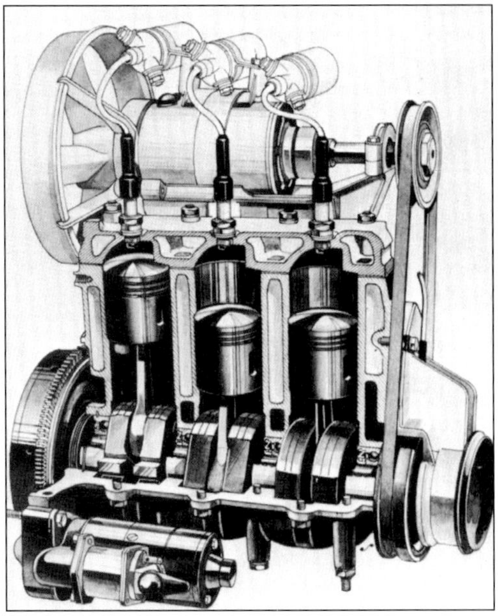

Cutaway drawing of the 750/800cc DKW three-cylinder engine installed in the Junior.

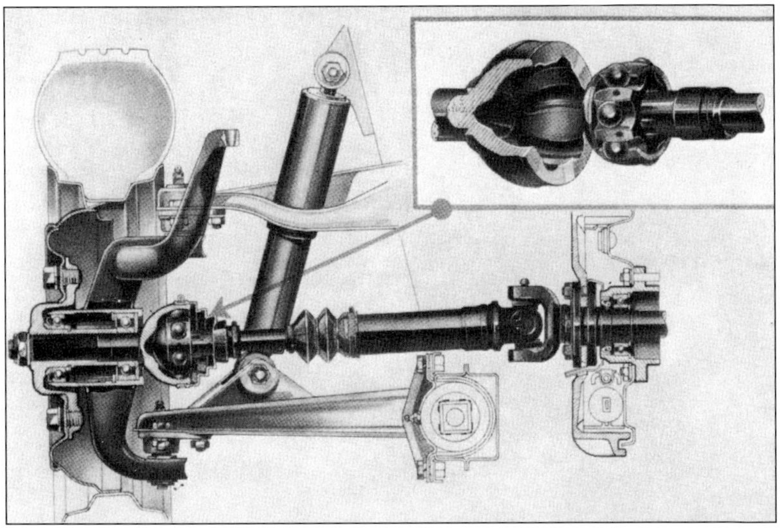

Front wheel drive in the Junior: large-angle constant-velocity joint outboard, universal joint inboard. Inboard Turbo drum brakes.

Front wheel suspension on the Junior: single wheel mounting on two swing arms; the lower affected longitudinal adjustable torsion bars. Telescopic shock absorber.

Auto Union built the Munga (multipurpose universal all-terrain vehicle with all-wheel drive as the Type F 91/4) from 1954 to 1968. It was initially powered by an 896cc three-cylinder engine delivering 38 or 40hp, and later by a developed version (bore 74mm) producing 44hp at 4,500rpm. It had a four-speed transmission and primary reduction gear, all-wheel drive (rear wheel drive could be turned off until 1956), weight 1110 kg, maximum speed 98kph. A plan to install the Müller-Andernach six-cylinder engine (see page 181) was not implemented, as the main buyer (Bundeswehr) did not renew its purchase contract.

The DKW F 102, a completely new medium class car, was unveiled in 1963 (and entered production in 1964). There were two versions, a two-door and a four-door limousine. Its three-cylinder two-stroke engine delivered 60hp at 4,500rpm (76x81 bore/stroke, displacement 1175cc). The first of a planned new generation of cars (of which something more than 52,000 were made) also had front wheel drive, but for the first time in the long series that began with the F 1, it had a self-supporting all-steel body. When production of the car ended in March 1966, it was also the end of the DKW automobile brand.

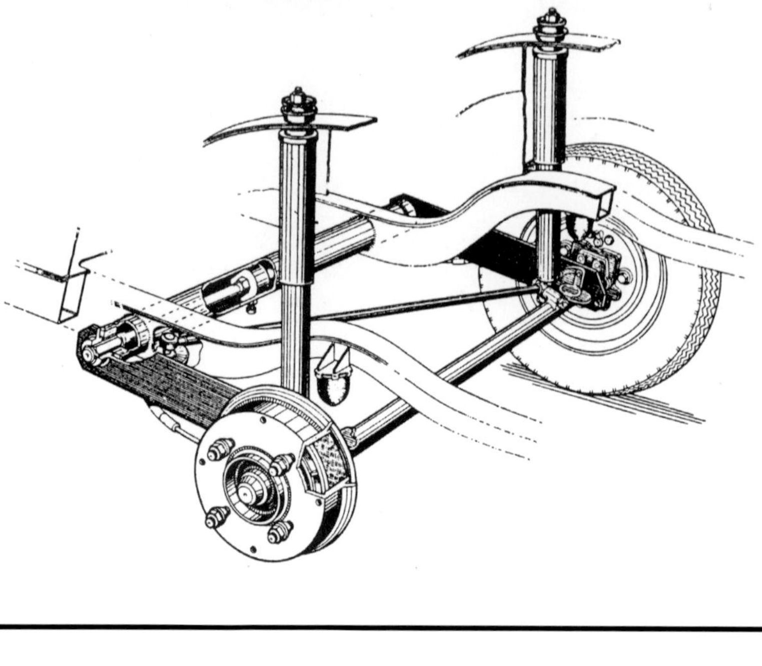

The DKW F 102 had a self-stabilizing torsion crank axle in the rear. It guaranteed consistent track and camber under all load states and wheel adherence even in extreme cornering situations. The slit axle tube was self-stabilizing, the transverse control arm from the axle tube to the frame ensured precise directional control of the wheels. Progressive torsion bar suspension with very long suspension travel and rubber buffer stop limitation. Together with the front disc brakes, the large Simplex drum brakes provided a high level of driving security.

DKW Racing Machines 1950-1956

Following up on the successful tinkering of the Wiesbaden DKW rider Döring (and his "tuner" Erich Wolf), the Ingolstadt factory (after hiring Wolf) initially began making 125cc racing engines with a double-piston cylinder and charging pump in the crankcase. With these machines Kluge, Wünsche and H.P. Müller were untouchable in their class.

Ewald Kluge during a victory lap on the 125cc charging pump machine.

Ewald Kluge (here in conversation with his team member Siegfried Wünsche, who also found his way to Ingolstadt) of course did not want to restrict himself to the smallest racing class for his old brand. He therefore moved heaven and earth to dig up a rotary intake valve machine that had survived the war. After several failed attempts he finally succeeded, and together with Erich Wolf he was able to make the his pride and joy operational again.

In 1950 (as long as the ban on superchargers did not apply to Germany, which had not been allowed back into the FIM, it had no effect on races held there) Ewald Kluge won many races in the 250 class.

H.P. Müller talks shop with Erich Wolf, the racing machine designer in Ingolstadt.

When the supercharger ban meant that additional charging pumps were no longer permitted on two-stroke engines, many saw it as the end of the two-stroke as a racing engine. Memories of the superiority of the Prüssing racing two-strokes before the war were still too clear – but also the opinion that without such considerable mechanical complexity it was not possible to make two-strokes superior to four-strokes. And the first experiments with crankcase-charged two-stroke racing engines, like this one derived from a standard 125cc DKW engine, seemed to confirm this view.

The first experiments with slot-controlled single-cylinder two-strokes with no charging pump (in keeping with the new rules) were followed by engines with radial flow slide intake valves – but their performance was far below expectations (this arrangement of slide valve control had no advantages over the simple slot control).

It was amazing, however, how quickly normal two-strokes could be skillfully doctored (as under H.P. Müller in the photo on the right). Indeed: where was a four-stroke competitor in the small class?

Above: Rudi Feigenheier with the piston-controlled 250 at the staring line of the Sachsenring Race in 1952.

Erich Wolf began experimenting further – with slot control for the intake and with rotary slide valve control on 125- and (as in the photo here) 250cc twin-cylinder engines. His success in achieving quite astounding performances was based on his knowledge of the possibilities of exploiting gas dynamics to quickly empty and fill the cylinder, even at high, power-generating revolutions. The muffler in this photo shows the first beginnings in this promising direction.

In 1951 Wolf built this twin-cylinder 250cc engine with piston-controlled intake and rotary magneto ignition.

DKW 250cc twin-cylinder racing engine with rotary slide valve intake and Bosch magneto ignition.

H.P. Müller at the starting line of the 1951 Rund um Schotten (Circuit around Schotten) on the DKW 250.

Like Ewald Kluge, Siegfried Wünsche also rode the twin-cylinder 250.

There was a sensation in 1952: DKW arrived in Hockenheim with an entry in the 350 class – the first time it had again entered a machine with this displacement.

Once, while sitting thinking in front of his twin-cylinder with the magneto ignition in the center of the crankcase, Erich Wolf had had an idea: there was room for a third cylinder positioned horizontally between the two outer, forward-sloping cylinders. And so the sensational 350cc three-cylinder DKW with three 116cc cylinders was born. A Bosch six-cylinder magneto ignition, driven via bevel gears with a 1:2 reduction ratio, was side-mounted.

The 250 ridden by Karl Lottes with rotary slide valve mounted in the center of the engine perpendicular to the crankshaft, where the axial flow resulted in improved effectiveness, and forward-mounted magneto ignition (precursor to the 350 triple).

Ewald Kluge rode the new triple, the "singing saw" (this machine was in fact the first to be given this name, which was later used so often).

Left: The exhaust system shows that gas dynamics had also been used here to get racing performance out of the "stinking simple" two-stroke. *Right*: But Wolf reached the limits of his potential – and tried to compensate for the lack of performance through extreme weight reduction. There were material failures – and when Dr. Eberan took over technical leadership in Ingolstadt there was a big quarrel: Wolf had to go and his place was taken by Helmut Görg. He was a DKW man from Zschopau, who had become involved with DKW engines before the war – but with stationary engines, not racing ones. But, with powerful financial support that Wolf never had, he succeeded in continuing the work and – with much effort – got the triple working and in particular made it reliable (with a not inconsiderable increase in weight). This is how the engine looked in 1954 after the switch to battery ignition.

The three-cylinder racing machine, which under Görg's direction underwent significant changes: with powerful brakes and short swing arm in front.

In 1956 the DKW triple was at the peak of its development – before DKW withdrew from racing and mothballed the precious racing machines.

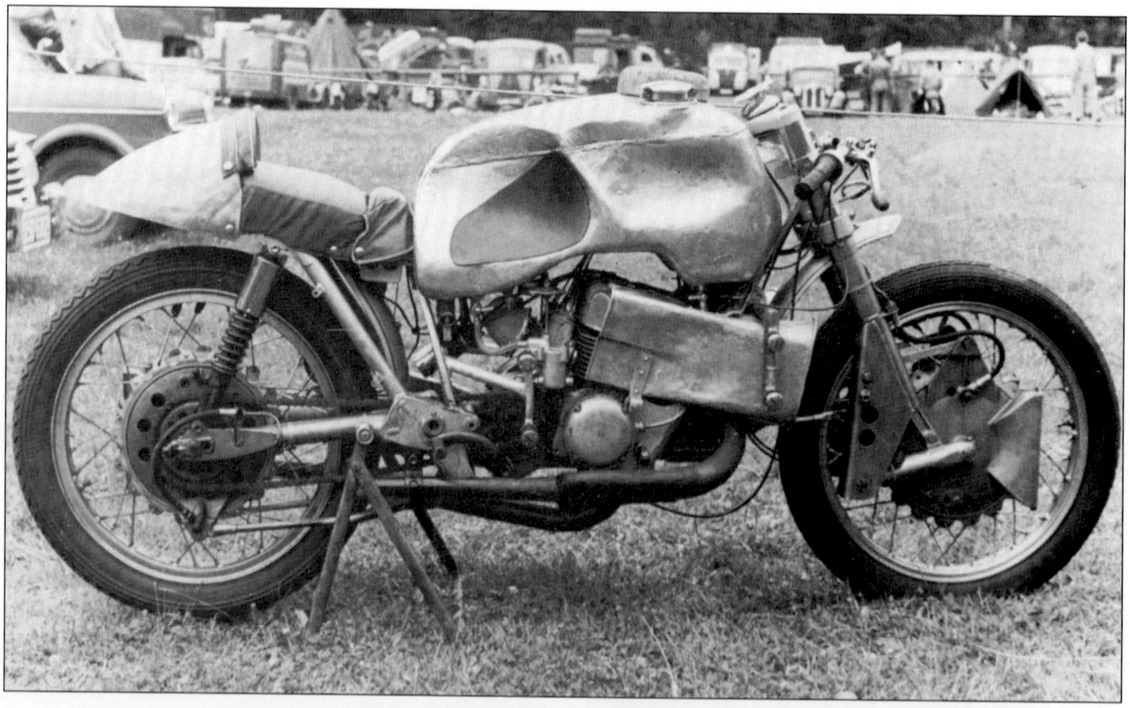

Ewald Kluge on one of the first 350 triples made by Erich Wolf.

The mechanically operated internal expanding brakes ultimately had to give way to hydraulic ATE brakes.

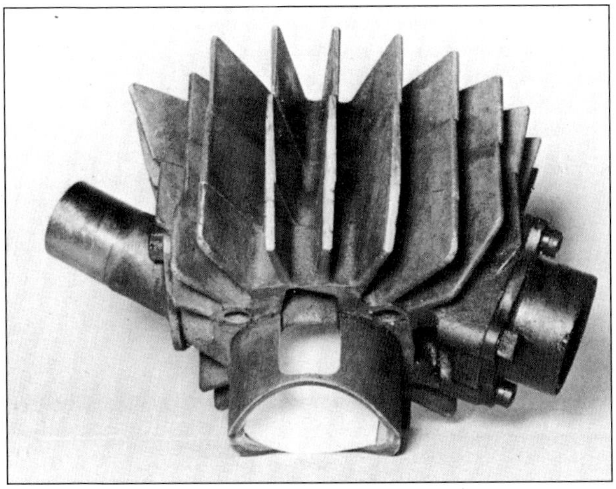

Individual parts of the DKW 350 triple. Above two views of the middle cylinder with lengthwise cooling fins (from which the single-cylinder 125cc racing engine was later derived). Opposite the combustion chamber in the cylinder head with single-sided "fold." Below left the four-bearing crankshaft with full small-diameter hub plates and crank pins staggered according to cylinder position (so that 120 degree igniter gaps resulted). Below right the triple interrupter of the battery ignition with interrupter camshaft positioned independent of the crankshaft (to shield the interrupters from engine vibration, which affected ignition precision).

During experiments to determine the output of the three cylinders, the astonishing finding was made that the middle cylinder's performance was the best. They quickly built a single-cylinder engine with a displacement of 116 cubic centimeters, whose horizontal cylinder sat where the three-cylinder's engine case had been, with the two outer connecting rods removed from the crankshaft. An example of this makeshift construction came into the hands of the Englishman Joe Ehrlich, who told the British press that the secret of the "high performance" of this new wonder engine (designed and built by him!) was the two engine case chambers on the sides. His English professional colleagues then went on to print his statement.

Because the thing worked so well, a "proper" 125 was made in Ingolstadt, with slightly increased bore and a small, light single-cylinder case. They now had an unbeatable 125 racing engine for the factory riders which delivered 17hp at 9,500rpm and had a top speed of 175kph. At the time no one could suspect that 20 years later it would be possible to obtain twice the power from a 125cc racing engine, not through technical complexity but rather the sophisticated utilization of gas dynamics.

The DKW racing machine with 125cc single-cylinder engine for the 1956 season.

Racing director Helmut Görg during test rides by August Hobl on the last 350cc triple as it appeared in 1956.

Five snapshots from the DKW racing department in Ingolstadt in the period 1954-56.

During the postwar years, when the production of motorcycle was again running at full blast (with a top figure of 8,000 motorcycles in a month!), DKW also participated successfully in off-road races and Motocross, which was growing in popularity. Here a DKW 250cc engine outfitted for off-road use.

The factory off-road team's motorcycles, ready for collection.

Here is Otto Sensburg, a successful DKW factory rider before and after the war. He looks a little nervous, because his son Manfred's DKW refuses to start at the check point of the six-day race in Garmisch (behind him: Zündapp's sports supervisor and manager of the German national team, "Schorsch" Weiss.

Under Nikolaus Dörner's direction, in the Ingolstadt motorcycle design bureau special machines based on production motorcycles were created for use in off-road and Motocross events: here is a 125cc off-road machine for the Danish importer.

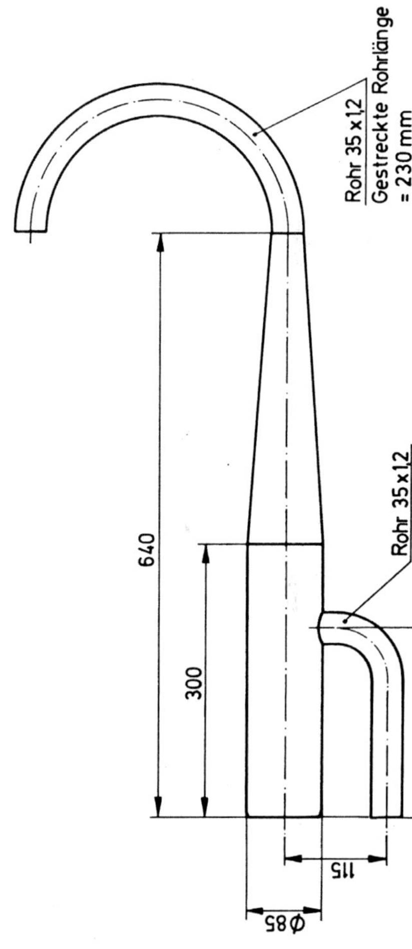

Auto Union provided tuning instructions to purchasers of the MC and GS models who wanted to take part in races with a chance of success – this resonance exhaust system, for example.

125cc rigid-frame off-road machine (1950-51).

125cc off-road machine with vertical rear wheel shock absorber (1954) and three-speed gearbox: output 7.2hp, maximum speed 95kph, tires 2.75x19 front, 3.0x19 rear, 150x25 drum brakes, weight 101kg.

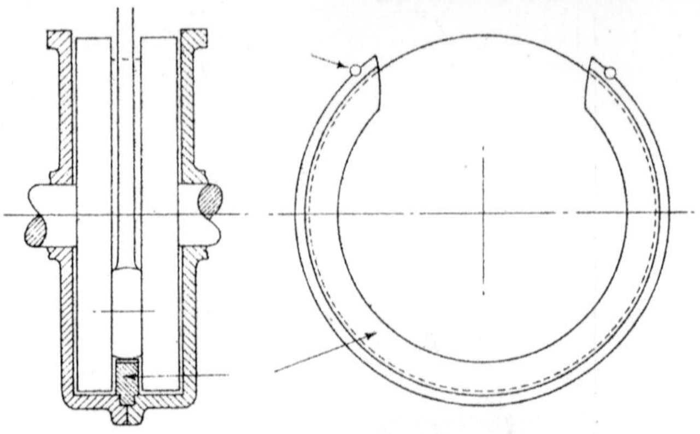

This horseshoe-shaped ring between the cam plates (well remembered by older "do-it-yourselfers") was one of the tuning recommendations made by the factory to reduce the crankcase dead space.

175cc off-road sport machine with vertical shock (1954-55) and swing arm (1956-57) rear wheel suspension and four-speed gearbox. Engine output 10.8hp, maximum speed 105kph, tires 3.25x19 front and rear, 180x25 drum brake in front, 160x25 in the back, weight 143kg.

250cc off-road sport machine (1954-55) with vertical shock rear wheel suspension and four-speed gearbox. Engine output 17hp, tires 3.25x19 front, 3.5x19 rear, weight 143kg.

250cc off-road sport machine (1956-57) with swing arm rear wheel suspension and four-speed gearbox. Engine output 18hp, tires 3.25x19 front, 3.5x19 rear, 180x25 drum brakes front and rear, weight 150kg.

This 350cc twin-cylinder off-road machine was produced in 1956.

Above: The MC 12 125cc Motocross machine with rear wheel swing arm and three-speed gearbox. Compression 9.5, sustained output 8.5hp, maximum speed 75kph, tires 2.75x19 front, 3.25x18 rear, 150x25 drum brakes, weight 92kg.

Below: MC 17 175cc Motocross machine with rear wheel swing arm and four-speed gearbox. Compression 9.5, sustained output 12.6hp, maximum speed 80kph, tires 3.0x21 front, 3.5x18 rear, 150x25 drum brakes in front, 150x25 in back, weight 114kg.

Further developed 175cc Motocross machine.

The Motocross version of the 250cc twin-cylinder machine was probably too tame for DKW rider Finkenzeller of Ingolstadt – he therefore souped up the engine himself.

A 350cc twin-cylinder Motocross machine was also developed from the production machine as a special version.

DKW Cars in Sports

In 1932 the four automakers Audi, DKW, Horch and Wanderer were combined to form Auto Union under the emblem of the four circles. All four had previously been active and successful in motorsports during their independence.

Early on Dr. August Horch had recognized the importance of sports, both as a tough material test and a form of experimentation for engines and vehicles. Before the First World War he personally took part in endurance races with his high-performance touring car made in Zwickau, Saxony. When, in 1906, Dr. Rudolf Stöss won victory in the second Herkomer Competition (named after the famous painter from Munich, the competition's sponsor) in an 18/20 Horch, it did much to boost the manufacturer's fame.

Dr. Horch also remained true to his sporting ambitions from 1909 in his Audi car. Driving the Audi 14/35 PS developed in 1911, he won the Austrian Alpine Competition three years in a row, and in 1914 the Audi team of Horch-Graumüller-Lange won the Wanderpokal once and for all. Then in 1931 Alexander Graumüller won his class for Audi in the AvD's 10,000 kilometer race through all of Europe in a 100 PS Zwickau. The Audi program later featured a front wheel drive car equipped with the six-cylinder two-liter Porsche engine (from Wanderer). In the 2000km Race through Germany in 1933 the Audi team of Momberger-Trübsbach-Loge reached the finish line first with a lead of two hours. They achieved an overall average speed of 80kph – quite an accomplishment considering the gravel roads of the day.

Later, in the Thirties, the Horch V 8 driven by the team of Count Sandizell, Trübsbach and Hinterleitner won the three-day race through the Harz Mountains and the East Prussia Race. At the 2000-kilometer race in 1934 the same team won as individual drivers and as a team.

Wanderer established a sporting tradition in the motorcycle sector early on, for the Chemnitz company was one of the best known German motorcycle manufacturers before the First World War (the successes achieved by Wanderer riders, like Albert Schuster of Chemnitz and Ernst of Breslau, in endurance and racing sport were continued until the company ceased making motorcycles in 1929). And when Wanderer also began making automobiles in 1905 (beginning with the legendary Puppchen), a growing number of Wanderer cars began competing in sporting contests. Karl-Friedrich Trübsbach, later head of Auto Union sports department in Düsseldorf, won the Saxony Championship in 1928, 29 and 30 with the 1.5- and 1.8-liter Wanderer. Later, as part of a team with Bernhard Bau of Chemnitz (who had flown with Baron von Oertzen in the First World War) and Dipl.-Ing. Hans Krügner, head of the Wanderer factory repair organization, he entered the Eight Mountain Race in the Upper Erz Mountains (where, almost unbelievably, they recorded an average speed of almost 100kph from the Polish border to central Germany – with no highways!)

Wanderer's great triumphs also included the AvD's 10,000-kilometer race through all of Europe. The former director of Wanderer (and later Auto Union) Claus Detlev von Oertzen (who brought his initiative to build racing cars with him to Auto Union) sent the team of Bau, Lippmann, Rudolf and Hasse (later driver of the Auto Union racing car) on the difficult endurance race in the 6/30 Wanderer. They became the only team to reach their destination, Berlin, with no penalty points. Then that same year Wanderer won the International Alpine Cup with the team of Graumüller, Bau and Hinterleitner, a feat it repeated the following year with the same team. In 1934 the Wanderer team of Count Sandizell, Trübsbach and Krämer won the Alpine Cup for a third time in the

Familiar names from the Wanderer and DKW sports era of the prewar period. From right: Trübsbach, Ove Rasmussen, Bau. Prüssing, Hans Rasmussen, Beckert, Fritsching, Kirchberg, Müller, Trägner.

Below: Our sports car from the Auto Union factory sports department in Chemnitz in action at the Loibl Pass.

8/40 six-cylinder. Incidentally the team of Bau, Prince zu Leinigen and Trübsbach won the first team prize in the Reichsfahrt in 1933 driving the same car, and Wanderer also had success in the 1933 and 1934 2000-kilometer races: Bernhard Bau with Ferry Porsche (present-day head of the House of Porsche) and Willy Krämer won the marque team prize with the Wanderer six-cylinder engine, a Porsche design.

In 1934 a fast man moved from the saddle of the DKW 250 and BMW 500cc racing motorcycles to cars: Heinz Meier of Chemnitz, later head of the Auto Union repair organization in Düsseldorf and subsequently in the same position with BMW in Munich. He immediately achieved success in his Wanderer car at many events. As part of the factory team of Lindner, Meier and Trübsbach, he competed successfully in the three-day Mittelgebirgsfahrt in the Harz, the cross-country race in Brandenburg, the winter competitions in Oberstaufen, Pottach-Egern and Altenberg-Geising as well as the East Prussian Race (to name just a few of the big races) until 1939. Admittedly his most successful period would not come until after the Second World War, when, driving the twin-cylinder and then the three-cylinder DKW as a factory driver for Auto Union, he won everything international long-distance and rally sport had to offer.

DKW's participation in motorsport began much earlier, however – the first 1.5hp engines were in Zschopau and riders from Zschopau won their first laurels on the

Avus circuit in Berlin (see page 64). It is impossible to compile a complete list of victories won by factory and private drivers in DKW production and special racing machines after 1921 – they were unparalleled, especially after DKW double-piston machines in the 175, 250, 350 and 500 cubic centimeter solo classes, as well in both sidecar classes, dominated national and international competition in national and international races before the Second World War. And even after the FIM banned boosting systems (charging pumps and superchargers) for motor sport (and many assumed that the end had come for two-strokes in racing), in Ingolstadt the company succeeded in developing new racing engines for the 125, 250 and 350 cubic centimeter classes – simple three-port two-strokes that were much closer to production standard than the earlier boosted engines from Zschopau – achieved new successes on the track. Modified DKW production machines were later always among the best in off-road events and the upcoming sport of Motocross until the production of motorcycles in Ingolstadt was abandoned.

Names like Toni Babl, Günter Bartels, Toni Bauhofer, Karl Bodmer, Karl Braun, Otto Dalker, Rudi Felgenheier, Heiner Fleischmann, Kurt Friedrich, Hermann Gablenz, Arthur Geiss, Xaver Gmelch, Walter Hamelehle, Willy Henkelmann, Wilhelm Herz, August Hobl, Karl Hofmann, Hans Kahrmann, Herbert Kirchberg, Josef Klein, Ewald Kluge, Rudi Knees, Otto Kohfink, H.P. Müller, Fritz Niemeck, Bernhard Petruschke, Bernd Rosemeyer, Hans Schumann, Hans Sprung, Karl Stegmann, Oskar Steinbach, Leo Steinweg, Hans Winkler, Walfried Winkler, Siegfried Wünsche and Ernst Zündorf belong to the history of DKW motorcycle racing, and yet they represent only a small segment of the many riders who were successful on DKW motorcycles for a long or short time.

***Above*: Chemnitz factory sports car (built with Wanderer and DKW engines) in action during a winter race. *Left*: Heinz Meier with Engineer Momberger, class victors in the prewar Liege-Rome-Liege long-distance race.**

DKW cars (with front and – center foreground – rear wheel drive) at the staring line of a small car race at the old Avus Circuit in Berlin (still without the banked north turn).

But it was not just in motorcycle racing that DKW, the company dedicated to two-stroke engines, won fame. In 1929 the drivers Gustav Menz and Gerhard Macher, who later enjoyed great success, entered the Monte Carlo rally in 1929 and reached the finish line in one piece in their small DKW 600cc twin-cylinder car with rear wheel drive and load-bearing wooden body. This was all the more amazing because the staring place in Königsberg could only be reached over the ice of the lagoon because of deep snowdrifts.

The first DKW front wheel drive car, on the other hand, was driven by Rasmussen's son Ove in the Eibsee Race in 1931 (see page 22). The performance of the car, which was still equipped with a provisional engine, against strong competition was impressive. It was running away with the race until it swerved into a snow bank. With no reverse gear Rasmussen was unable to get the car out, and the sensational demonstration came to an end.

Thousands of successful entries followed. From then on DKW cars were among the most popular racing vehicles, especially after a largely independent sports department was installed in the Chemnitz Rößlerstrasse factory, where competition vehicles – based on production automobiles, but built with special bodies suitable for off-road use and DKW and Wanderer engines – were built for factory and private drivers and official use. Wanderer provided the four-cylinder engine from the W24 and the six-cylinder from the W26. Also used were the 700cc twin-cylinder and the 100 four-cylinder V engine (from the Schwebe- and Sonderklasse) from DKW.

Whether in the East Prussian Race, the Three-Day Harz Race, the Brandenburg Off-Road Race, the Liege-Rome-Liege race, mountain races in all of Europe, the International Alpine Race – especially the 2000km races in 1933 and 1934 – DKW cars (production vehicles and ones from the sports department in Chemnitz) were always in front and were class winners, taking special and team prizes. In the 1933 2000-km race, Zentzytzki finished in first place, five hours ahead of his closest competitor, and at the 1934 2000-km race DKW drivers won no less than 60% of the gold medals.

Left: **A few months after the start of the series, in 1931 Arne Rasmussen started the Berlin-Paris-Barcelona-Madrid-Lisbon-Riviera-Rome-Munich (first non-stop stage) and then via Salzberg-Katschberg (at that time still a 28° uphill gradient)-Sarajevo-Belgrade-Budapest-Vienna-Prague-Berlin 10,000km race and recorded no penalty points.** ***Right***: **in 1934 the DKW factory team, of which the three Rasmussen sons Hans, Ove and Arne were a part, won the team prize in the 2000km race. They reached the finish line in Baden-Baden two hours before the allocated time.**

The front wheel drive DKW cars proved themselves in the notorious winter races. Gustav Menz, Fritz Trägner and Walter Fritsching formed the feared "Golden DKW Team," which repeatedly won the Through Bavaria's Mountains, The Frankish Jura and the Three Heath races. Hans and Ove Rasmussen, W. Henning, Herbert Kirchberg, Dr. Nieders, Karl Trübsbach, Franz Kosel, E. Keidel, H. Meffert, Eduard Voigt – these are just a small selection of the successful competition drivers in DKWs from those years.

Preparations for the planned big long-distance race from Berlin to Rome in 1939 were in high gear, two-seat streamlined sedans with streamlined light metal bodies had been prepared by all four marques (twin-cylinder four-piston engines with double-action charging pump, variants of the big motorcycle-sidecar engines, powered the DKW front wheel drive cars) – then the war broke out and all sporting ambitions came to an abrupt end.

But soon after the end of the war, initially based on private initiative, motorcycle sport began again in both parts of Germany, and before long the first factory riders from Zschopau and Ingolstadt were entering racing machines produced in the factories – in West Germany DKW was again represented in automobile racing in

One of the light metal coupes prepared for the 1939 Berlin to Rome long-distance race. This is the DKW version with front wheel drive and the four-piston two-stroke engine with charging pump.

1951 – although again more or less on private initiative. Heinz Meier won the first gold medal at the Garmisch-Partenkirchen winter race in 1951 driving the DKW F 89 made in Düsseldorf (the "new" Meisterklasse with 700cc twin-cylinder engine and front wheel drive).

This feat was repeated in 1952 and 1953, continuing the success achieved by Gustav Menz in the new DKW Sonderklasse (three-cylinder engine, also with front wheel drive). Together the two drivers went on to win the International Rally in Travemünde and the Düsseldorf Rally. Together with Karl Trübsbach, Heinz Meier won overall victory in the Weser-Ems eight-day race in 1953 (in the twin-cylinder model, by then with a four-speed transmission), finishing with an average speed of 103 kph over 800km. This successful year was capped by Meier's first use of the F 91 three-cylinder car and victory in his class in the 5th Tour de Belgique, a feat he repeated against international competition twice in the following years.

In 1954 the factory sports department was installed in Düsseldorf. Karl-Friedrich Trübsbach took charge and immediately set an ambitious goal: the European Touring Car Championship. The DKW three-cylinder F 91 and the team of Gustav Menz, Heinz Meier and Walter Schlüter seemed sure to succeed. Heinz Meier opened the season by winning the Monte Carlo Rally, the Great Britain Rally, Wiesbaden, Mitternachtssonne, the Tulip Rally and the Geneva Rally, and in the Tour de France the DKW was the best European touring car in any class.

Schlüter, Menz and Meier – Auto Union's successful DKW team.

In Schlüter and Menz's series of successes in 1954, Auto Union took the first three places in the European Touring Car Championship "all against all." Heinz Meier also won the 1000cc class at the Mille Miglia and a number of national races as well as the Tour de Belgique. In addition to these victories, the team of Mantzel and Hopfen won the Rallye Soleil in the general rankings, and at the Rallye Solitude Eberhard Mahle won class victory in the three-cylinder DKW, while the team of Mantzel, Schulz and Vogt finished as the best marque team.

As well, the Dutch driver Gatsonides was the overall winner at the Rallye Limousin, and the DKW F 91 three-cylinder was the class-winning car at the Rallye Maroc and second in the general rankings at Hue-Monod.

The factory team continued its success in 1955. Sven von Schroeter became German Touring Car Champion. Heinz Meier, now driving with Hermann Luba, was knocked out of the Liege-Rome-Liege long-distance race by a serious crash in the Gavia Pass. Meier's bad luck continued and in the penultimate hour he was forced to withdraw from the 24-hour race in Le Mans because of fuel pump failure. Nevertheless, he achieved third place in the European Championship that year, behind cars with much more powerful engines.

The three victorious DKW cars – with no breakdowns, no dents – at the finish of the Monte Carlo Rally in 1953.

The DKW three-cylinder engine proved particularly well-suited to performance enhancement, and many two-stroke experts in and outside the factory busied themselves with tuning this engine, whose design was so simple. There were various performance stages, up to more than 100hp. The photos on this page show details of the engine that famous tuner and racing driver Gerhard Mitter of Leonberg prepared for a Lotus racing car chassis. He installed a six-speed gearbox in the flange-mounted VW transmission case.

With their success, the DKW factory team had not only brought life to the international sporting scene but also encouraged private drivers. Factory sport was therefore more and more restricted in favor of private race drivers. In Düsseldorf they concentrated on the big events – Monte Carlo, Le Mans, the Acropolis Rally, the Deutschland/Wiesbaden Rally and the Midnight Sun Rally, which were won by Meier, Schlüter and Menz in their class and sometimes also in the general rankings. The top six or more finishers were often now DKW drivers, with 20 to 30 DKW cars at the starting line. Among the most successful drivers of the day were the Swiss master Stefan Brugger, Robert Meyer and Fausto Meyrat, Alfred Hartmann, Gustav Schmutz, Willy Weber, the Belgian master Emile Holvoet, Julian of Paris, Francis Petit of Belgium, A.W. Mantzel, Eberhard Mahle, Hermann Vogt, Wolfgang Levy, the Luxembourg master René Bintner, the Norwegian master Leif Vold-Johansen, the Swede Greta Molander, Madame Wagner and Madame Blanchent, Siegfried Eikelmann, Otto Brindl, Grosgogeat (Nice), Hans Schallhas, Helmut Sinn, the Dutchmen Jan Flinterman and Henk van Zalinke, Vlanden of Munich and Walter Schatz from Innsbruck. Herbert Brand was especially successful in special touring cars produced in the Ingolstadt factory under his supervision.

The idea of using DKW cars for record attempts was a private initiative. Heinz Meier and Günter Ahrens made the preparations, and in December 1956 they were ready: the team of Meier, Ahrens, Theiler and Barbay took a DKW 3 = 6 (900cc) with a plastic body onto the track at Monza and set new world records in the G Class – 4,000 miles, 48 hours, 5,000 miles, 10,000km and 72 hours, easily surpassing the previous best performances. In the 48-hour category, for example, they recorded an average speed of 140.961kph, more than 16kph better than the previous record.

The team that set a series of world records at the Monza Autodrome in 1956 with the DKW 3 = 6 with plastic body. From left: Meier, Ahrens, Barbay, Theiler.

The promotion of private racing was crowned in 1958 when Auto Union announced a DKW Trophy, and the number of active DKW sports drivers grew rapidly. Meanwhile DKW continued to pile up successes in Europe and overseas. In the decade until 1964 alone, DKW drivers won more than 100 championships, 150 overall victories, 25 first championship victories and about 2,500 class victories.

From 1960 until the cessation of sporting activities with DKW cars, each year the most successful were featured in an honor roll, whose changing names provided proof of the DKW three-cylinder two-stroke car among those private drivers interested in motorsports.

Successful Years – Then the End of the DKW Marque

After it became apparent that Hermann Weber, chief designer in Zschopau, would be unable to assume his previous position, while the DKW motorcycle program was to undergo significant expansion, the Auto Union GmbH board of directors placed Nikolaus Dörner (previously active in the central research department in Chemnitz) in charge of the motorcycle design department. He was also no DKW man – but now he was part of a "triumvirate" with Ing. Herbert Kirchberg (head of motorcycle research) and Ing. Franz Ischinger (head of motorcycle production), both crafty DKW and motorcycle experts. The DKW motorcycle division was once again in the best of hands – the rising production and sales figures (up to 8,000 per month) showed that the DKW motorcycle models, like their prewar predecessors, were in line with market conditions.

Development of racing machines began once again, parallel to the development and production of series machines, though initially on a much more modest scale than in prewar Zschopau. Erich Wolf, whose successful tuning work on privately owned DKW engines (including those of Carl Döring) had demonstrated his skill, was brought from Wiesbaden to Ingolstadt for this purpose. Until the FIM ban on superchargers in 1951, new racing machines for the 125 class, with double piston engines and auxiliary charging pumps, were created under his leadership. Then, beginning in 1951, he oversaw the development of single- and twin-cylinder racing machines without boosting systems – something originally thought impossible. Some of these machines turned in amazing performances.

Then, in 1953, Wolf produced a great success with the 350cc three-cylinder racing machine. Wolf was forced to hand its further development over to Helmut Görg on orders from the new technical director, von Eberan. Görg was able to finish Wolf's work and made the three-cylinder machine equal and often superior to the four-stroke competition. Finally, before the company abandoned the racing department in 1956, it produced a very fast 125cc supercharger racing machine from the three-cylinder concept.

Over the years, however, Ingolstadt also produced new and successful machines for other purposes besides road racing. By modifying standard 125-, 175-, 250- and 350cc machines, Dörner's design bureau produced motorcycles for use in off-road and Motocross competitions until 1958. They represented the DKW marque at national and international events just as well as the prewar machines had.

The year 1951 saw the arrival of new motorcycle types. Over the years the RT 125 W (originally almost identical to the prewar version) was developed in several stages and its performance improved – more than 30,000 of these bikes were made in 1951 alone. That year the RT 175 and RT 200 were added to the program, and more than 12,000 units were completed in 1951. Toward the end of the year they were joined by a new design, the RT 250 – like the other two, it was equipped with a single-cylinder two-stroke engine and retained typical DKW features.

And while more than 7,000 examples of the high-speed truck were delivered in 1951, the new Düsseldorf factory, which had come on line the year before, produced just under 15,000 cars.

On 25 June 1951, Dr. Bruhn's 65th birthday, the just-completed large factory hall in Düsseldorf was opened (it was named after him). Auto Union seemed to have reached a zenith in its postwar development and the portents for further upward development appeared good.

But the gleaming façade was somewhat deceiving. The German economy, whose rebirth few had thought possible, still gave no cause for concern – the "German economic miracle" was still in its full splendor. But Dr. Bruhn was not the only one burdened with the worrisome knowledge that Auto Union's internal structure was not what it should have been to deal with the competition in the motor vehicle industry, which was undoubtedly becoming stiffer. The old two-stroke/four-stroke dualism was making itself more and more obvious. The technical apparatus, especially as it affected automobile production, was overwhelmingly occupied by former employees of the Horch organization – and it would have been surprising if their prewar mentality failed to surface sooner of later.

In contrast to this divergence within the circle of technicians was Dr. Hahn as leader of the sales organization. Not only had he been convinced of the future promise of two-stroke technology and front wheel drive from an early age – he also had the unique ability to transmit his convictions and enthusiasm to others. There is no doubt that much of the upwards impetus of the postwar years came from the circle of people around Dr. Hahn, who felt bound to the DKW marque.

But nevertheless the leaders of the company probably felt that what they had achieved so rapidly only needed consolidation and a precise technical plan for the future. And so in 1951 a central design bureau was created and placed under a new addition – but that proved to be a mistake, and in 1955 the company parted ways with this employee without having set concrete goals for the future.

Dr. Hahn fell seriously ill in 1953 and he was damned to inactivity for some time. That same year Prof. Dr. Eberan was appointed to the company management to add technical weight at the management level. Before the war Dr. Eberan had occupied a leading position in Auto Union's racing department and then held a position as a professor at the Dresden Technical College until the end of the war. After the war he gained additional experience working in the British automobile industry. But before the measures he introduced (including development of a plastic body) could bear fruit, the economic situation in Germany changed.

First the sales of motorcycles began to fall. Only about 3,500 examples of the RT 125 were sold in its last year of production. The RT 175/200 reached its highest production level in 1954, with approximately 30,000 being built, but the weakening motorcycle market caused this to drop to 21,000 in 1956. It was no different with the RT 250: it reached its maximum production rate in 1953, with 27,700 completed, but by 1956 this had sunk to about 9,000 motorcycles. Approximately 4,000 examples of the RT 350, a sporty twin-cylinder machine and the last added to the program, whose production startup in 1953-54 had been accompanied by a number of technical difficulties, were delivered in 1955, but the following year production totaled just slightly more than 1,000.

The heyday of the motorcycle appeared to have passed – at an economic press conference in Schweinfurt, Ernst Wilhelm Sachs said bluntly: "The motorcycle is dead." These vehicles, which had been the primary agents of motorization after the war and which had accompanied the economic and personal rise of so many, were hit hard by the repercussions of the economic miracle. It was no longer considered sporty and an expression of Spartan toughness to expose oneself to the wind and weather with almost no protection – in particular it was women, rather than men, who preferred the company of someone who could at least offer his passenger a roof over their head, even if in a primitive four-wheel vehicle rather than a "proper" car.

Development of the DKW Hobby, a scooter, came just as late as the attempts by the competition to offer something that provided a little more protection against the weather. Production of the Hobby-Roller, with its fan-cooled 75cc engine and infinitely variable belt system, began in 1954, when about 1,000 were completed. Approximately 26,000 were made in 1955, but in 1956 the production of scooters was transferred to the French Manurhin company, which completed about 14,000.

Small Cars, Scooters and Mopeds

Prof. Dr. Eberan left the company in 1956, soon after Dr. Werner (the former technical board member of the prewar Auto Union) joined the management of Auto Union. Promising tests with the small car, initially with three and later four seats, with plastic body, which was supposed to replace the motorcycle were not continued. Instead, mainly on the initiative of Dr. Hahn (who after recovering from his illness seemed to be the old Dr. Hahn, but who in 1957 retired on the advice of his doctor, and then died in 1961), in 1957 the first DKW moped was offered, much to the consternation of the established competition. The Hummel (bumblebee) was the first moped with a three-speed gearbox. (Hummel was to have been the name of a small pedal machine. Had the war ended differently, it was supposed to have had a "motorized rear wheel" – like the Saxonette by Fichtel & Sachs. A new factory was proposed near the Bernd-Rosemeyer complex in Chemnitz and initial production would have been 1,500 per day – see page 55.) In any case, approximately 20,000 examples of the Hummel were completed in the first year, and by the time the production of two-wheel vehicles ended in 1958, roughly 177,000 Hummel mopeds were delivered by the factory in Ingolstadt. In this case, too, the company was too late, for after several boom years the moped experienced its first descent into the valley. And later, when there was a revival of interest in the moped (or mofa), all that was left of the Hummel – now in Nuremberg – was the name.

Production of the F 89 P automobile had begun in the Düsseldorf factory in 1950. Unlike the prewar models, the "new Meisterklasse" had the traditional DKW front wheel drive engine in front of the forward axle – like the high-speed truck – instead of behind it. A light metal cylinder head with modified combustion chambers, downdraft carburetor, a modern exhaust system with muffler directly behind the exhaust manifold and other detail changes resulted in 23hp instead of the previous 20hp. The 700cc twin-cylinder also had an improved torque curve, better revving in the gears and better fuel consumption. The change from a three- to a four-speed transmission in 1953 was a much more important change, as was the switch from the motorcycle-like multi-plate oil bath clutch (lubrication of the primary drive, which included the wet clutch, was very tricky) to a single-plate dry clutch. The postwar version of the DKW-typical Dynastart system, built by the Chemnitz Electrics Works on Rösslerstrasse before the war, underwent considerable redesign. Made in the Spandau factory (where gear production also took place), it no longer had the bell type armature with the flat trajectory collector in its base. Instead it had a smaller drum armature and external field coils for the generator and starter functions.

The earlier plywood body covered in faux leather had been replaced by an all-steel body, which had been designed before the war in the ZKB (central design bureau) Chemnitz for the projected three-cylinder F 9 car and for which the pressing tools were available in West Germany.

In 1953 the F 89, of which about 60,000 had been built, was replaced by the F 91 – which for the fourth time in the history of the DKW automobile bore the name Sonderklasse. This model had been created before the war in the ZKB as successor to the F 8, and was supposed to have entered production in 1940. The 900cc three-cylinder engine (32hp, later 42hp) had the flange-mounted four-speed transmission and differential ahead of the front axle (like the twin-cylinder engine of the F 89). Like Dr. Porsche's Auto Union racing car, the power flow went from the crankshaft with the dry clutch through the differential into the four-speed transmission (with freewheel) and from it back to the differential, from which the two side shafts with homokinetic joints led to the front wheels. This fast and sleek vehicle was built in six different models until 1955. Then it was replaced by the Grossen DKW 3 = 6, a Sonderklasse widened by 10cm with a more powerful engine. It was made until 1959.

In 1953 Auto Union began production of the MUNGA, a four-seat, four-wheel-drive all-terrain vehicle. Against strong competition it won the contract to supply the Bundeswehr. The vehicle, which never appeared under the DKW name, also found civilian buyers.

Dr. Bruhn retired in 1956. His successor was Dr. Henze, who managed the company together with Dr. Werner.

Daimler-Benz Comes on Board

On 1 January 1958 the Daimler-Benz AG took over all the shares of the Auto Union GmbH. Production of transport vehicles was sold in its entirety to the newly-established Nürnberger Zweirad Union. The new company also acquired motorcycle production (which, since its resumption in Ingolstadt, had made a total of 519,000 motorcycles and mopeds) with the right to use the DKW brand name for two-wheel vehicles. Ing. Ischinger and a small cadre of designers joined the new company in Nuremberg.

The elements of racing machine production that had not disappeared or been scrapped in Ingolstadt also went there – still many parts and several complete machines, which were then sold without any illusions in Nuremberg.

After the collapse of the motorcycle market in Germany and elsewhere (from which such tradition-rich Nuremberg marques such as Victoria, Triumph and Zündapp had disappeared), those in Nuremberg were, understandably, ill disposed towards continuing, even partially, the production of motorcycles in Ingolstadt. During the first year, therefore, the designers from Auto Union left Nuremberg and returned to Ingolstadt to take on other duties.

DKW in Nuremberg

Initially, the DKW name lived on in Nuremberg only in several models of moped and small motorcycle (which were also sold under the Victoria name), later also in a 125cc street model and off-road and motocross machines. All were equipped with engines made by Fichtel & Sachs. And even when, on Ischinger's initiative, a series of 50-, 75-, 100- and 125cc single-cylinder engines of his own design in a nice twin tube chassis was displayed at the IFMA 1962 (only the TS 159 with the 50cc engine was left for series production), the concept did not last: the Zweirad Union also proved incapable of surviving. Fichtel & Sachs took over in Nuremberg and its subsidiary, the Nuremberg Hercules Company, moved from Fürther-Strasse into the more spacious and expandable factory complex in Nuremberg's Nopitsch-Strasse. Its first move was to replace the DKW engine in the TS 159 with a Sachs engine.

Under the prevailing conditions in Nuremberg, a continuation of DKW racing motorcycle development was also out of the question. Dr. Ischinger did recall Erich Wolf and tasked him with designing a 50cc racing engine for use in Grand-Prix. With modest means, Wolf (who for years had been out of two-stroke engine development, which had made enormous strides) tried to do so with an engine whose inlet valve was controlled by a rotary slide valve. It was a hopeless undertaking that was soon abandoned in favor of several prototypes of slot-controlled racing engines, especially as Ischinger had retired to his home on the outskirts of Ingolstadt. Erich Wolf, on the other hand, was busy with a no less hopeless task: a two-stroke differential-piston diesel engine, which was to replace the Goggomobil or BMW engine used in the Kraka (the Zweirad Union's Kraftkarren, or factory truck). Erich Wolf died in 1970.

Nuremberg was the last stop for DKW motorcycles, however. There was no one – not in Ingolstadt, not in Nuremberg and of course not in Untertürkheim – who would have given a red cent for the future of the motorcycle at that time. The chance of preserving a small cell for the day (as a handful of "hardheads" believed) when the motorcycle would make a comeback was wasted in Ingolstadt and Nuremberg just as in Neckarsulm. The field was left open, without a struggle, to the Japanese, who were much more farsighted.

And so DKW, once one of the most famous makers of motorcycles in the world, disappeared without fanfare after forty glorious years.

Dr. Ischinger tried once again to revive the true DKW tradition with the Zweirad-Union in Nuremberg. Of the planned modular series with 50-, 75-, 100- and 125cc engines (displayed at the IMFA), only the 50cc variant survived (under the model designation 159).

This vehicle, inspired by the new DKW concept prototype developed in Ingolstadt (see page 200), was built in Nuremberg. It was sold under both the DKW and Victoria brand names, however it failed to make much of an impression on buyers. Detractors called it "The Metal Banana" and one motorcycle magazine wrote that it came with "the engine in a basket and the headlight in a bag." Technologically, however, it was an interesting design.

When Hercules (Sachs) took over the Victoria and Zweirad-Union factories on Nuremberg's Nopitsch Strasse, the DKW engine was immediately replaced by a Sachs engine, which sat in a modified Hercules backbone steel tube frame (with bolted-on under beams).

Later the 159 TS reappeared as the RT 159, again with a 50cc Sachs engine.

For a time Hercules sold its (later used in off-road sports as "Sachs") GS and MC models in Italy under the name DKW.

And this "RT 125" from Nuremberg of course also had a Sachs engine – the tank emblem and the RT designation were the only reminders of a once-famous German motorcycle marque.

• • •

As Daimler-Benz had other use for the Düsseldorf factory, construction of a new factory "in the open countryside" in Ingolstadt was begun in 1958 – a highly modern automobile factory. And while production of the Auto Union 1000 models (of which more than 58,000 were made between 1957 and 1962-63) was continued and finally brought to an end, in the "new factory" in Ingolstadt (built in just a year and a half) production of the DKW-Junior began in August 1959. More than 60,000 cars were completed in 1960 alone.

In 1961, the Junior program was expanded through the addition of the Junior de Luxe (with an 800cc three-cylinder engine in place of the previous 750). In 1963 the F 11 replaced the Junior, and the F 12, with a 900cc three-cylinder engine, left the production line in Ingolstadt until 1965. The new three-cylinder engines all had a shorter stroke than the models in the "pre-Junior" period, during which a total of about 350,000 DKW front wheel drive cars were built.

VW Takes Over

In 1962, Dr. Werner left the company management and his place was taken by Hans A. Stoehr. Jörgen Skafte Rasmussen and Dr. Bruhn (on 8 July) both died in 1964. Auto Union's share capital was raised to 160 million. The additional shares were purchased by Volkswagenwerk AG, which later also acquired Daimler-Benz's shares, and ownership of the Auto Union GmbH (less the Düsseldorf factory) passed to VW (Audi NSU Auto Union AG).

A newly developed DKW front wheel drive car with a three-cylinder two-stroke engine entered production in 1964. It was the F 102, with a displacement of 1175cc and a power output of 60hp. For the first time in the history of DKW front wheel drive cars, it did not have a chassis frame, having a load bearing all steel body instead.

Production of the AU 1000 models finally came to an end in 1965 (after about 194,000 units had been delivered), likewise the F 11 and F 12 models.

That same year Dr. Henze and Hans A. Stoehr left the management of the company. Their places were taken by Rudolf Leiding, later head of Volkswagen, and Ludwig Kraus, who had been deputy managing director (for development) since January 1964. Under his watch was developed the four-cylinder four-stroke engine that replaced the two-stroke engine of the DKW F 102 in the new Audi (72hp) that began leaving the Ingolstadt production line in September 1965.

Production of the F 102 ended in early 1966. This marked the end of the DKW marque's automobile production, after the postwar Auto Union alone had built almost 1,000,000 DKW front wheel drive cars.

DKW – The Pioneer of Two-Stroke Engines, and Front Wheel Drive

Two technical concepts that were unusual for their time and the vehicles in which they were used clearly determined the course of DKW history.

One was the two-stroke engine. When Jörgen Skafte Rasmussen built his first two-stroke based on the ideas of Hugo Ruppe in 1919, its working principle was already well known. And there had already been many vehicles, especially motorcycles, which, equipped with two-stroke engines, were produced industrially and used all over the world. But in the roughly fifty years that DKW two-stroke in engines were used in motorcycles, power units and automobiles, there was no other two-stroke brand that came anywhere close to the numbers made by DKW. And anyone who did come close to these figures – at any time – was only able to do so because Rasmussen's DKW engines had removed the odium of being technically primitive, noisy, fuel guzzling and short-lived that had afflicted this working principle.

This was possible in large part after DKW was able to come up with the technically simple but logical and effective loop scavenging system for its two-stroke engines. The determined efforts by most of DKW's competitors to also use this advantageous scavenging system in their motorcycles were proof of the level of improvement that Schnürle loop scavenging brought to the simple three-port two-stroke. Its universal acceptance (and development) in international motorcycle engine making after the expiry of the patent proves that there was nothing better than what DKW held with this scavenging system as its trump card after 1932.

Today there is little argument that a two-stroke gasoline engine built in this way is superior to the four-stroke engine, which is less economical in terms of mechanical complexity, size and weight, and working principle, for everyday use in a multitude of roles. Hardly anyone who considers the technological effort with which the DKW two-stroke racing engines were built (and were superior to the four-strokes), and the complexity with which they had to be made in order to make up for the handicap of the shorter stroke in the two-stroke operating cycle, believed that a two-stroke engine in its simplest form as a single-piston engine of single-or multi-cylinder design could not only be equal to but superior to the four-stroke as a high-performance (racing) engine. And when, under pressure of the FIM's ban on the use of superchargers in motorcycle racing, all boosting systems were also banned in Germany, it appeared that the two-stroke's superiority to the four-stroke in this sector was over.

But it didn't happen. Exploitation of the gas dynamics in the engine (including carburetor and exhaust system) enabled the creation of two-stroke engines which, while retaining the mechanical simplicity of prewar two-stroke engines, left the displacement performances of the prewar two-stroke engines far behind. And DKW engines (like Erich Wolf's legendary three-cylinder engine) were once again the first, based on the new concepts, to retake the lead over the four-strokes.

It is impossible to diagnose here why Auto Union – and almost the entire European motorcycle industry – missed the transition to a new motorcycle epoch and had to leave the field largely to the Japanese. On the other hand there is more to say as to why the promising development of the two-stroke engine – especially as an automobile power plant – was not followed up.

DKW was also a pathfinder in the field of front wheel drive. Internationally, there had been vehicles designed and built with this technical concept when Rasmussen built his first front wheel drive car in 1930. But once again it was tireless DKW advertising that educated the public that it was more logical to pull a vehicle than push it. And while more and more people became ready to accept this argument for smaller, less powerful vehicles, it was DKW which, in the course of front wheel drive development, demonstrated with its medium class cars that there was virtually no displacement limit beyond which the justification for front wheel drive ceased. What DKW itself was unable to prove in this sector was taken up by those who initially were not prepared to accept front wheel drive for anything but the lowest displacement class: today the majority of automobile makers around the world have at least one front wheel drive car in their program, and more than two-thirds of all new registrations in Germany are for cars with front wheel drive.

Why the Two-Stroke Automobile Engine in Ingolstadt Had to Die

It is no longer a secret that a number of leading international automobile and engine makers have long been working hard on the development of the two-stroke engine as an automobile power plant. This may sound amazing to some, taking into account certain inherent disadvantages of the two-stroke operating principle, which today more than ever appear to make the two-stroke engine less suitable as an automobile power plant than ever. But those who are working on the two-stroke automobile engine have long known that a correct two-stroke concept can hold advantages of this operating principle that can secure it a clear advantage over the traditional four-stroke engine. Such a "modern" two-stroke concept would of course look much different than the last three-cylinder engines from Ingolstadt (as they ultimately represented nothing more than refined motorcycle engines). The "correct" two-stroke concept for the purpose at hand would defeat the four-stroke engine in all decisive points: in mechanical complexity, size, weight, performance characteristics, fuel consumption and pollutant emissions – while requiring less maintenance and having a similar operating life.

From these points of view, the question posed at the start of the chapter, why the two-stroke automobile engine in Ingolstadt had to die, becomes all the more relative when most of the development offices and the men working on the coming automobile two-stroke do not come from the two-stroke scene in the old sense. Is not the obvious question why could the DKW tradition not have formed the promising starting point for the undoubtedly coming automobile two-stroke?

While not a comprehensive answer to this question, the following article by an engineer (now deceased) who, though "outside," was intimately involved in the development of the DKW three-cylinder engine, sheds light on the failure to support the two-stroke concept in Ingolstadt. It was published in a German magazine in 1966:

> "In recent years the two-stroke engine has not received much praise from motoring magazines and the auto makers themselves as a gasoline engine for automobiles. Auto Union, handicapped by inept management and miserable leadership of the so-called "research department," sold fewer of its two-stroke automobiles from year to year and therefore, at the wish of its new owner, found itself in new hands to whom the two-stroke engine was less of a concern than the previous owners.
>
> Why did this development take place at a time when elsewhere they were willing to invest millions in a completely new and risky engine operating principle, namely the Wankel? Why was it that the equally simple and ingenious two-stroke engine came into such disrepute that it was not even possible to get a fully developed two-stroke six-cylinder V engine, which had demonstrated sensational power and torque values, into series production? Was it due to the engine system – or an artificially generated mass psychosis – or why else?
>
> If we are honest: the example of Auto Union showed that even a fanatical following could not save this car. Auto Union, whose cornerstone was once the DKW factory in Zschopau, had been able to give the two-stroke automobile an almost legendary reputation. DKW cars had become famous for their reliability, comfort and handling. The small 600- and 700cc cars were also nice to look at, extremely potent for their performance class and very cheap. Anyone who had ridden a motorcycle could quickly familiarize himself with their technology.

Naturally it was inevitable that, in addition to the cheap car for the "common man," Zschopau would also interest itself in a larger type. Its four-cylinder engine with two double-action charging pumps was considerably faster and also had good acceleration – but, if you will pardon my saying so, it consumed fuel barbarically. This engine thus became Auto Union's first setback. In the 1930s, however, they were very versatile at DKW. The Schnürle loop scavenging system brought considerable improvements in performance and fuel consumption, and eventually the first three-cylinder engine based on this principle was created in Zschopau. Exploitation of the pressurization effect on the exhaust side allowed extremely good values to be achieved. This engine did not enter production before the war began, but it was revived after the war both in the DDR (as the F 9) and by the new Auto Union in West Germany. The DKW F 91 appeared in Ingolstadt at the end of 1953, still with the body of the F 89 (with the 700cc twin-cylinder engine), but with the 900cc three-cylinder engine producing 34hp. One year later East Germany produced the Wartburg, also with a 900cc three-cylinder.

Many will remember well that the F 91 became like "a pike in a fishpond." Its performance was similar to that of four-stroke automobiles with 1300-1500cc engines, and because of their excellent road handling these DKWs could be driven so sportily that even much larger automobiles couldn't do much against them. It was also taken for granted at sports meets of the day that the DKWs would "come and conquer." They won the European rally sport championship a number of times and often returned home the overall winners.

A few years later the F 91 became the F 93, a car that had become significantly wider and therefore more comfortable. It was powered by a 900cc engine that initially delivered 38 and later 40hp. But this F 93 was already too big and too heavy for the available engine power. But it had excellent fuel consumption and this allowed the company to retain customers and also add former four-stroke owners. Nevertheless, Auto Union soon found itself in the position of having to do something for the vital aura of its "for its class especially temperamental" car. They made the AU 1000, with 1000cc and 44hp, soon followed by the AU 1000 S with 50hp. The body was essentially that of the F 93 (but also with its weight), but they had something that made the customers happy. The AU 1000 S ran at about 125-130kph, fast examples even attained 135kph – a notable achievement for a car with an engine displacement of just 1000 cubic centimeters. Unfortunately Auto Union did not take sufficient care to ensure that the new types retained the brand's famed reliability. Some suppliers, of the crankshaft for example, proved unsuitable, and experiments were carried out with a crankshaft made by the company itself – initially with negative results. The rumor began to circulate that the DKW was trouble-prone and that crankshaft failures were the order of the day. Obviously the competition fed these rumors in discussions with customers. The press also began what soon became an endless criticism. There was also the fact that, despite a reduction in mixture ratio from 1:25 to 1:40, the mixture-lubrication engines left behind a clear smoke trail at idle and in city traffic. At higher loads, those driving behind the vehicle had to endure a penetrating, stinking smell of exhaust gas.

Auto Union had to do something; and it did, developing the clean oil regulator (which Dr. Venediger had earlier proposed in Zschopau), which unfortunately was put into production much too soon (because it wasn't perfected). This system had an interesting psychological effect: the press stated that the smoke was gone, as well as the smell (which was only partly true). But then came the horribly cold winter of 1962 and unbelievably many of the DKW engines died – from oil starvation. No one had probably considered that, made more viscous by the cold, the oil would be unable to flow in the narrow oil tubes. That winter there were probably almost as many warranty claims as cars sold – and once again the competition had material for their sales talks and the press again reason for destructive criticism.

There was also the fact that, at the time, crankshaft bearings were used that were supposed to counter the fear of cold corrosion in the anti-friction bearings. They encapsulated the "lifetime" bearings and lubricated them "for life." But they took a wrong design path, and the lubricant that was supposed to work "for life" often ran out after fifteen minutes on the test bench, causing the bearings to run dry. Technicians could only shake their heads and ask how such a design error was possible, but it happened. Like the premature introduction of the clean oil regulator, it was the fault of the department that pompously called itself the "research department" and had given its approval for the bearings to be used on the production line.

The DKW Junior had come onto the market prior to 1962 (1959). Despite all the good experiences with the three-cylinder engine, it had been designed with a 660cc twin-cylinder. They realized in time, however (after much money was unnecessarily spent), that it had to be a three-cylinder, which could also guarantee acceptable fuel consumption because of its reciprocal barrier pressure. And so, after several years of laborious preparation time, the first DKW Junior to be sold appeared with a 750cc engine that delivered 34hp. The engine, which still had mixture lubrication in the beginning and weighed just under 700kg, gave the car a really impressive performance. The car's body lines, however, were not very pretty: the "frog's eyes" and the steep windscreen were the opposite of what was understood by "streamlined." It was, however, quite roomy and received a positive reception from the market. Certain shortcomings in road handling were resolved relatively quickly.

The DKW Junior de Luxe, now with the clean oil regulator, arrived on the market as a car whose engine had been upsized to 800cc with an improved torque curve at the same power. The DKW Junior and its successors could never, however, make up for their shortcomings in streamlining. It is an old rule that two-stroke vehicles should be as streamlined as possible because they consume rather more fuel at full power than four-stroke engines. In those days that was the only way to achieve fuel consumption values that were not excessive; but obviously the generation of people who knew that had been replaced in the course of the takeover by Daimler Benz. The fat pencil of the senior technician of that era, William Werner, had also had a hand in making the DKW's streamlined front end into a "baffle plate." William Werner was also responsible for the "Baby Thunderbird," the AU 1000 SP, a boulevard sports car whose stylish headlights and 55hp engine could not make up for what its stylist had botched.

The setback of the winter of 1962, which even the DKW Junior did not completely escape, affected production numbers significantly. Even improved equipment quality could not make up for the car's technical failings.

They then tried to make a virtue of necessity. The Junior was also improved. It was given a 900cc (40hp) engine and was renamed the F 12. In doing so, they forgot that merely changing the body's roofline was not enough to escape the bad smell that had developed around the 1000 types and the automatically lubricated Junior de Luxe. If they had given the F 12 a new, more pleasing body shape with better streamlining, then perhaps the subsequent history of Auto Union would have been different. It would have been so easy to give the F 12's standard 900cc engine at least 50 stable horsepower – but here too the "research department" failed. Even the step to 45hp in the later F 12 Roadster was celebrated as a major feat.

The AU 1000 and the AU 1000 S, however, slowly faded away. The company was convinced that it had to come up with something completely new and began designing an entirely new automobile in keeping with the increased demand for prestige – the F 102. This car was displayed at the auto show in 1963 and appeared on the market in the spring of 1964. It was a difficult birth, for contrary to all previous experience they had given the engine a total displacement of 1175cc, or 392cc per cylinder. They should have known that the Schnürle loop scavenging system can become unstable in large cylinder units, resulting in poor fuel efficiency. They had also retained the same overall length of the engine block – despite an increase in bore from 74 to 81mm, which made the cylinder walls dangerously thin and reduced water spaces unacceptably. The result was that the early engines seized more than they ran and also developed an unquenchable thirst for fuel. The car was demonstrated to dealers in Wiesbaden shortly before the automobile show in September 1963, and its design received high praise. In fact it was one of the most beautiful cars in its class, and its road handling maintained the good DKW tradition – but the engine was a nightmare for the company's management. While the car as a whole was praised, engine performance and fuel consumption received little applause. And so "the best DKW there ever was" joined the competition battle with a terrible handicap. It also did not help much that better fuel efficiency figures were achieved before deliveries of the car began in spring 1964 – they were achieved in part at the cost of engine performance, and the publicized 60 DIN horsepower existed only in the prospectus. Only a few engines came close to this value, many were considerably beneath it.

Despite promises made to dealers and customers, production of DKW types ended after VW took over in autumn 1964. An attempt was made in the spring of 1965 to revive the F 12 by giving it the Roadster's 45hp engine with a properly functioning clean oil regulator with oil pre-heating as in the F 102, plus a mechanical water pump. Despite a clear rise in sales, the car, which was properly priced, died for good in early 1966.

At that time those in Ingolstadt who still advocated the two-stroke principle were viewed as near-criminals. The engine principle was blamed for the demise of Auto Union instead of thinking that personal inability alone was responsible for the debacle. For there were more than enough proposals that could have given Auto Union fresh impetus and secured its marketability – except that they came from people the industry liked to dismiss as "outsiders." One of these would have been good enough to develop the engines that in previous years had won more than 1,000 race victories and countless championships. These engines were commissioned, but despite many promises never entered production. Instead their creators reaped defamation and financial losses.

The Auto Union of the postwar years never lived up to its original pioneering role in the two-stroke sector. Instead it proved that one can kill a good principle if one allows things to be run by a sufficient number of incompetents, whose personal vanity is more important than the well-being and future of the company entrusted to them."

DKW in Color

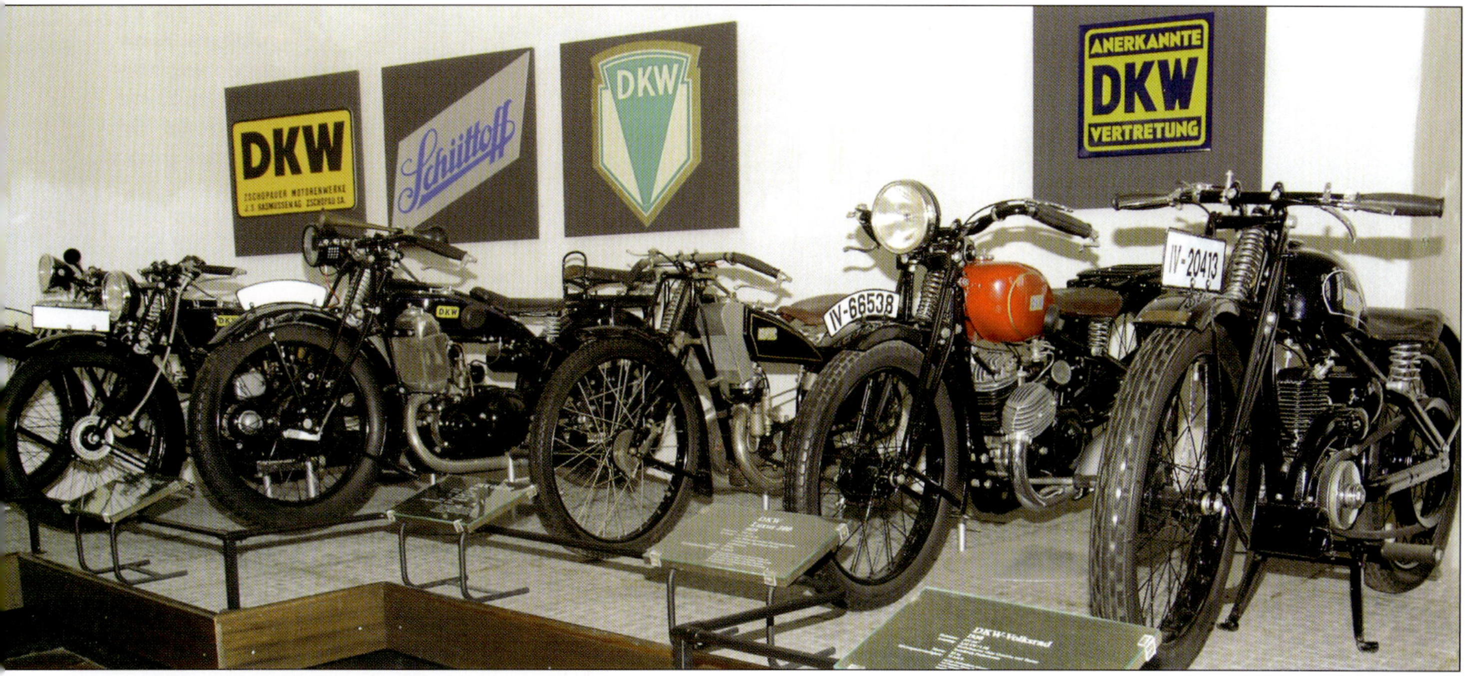

Above: The motorcycle museum at the Augustusburg near Chemnitz contains almost every model of DKW motorcycle built before and during the Second World War.

Left: The Reichsfahrt model was the first motorcycle made in Zschopau, with production beginning in 1922. Various models with 1.5 to 2.5hp engines were made until 1925.

Below: The DKW marque's rise began with the auxiliary bicycle engine in 1919.

The Golem armchair motorcycle can be seen as the true forerunner of later motor scooters.

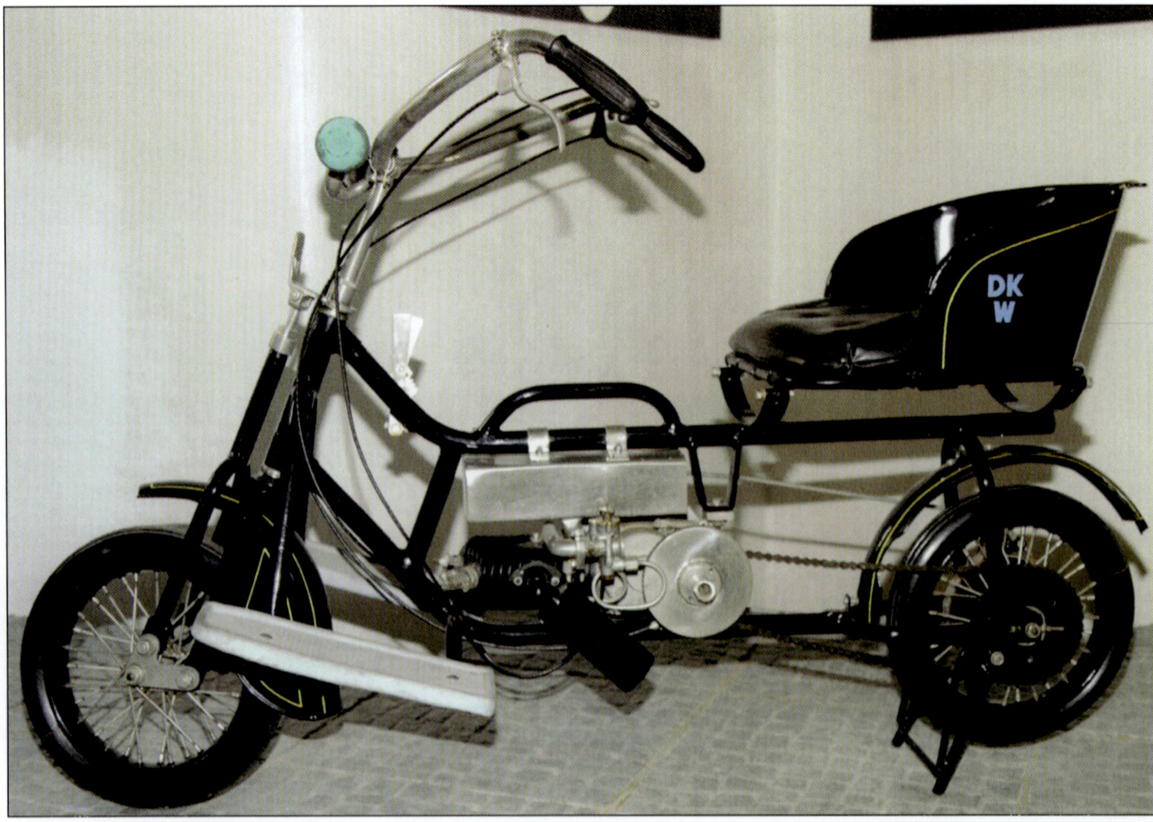

Below: The so-called "steel model" of the mid-1920s followed the upcoming style of frames with integrated fuel tanks.

Many DKW motorcycles, like these charging pump racing machines, can be seen in the Museum of Saxon Vehicles in Klaffenbach Castle near Chemnitz.

This E 200 from 1928 is fitted with many accessories not found on production machines, such as headlight, tachometer and passenger seat.

This recreation of the E 200 assembly line may also be seen in Klaffenbach. The E 206 and E 200 were the first German motorcycles produced on an assembly line.

The E 200's powerplant seen from the fan side. The shift lever allowed the rider to select two gears in the crank chamber.

A Spezial 200 from 1929. (Photo: Rasmussen GmbH)

The Luxus 500, made between 1929 and 1931, was the most economical entry into the heavy class, with a price of 1,095 Reichsmarks. In 1931 a Sport 500 cost an additional 100 Marks but came with liquid cooling.

A Super Sport 500, year of manufacture 1929. This motorcycle belongs to DKW collector Hermann Bargmann, who owns examples of all DKW production motorcycles and various racing machines from Zschopau and Ingolstadt.

Another Super Sport 500 with the drive train and an interesting paint job exactly like the one applied on production machines.

On 1 April 1928 a tax exemption took effect in Germany for motorcycles with a displacement of 200 cubic centimeters or less. Among the various DKW motorcycles in this class was the Luxus Spezial 200, which was made from 1929 to 1932.

In the mid-1930s the SB 350 (here a 1934 model) was in the elevated class, which few could afford. One of the most striking features of SB models from the first series was the almost fully chromed fuel tank.

On the second SB model series only the sides of the tank were chromed. With their lengthened chassis and teardrop-shaped tank, the later SB motorcycles cut a fine figure.

Above: On the luxury models, the "A" stood for Anlasser, or starter, which is clearly visible in this photo of a 1936 SB 200.

Right: This close-up depicts a KS 200, after the RT 3 PS the most-produced DKW motorcycle of the prewar period. It was a true bread and butter vehicle that sold for 540 Reichsmarks.

Above: On 6 February 1939 an SB 500 (not the machine illustrated here, which is a 1937) became the 500,000th DKW motorcycle.

Ready for an old timer's ride on a 1939 NZ 350.

This US 250, a double-piston, supercharged machine, was made in 1939. Its engine delivered 35hp. (Museum Mobile)

Also made in 1939 was this SS 350 with twin-cylinder double-piston engine and classic charging pump. This motorcycle, which was available to private buyers, delivered 32hp.

The DKW factory race team employed the ULD 250 with great success from 1937 to 1939. In 1938 Ewald Kluge won the European Championship on such a machine.

Museum piece: this UL motorcycle-sidecar of 1937 was obviously the only complete racing combination to survive the war and avoid being shipped off to Russia.

The RT 125 was both the last civilian development and also a true milestone in motorcycle history. 21,000 examples of this motorcycle were built in 1940-41.

Above: This pleasing display of DKW motorcycles used by the German military may be seen in the Museum Mobile in Ingolstadt. In the foreground the RT 125-1, behind it the NZ 350-1.

Right: Not until 1944 did those responsible for the Wehrmacht switch from complicated and heavy four-strokes to the lighter and easier to repair NZ 350. By then the war was lost.

Right: Auto Union resumed the production of motorcycles in Ingolstadt in 1949 with the RT 125.

Below: Many postwar DKW motorcycles, such as this RT 250 H of 1952, are on display in the Museum Mobile in Ingolstadt.

The off-road version of the RT 125 from 1956. DKW motorcycles had been competing successfully in off-road competitions since the 1920s.

The Hobby, a 75cc scooter, was one of the most popular German scooters from 1954 to 1957. It became one of the best-selling DKW two-wheelers.

Below left: The RT 350, just 5,290 of which were made in 1955-56, is one of the most sought after and expensive vintage DKW motorcycles.

Below right: Very sporty looking, but not production standard. The RT 350's twin cylinders were only fed by one carburetor.

Color factory photos were not the norm in the 1950s. DKW made an exception for the last RT 200 VS models in order to show off their eye-catching paintwork.

The 250cc "Kuhnke DKW" had a twin-cylinder, opposed piston engine to counteract the supercharger ban imposed in 1950.

Below: The final version of the RM 350 racing machine, with which August Hobl became runner-up world champion in 1956.

Sissi Wünsche was permitted to make a lap of honor at the 1988 TT.

Veterans reunion: In 1968 August Hobl, Siegfried "Sissi" Wünsche and Hans Bartl (from l. to r.) pose with the 1955 model of the RM 350 at a small reunion.

For more than thirty years, DKW enthusiasts have been gathering in the small town of Garitz in Saxony with their vehicles at the beginning of June. Nowhere else can one find as many prewar DKW cars.

Above: The P 15 with two-stroke engine, wooden body and rear wheel drive was the first DKW car and entered production in 1928.

Right: The most common models of the P 15 were the roadster and the convertible with two fold-down seats. The car in the photo was made in 1928, the first year of production.

Above: Made in 1931, this 4=8, V 1000 is extremely rare today. Slightly less than 3,000 of these vehicles were produced. The rear wheel drive car was powered by a V-4 two-stroke engine.

Right: Although just 4,353 examples of the F 1 were built in 1931-32, this first DKW front wheel drive car is once again a relatively common sight.

For example at the annual Auto Union veterans meet, as here in Ingolstadt.

Many DKW cars from the prewar period may be found in the August Horch Museum in Zwickau. Some are very rare vehicles, such as this Sport Roadster based on the Sonderklasse ...

... or this Schwebeklasse model. DKW sold the rear wheel drive Schwebeklasse from 1934 to 1937.

The Front Luxus Cabriolet, production of which began in 1935 (Type F 5), has long been one of the most sought after two-strokes from Zwickau.

In previous decades, DKW automobiles with faux-leather-covered wooden bodies were not considered worth collecting. Today a beautiful 1936 F 5 sedan is a real rarity.

There had been two-seat convertible sedans since the F 2. These body variants were offered in a wide variety of variations until the F 8.

A Meisterklasse convertible sedan, four seat, Type F 5.

Below: The Front-Luxus two-seater is seen as the most beautiful of all DKW cars. Just 400 examples of the car, which was generally referred to as the "F 5 Roadster," were made.

Surviving Roadsters are either not for sale or priceless. The latter even applies to cars that are little more than piles of junk.

If you like: homemade roadster based on the 1937 F 7.

Above: Equally hard to find is this Sonderklasse-Kübelwagen, for it never went into production.

Left: Almost 3,000 F 8 Front Luxus-Cabriolets were made from 1939 to 1941. This model had a four-seat body made the Baur Company of Stuttgart.

Below: In addition to the delivery van, the F 8 utility vehicle program also included a platform truck.

Not rebuilt, but also not fully authentic: an F 8 Combi as a "barn find."

The new Auto Union resumed making autos in Ingolstadt in 1949. Its first product was the F 89 L fast truck. This model, from the Museum Mobile, was built a year later.

The first DKW car made in West Germany after the war was the F 89 P, which was built in Auto Union's branch factory in Düsseldorf. (Museum Mobile)

In autumn 1955, further development and a switch to a three-cylinder engine resulted in the F 93, which was also called "the big 3=6."

From the end of 1957, the improved 3=6, a four-door sedan with center-hinged doors, was called the Auto Union 1000.

The F 102 appeared on the market in 1964. It was the last two-stroke DKW car with the four rings on the grille. It was also the first DKW with a load-bearing all-steel body.

The Munga was built for the Bundeswehr until December 1968 and was the last two-stroke representative of the DKW marque. The all-wheel crawler is still suitable for family outings.

A nice collection of Auto Union 1000 Universals, photographed at a spring meeting of the Auto Union Veterans Club.

The body style derived from the F 9 Hohe Klasse eventually featured doors hinged at the front.
The Auto Union 1000 S with panoramic windows front and rear.

Most DKW postwar models can be seen in the Museum Mobile in the Audi Center in Ingolstadt. Like this 1960 DKW Junior.

A smorgasbord: DKW F 12 Roadster, IFA F 8 Cabriolet, DKW F 8 flat bed – the meet in Garitz covers the entire spectrum of DKW automobiles.

Beginning in 1964, the F 12 Roadster was supposed to counteract the negative image of the two-stroke. In any case it was a beautiful car.

One of the highlights of the IAA 1957 was the unveiling of the Auto Union 1000 Sp. With a price of 11,960 Marks, however, this model was twice as expensive as the 3=6 two-door sedan.

Index